I0799904

IMAGES
of America

LANSINGBURGH

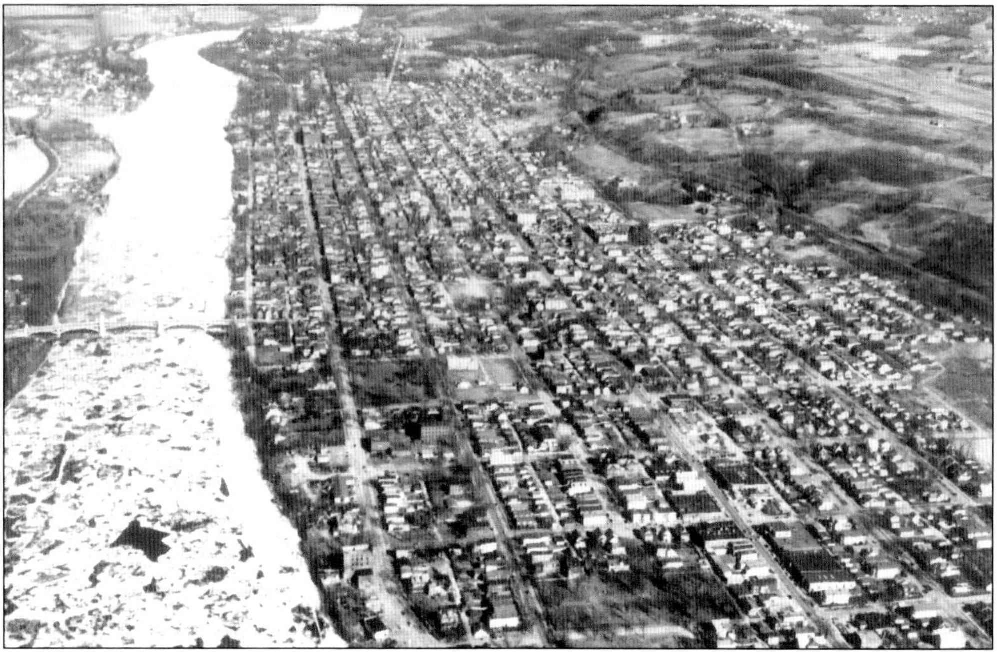

LANSINGBURGH, 1950S. This wintertime aerial view shows all of Lansingburgh laid out on the Hudson River flood plain. Both the Cohoes and Waterford Bridges can be seen crossing the river. Lansingburgh was laid out in this rectangular fashion in 1771, making it 30 years older than the city of Troy.

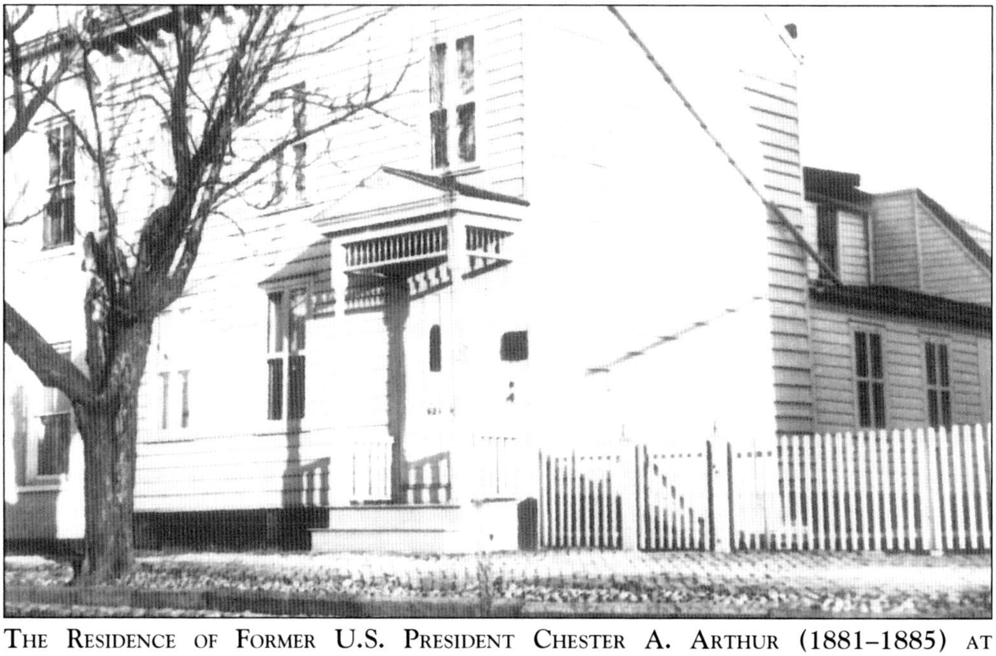

THE RESIDENCE OF FORMER U.S. PRESIDENT CHESTER A. ARTHUR (1881–1885) AT 626 FIRST AVENUE IN 1846. Arthur went to Union College in Schenectady at the age of 15 in 1845, and taught school in the one-room brick schoolhouse (still standing) of School District #14, in the town of Schaghticoke on Verbeck Street. By doing so he earned $15 a month.

IMAGES
of America

LANSINGBURGH

Don Rittner

ARCADIA
PUBLISHING

ISBN 978-0-7385-0089-8

Published by Arcadia Publishing
Charleston, South Carolina

Printed in the United States of America

Library of Congress Catalog Card Number: 99-62499

For all general information contact Arcadia Publishing at:
Telephone 843-853-2070
Fax 843-853-0044
E-Mail sales@arcadiapublishing.com
For customer service and orders:
Toll-Free 1-888-313-2665

Visit us on the Internet at www.arcadiapublishing.com

To Frances D. Broderick
Longtime Lansingburgh Historian

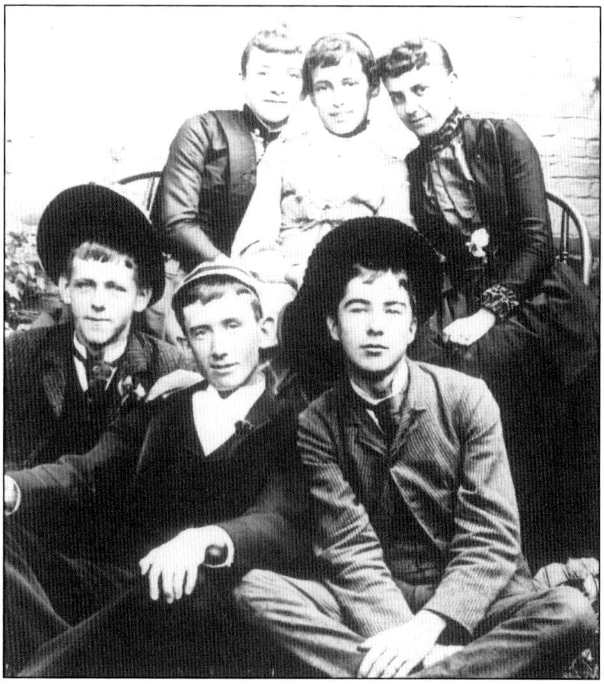

COVER: MEMBERS OF THE LANSINGBURGH ACADEMY CLASS OF 1890. If there is one structure that represents continuity it is the Lansingburgh Academy. The academy was an important educational institution in Lansingburgh for almost 150 years. Chester A. Arthur and Herman Melville attended. The building is still in use today as a public library.

Contents

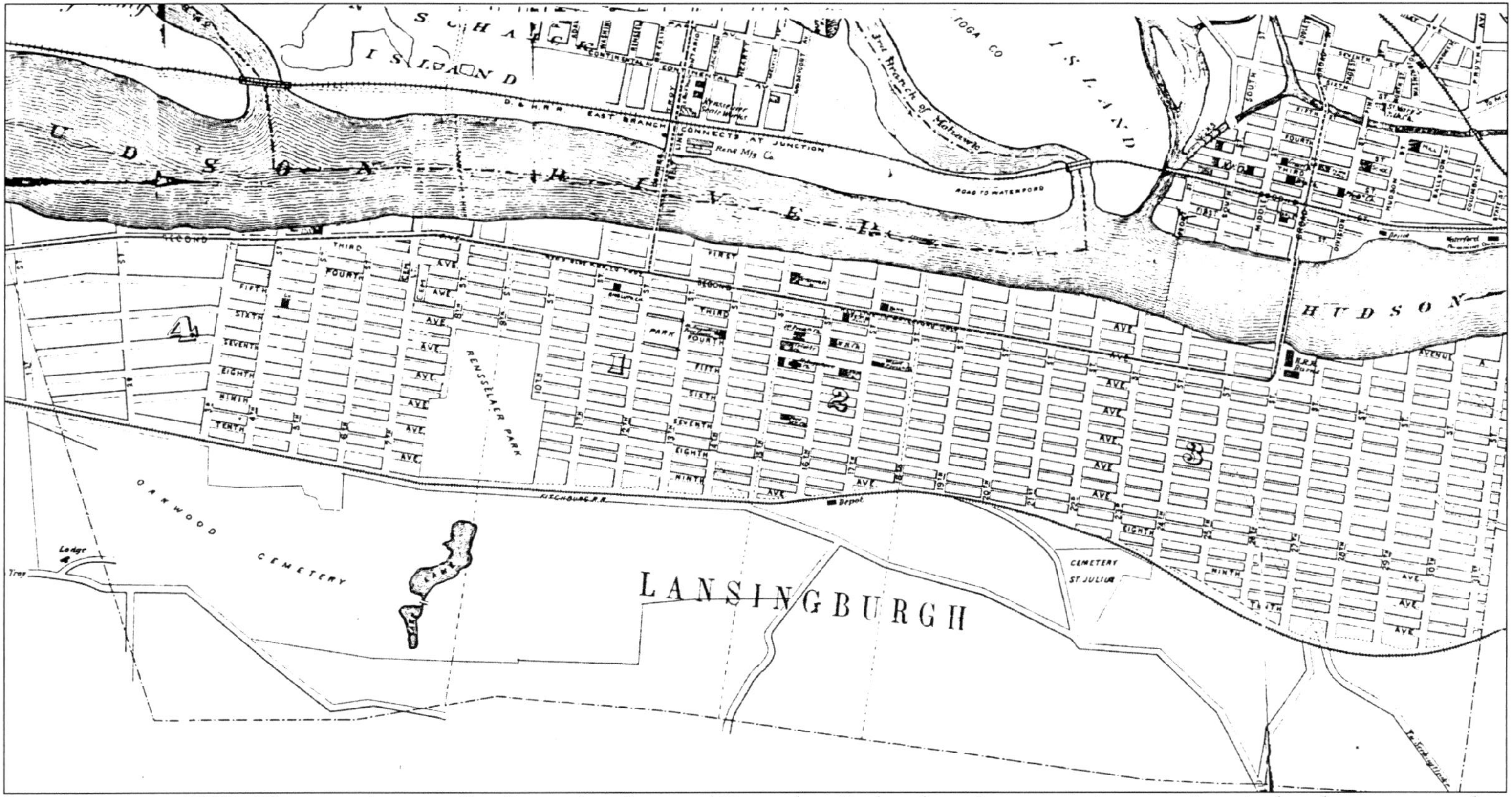

LANSINGBURGH, 1897. This map shows trolley lines, churches, and Rensselaer Park, a longtime recreation area. Lansingburgh was annexed to the city of Troy three years later.

INTRODUCTION

To be ignorant of what occurred before you were born is to remain always a child. For what is the worth of human life, unless it is woven into the life of our ancestors by the records of history?

—Cicero

The name Lansingburgh is best known today as the northern suburb of the city of Troy, New York. It is located about 150 miles north of New York City, and occupies the east bank of the historic Hudson River. However, the village of Lansingburgh was in existence almost 30 years before Troy was incorporated in 1798.

Lansingburgh is the oldest settled region and first chartered village in New York's Rensselaer County, an area of hills, forest, and river plains covering about 658 square miles. Lansingburgh was a thriving mercantile village before the American Revolution, when today's city of Troy was still farmland.

Abraham Jacob Lansing established the area that encompasses Lansingburgh, originally called Tascamcatik by local Native Americans, in 1763, as a 5,000-acre farm. Only eight years later, in 1771, Lansing laid out his land into a square of 2-by-1.5 miles with 288 building lots, streets, alleys, and an oblong square village green in the center. He named his new proposed city Lansingburgh. Instead, it became known as "Niew Stadt," or New City, as opposed to Albany, or "Old City," south of it. Lansingburgh quickly grew into a thriving village thanks to an influx of New England entrepreneurs.

The "Burgh," as it is called today, was annexed to the city of Troy in 1900, but present-day residents of Lansingburgh still have a deep sense of a separate identity and their own claim to fame. Lansingburgh has made its own contributions to national politics, literature, and sports.

Residents are eager to point out that on April 17, 1775, 46 of their leading inhabitants signed a proclamation opposing England's rule that may be the first Declaration of Independence signed in the country, a year before the historic July Fourth proclamation of the Colonies.

Chester A. Arthur, the 21st President of the United States, lived and was educated here and taught locally. His father was a well-known local preacher.

Famed novelist Herman Melville, best known for *Moby Dick*, also spent his youth here. Melville's boyhood home, now the Lansingburgh Historical Society, is where he wrote his first two novels.

A part of American baseball history began in Lansingburgh. The Union "Haymakers," an early Lansingburgh baseball team, was the beginning of what later became the New York Giants, now located in San Francisco. Four of the ballplayers are in the Baseball Hall of Fame.

The Lansingburgh Academy was an important educational institution that lasted 150 years. Lansingburgh still maintains its own separate school district, keeping with tradition.

The products of early Lansingburgh industries, including oilcloth, brushes, valves, knit goods, beer, crackers and biscuits, scales, carriages, and shirts and collars, were world famous during the 19th century, and continued to be even after the village became part of the city of Troy.

Within this book you can relive some of the events and view images of Lansingburgh in the late 19th and early 20th century. There are more than 200 photographs, most from the archives of late historian Frances Broderick, that show the businesses, landmarks, people, and events that give Lansingburgh its proud history. No photographic book can do complete justice to the history of any community. To learn more about the history of Lansingburgh, try reading *History of Rensselaer County, New York* by Nathaniel B. Sylvester (Philadelphia: Everts and Peck, 1880) and/or *Landmarks of Rensselaer County, New York* by George B. Anderson (Syracuse: D. Mason and Company, 1897).

Lansingburgh is a 228-year-old community. To this day, it is considered a beautiful village along the banks of the Hudson River with friendly people and architecture worth admiring. The residents of the "Burgh" should be proud that they have been able to maintain their identity for more than two centuries. Let's hope that they make a new commitment to preserve this wonderful history as we enter the next millennium.

I would like to extend my appreciation to Warren Broderick for the use of the superb photographic archives of his mother, late historian Frances Broderick, and for his review of the captions for accuracy. Also, my appreciation to Stacy Draper, Kathy Sheehan, and the staff of the Rensselaer County Historical Society, for the use of their pictorial archives (photos on pp. 2, upper; 19, upper; 35, lower; 77, both; 38, lower; 54, lower; 92, upper; and 122, lower). Richard T. Zeller was an excellent source of information on Rensselaer Park and I thank him. Any errors are my own.

If you have any Lansingburgh history you would like to share, please contact me by e-mail at drittner@aol.com, or P.O. Box 50216, Albany, NY 12205.

—Don Rittner
February 1999

One

Villagescapes, Landmarks, and Views

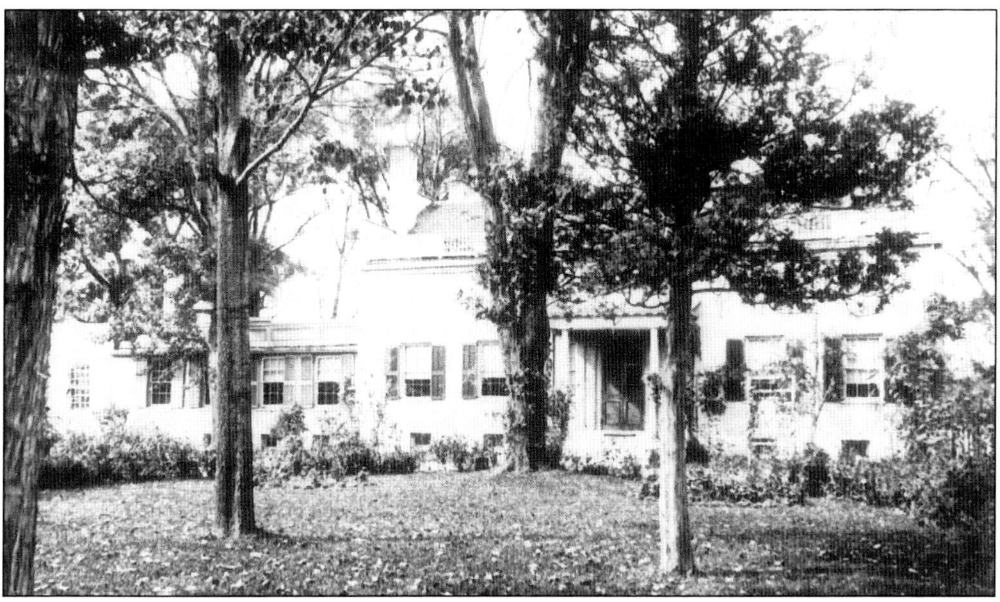

The Village Home of Abraham Jacob Lansing, 405 Second Avenue. Lansing, the founder of Lansingburgh, had this home built in 1749. It was demolished for a supermarket in 1962. One must question how our history can be so easily scraped away for corporate greed. How many other landmarks in Lansingburgh will be destroyed before its citizens say no more?

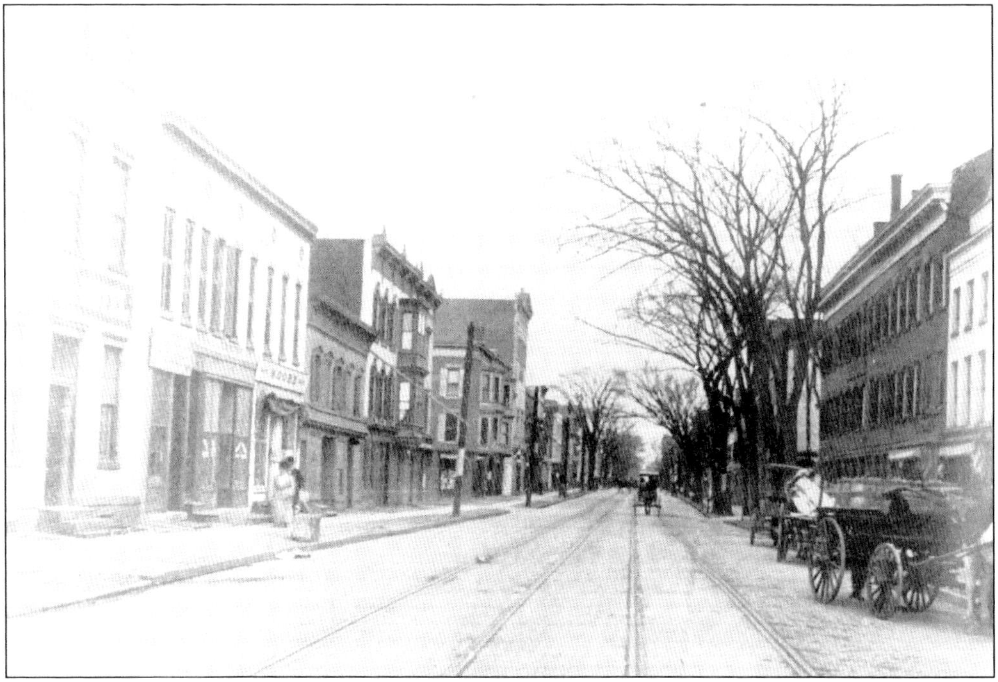

SECOND AVENUE LOOKING NORTH TOWARD 116TH STREET. The Brunswick Hotel is on the left, the Phoenix Hotel is on the right, and trolley tracks run through the middle. Second Avenue was a major thoroughfare that connected to Troy's River Street.

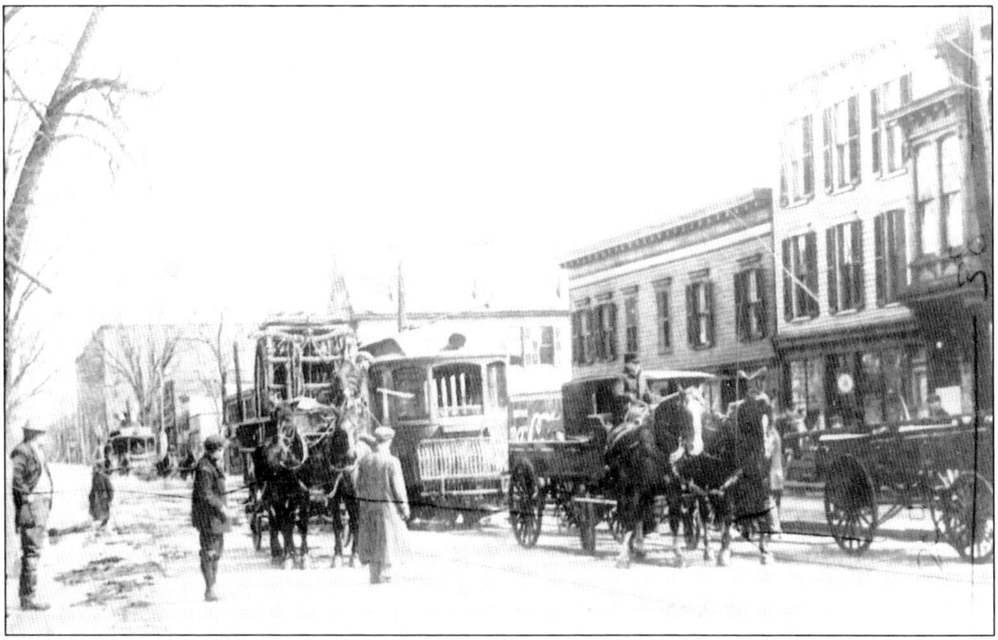

A TRAFFIC JAM ON SECOND AVENUE, LOOKING NORTH FROM 118TH STREET. Trolleys and horses are competing for the street. As automobiles became more popular, scenes such as this became less frequent. The last trolley ran in Troy in 1933.

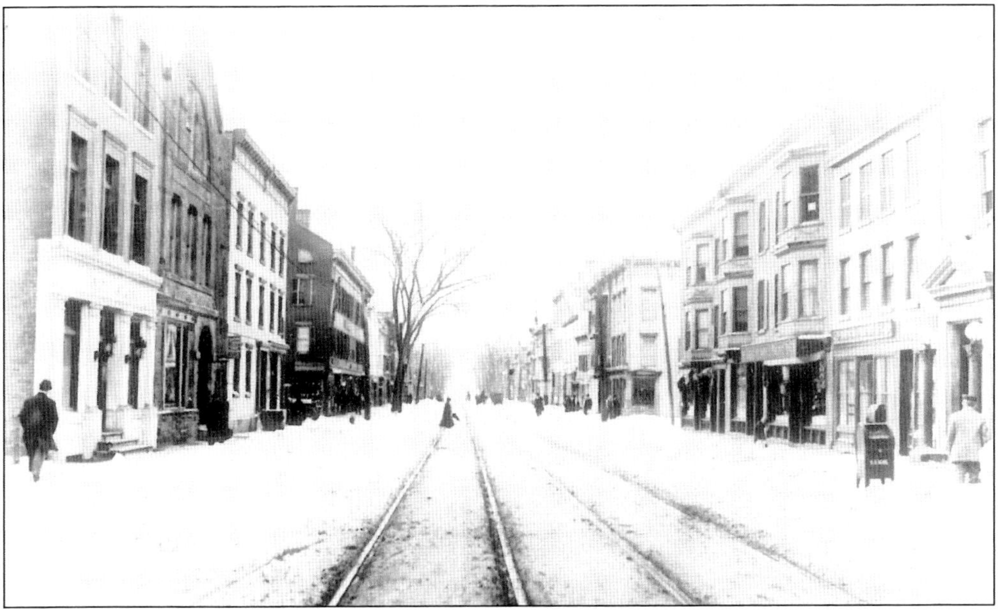

WINTERTIME ON SECOND AVENUE LOOKING SOUTH TO 116TH STREET. The building that housed the police department (on the left) is still standing, but the People's Bank next to it is no longer. Take away the trolley tracks and a few buildings and this view is basically the same today.

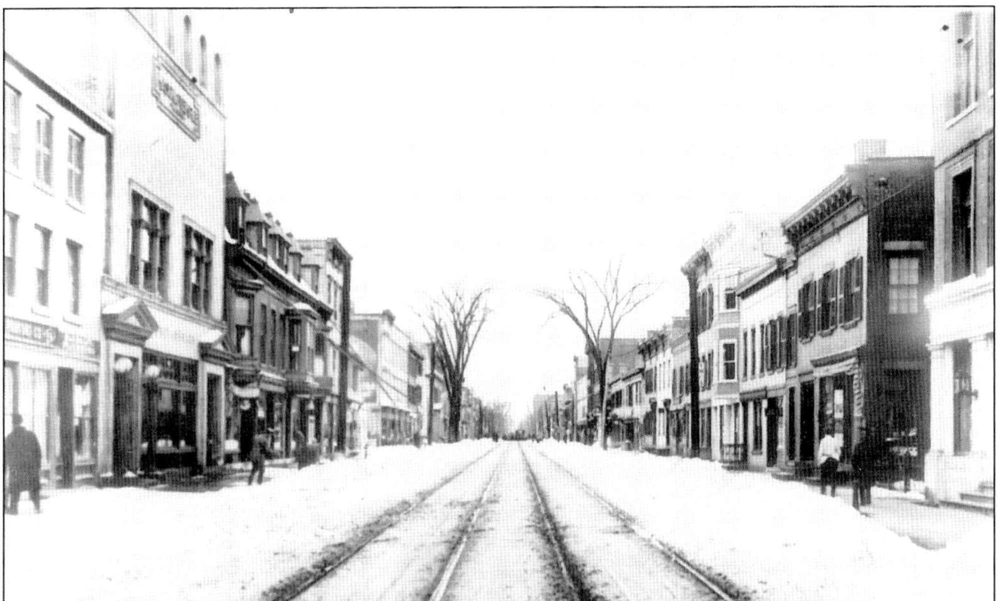

AN OPPOSITE VIEW ON SECOND AVENUE LOOKING NORTH FROM 116TH STREET. The post office, located in the Masonic Temple building, is on the left. A few buildings north is the YWCA. The trolley car tracks have been plowed. Both the Masonic Temple building and the former police station remain in use today, though for other purposes.

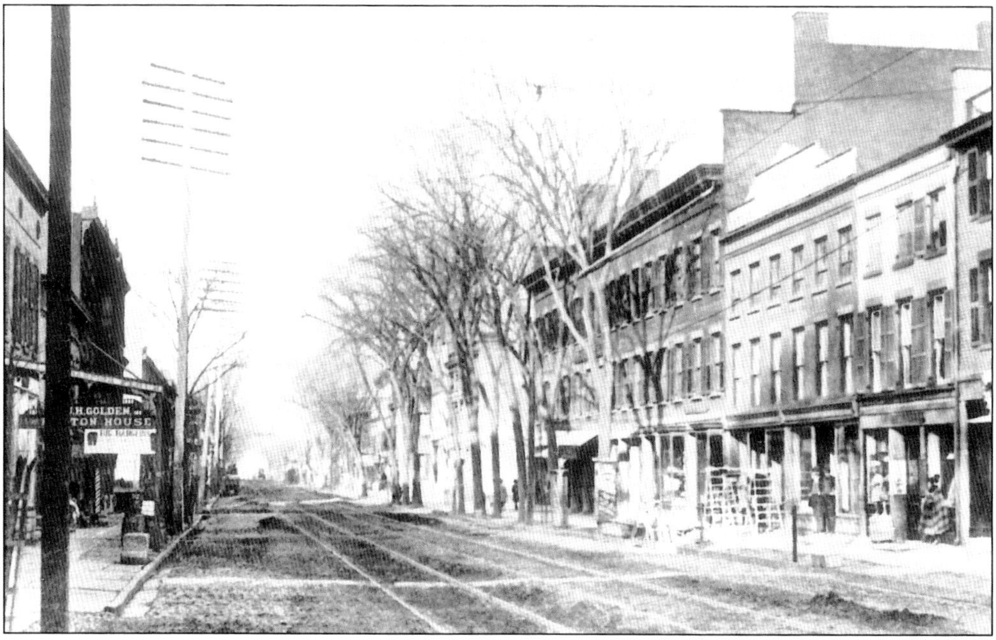

SECOND AVENUE LOOKING NORTH TOWARD 116TH STREET AND WATERFORD. The Phoenix Hotel is on the right, along with Mason's, an undertaking business no longer in existence that also sold furniture. Next to Mason's is a cigar store and a cigar-store Indian. The post office was in the hotel. North of the corner is the Fox Cracker Factory; trolley car tracks are visible in the center of the photograph.

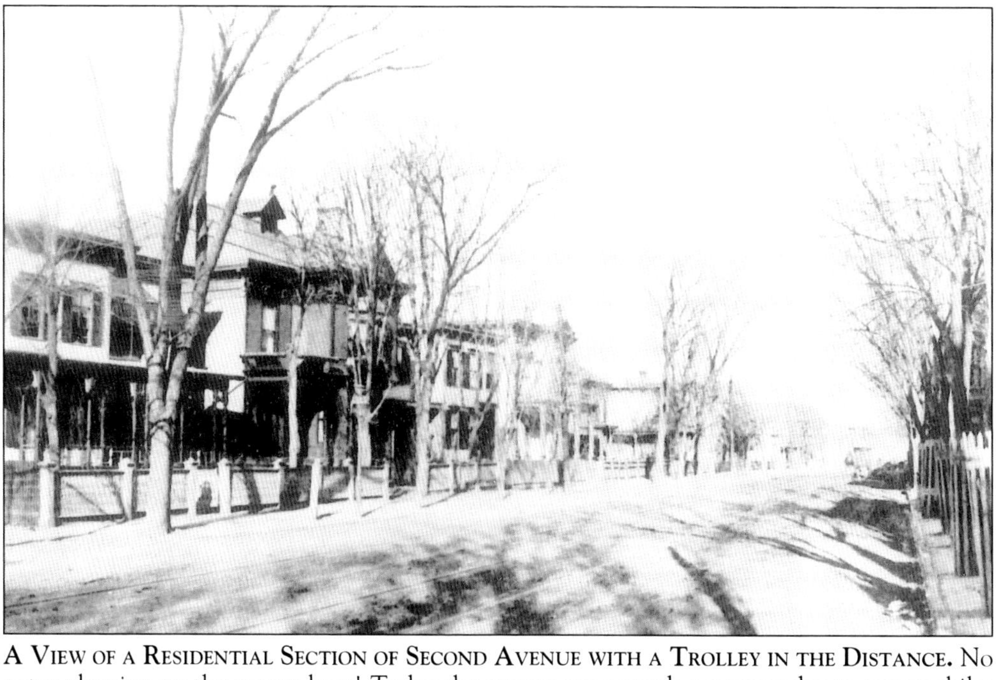

A VIEW OF A RESIDENTIAL SECTION OF SECOND AVENUE WITH A TROLLEY IN THE DISTANCE. No autos clogging up the streets here! Today the streets seem much narrower due to automobiles parking along the sidewalks. Much of Lansingburgh still maintains this quiet charm and peaceful residential setting.

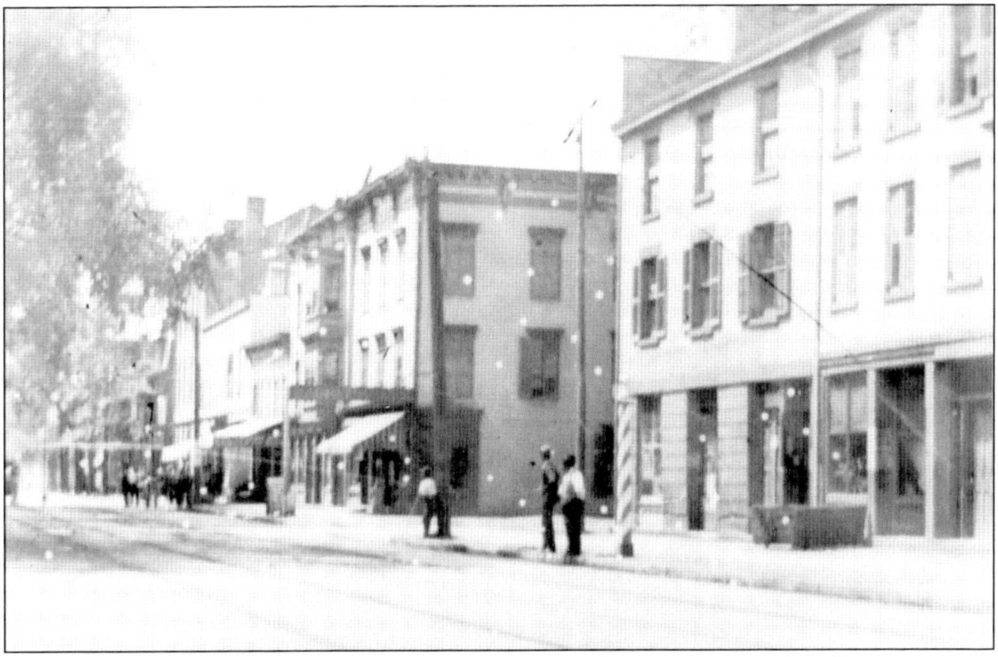

A Building on the Northeast Corner of Second Avenue and 116th Street with a Steep Pitched Roof and End Gable. This structure was mentioned in many early records but is seldom seen in street views. Notice the barber pole in front of the building. It seems that there were always people milling in the streets and socializing during these times.

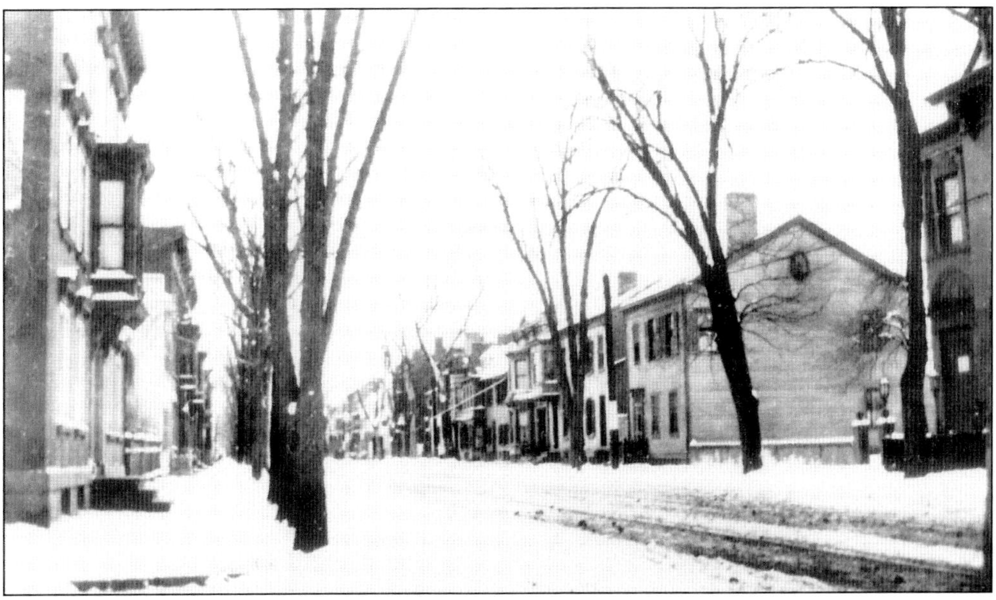

Second Avenue Looking South from 114th Street. Barton Arms, an apartment house, is on the left. Federal-style brick-and-wood homes built in the 1860s line the streets.

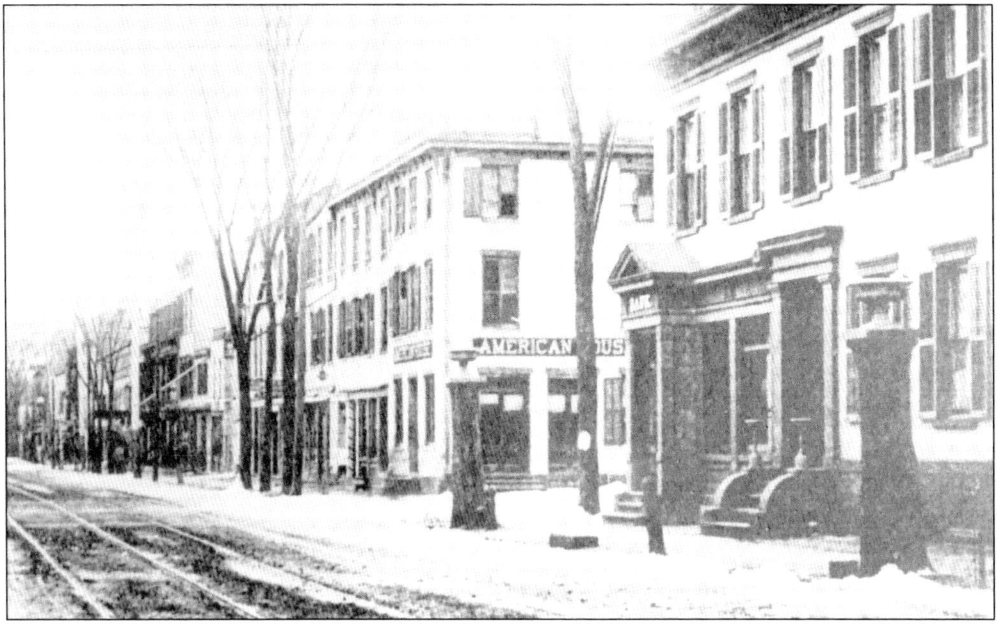

LOOKING SOUTH ON SECOND STREET FROM THE BANK OF D. POWERS AND SONS, JUST NORTH OF 117TH STREET. American House, a Federal Period hotel, is on the other corner at 629 Second Avenue (Edward H. O'Neill was the owner). The Powers Bank, owned by Deborah Powers and two sons, was the only bank in the village for years.

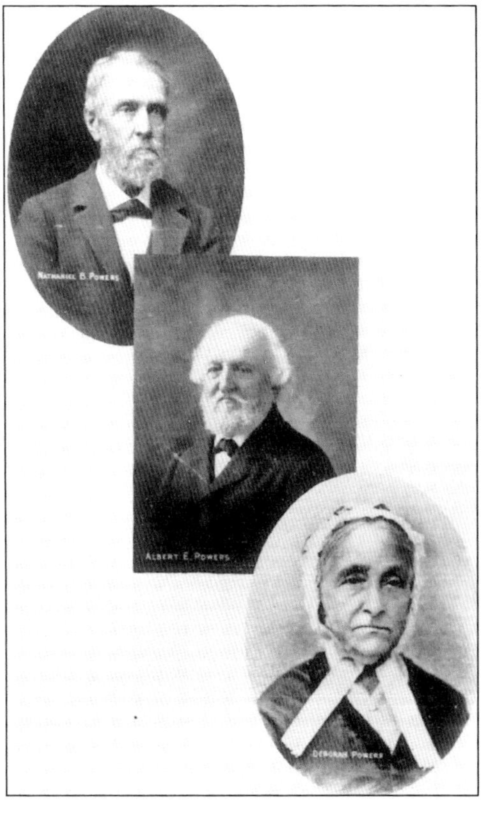

DEBORAH POWERS AND SONS. A school, a park, and an old ladies home were named after the Powers family, prominent participants in the oilcloth business. Deborah's husband, who was killed in a factory accident, began the business; Albert E. and Nathaniel B. Powers took over operations when Mrs. Powers died.

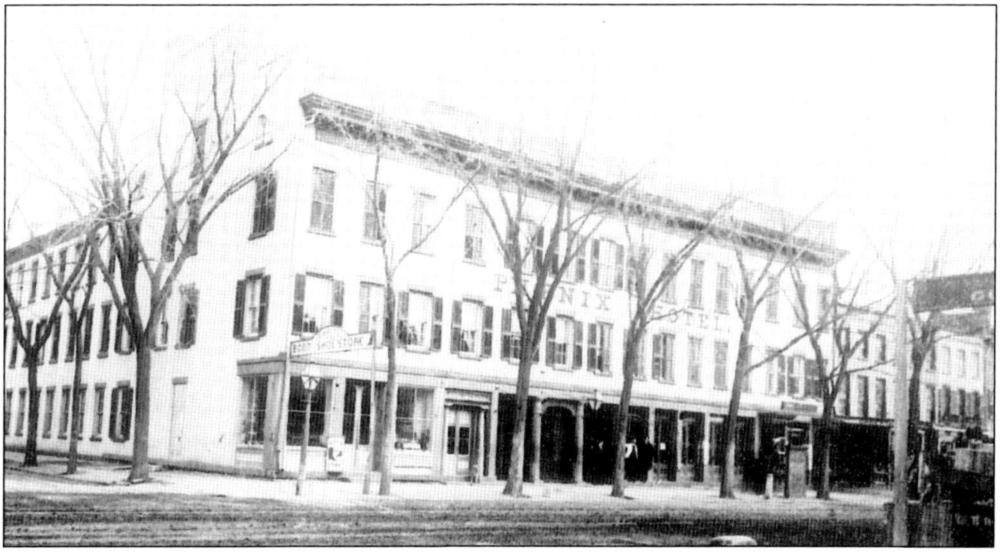

THE PHEONIX HOTEL, SECOND AVENUE, AND 116TH STREET. The Pheonix Hotel was built in 1834 by Esek Hawkins on the site of the Village Tavern, which had burned earlier that year. The original hotel on the site, built in 1780, was owned by Ananius Platt, and was known at various points as the Village Inn, Haner's Inn, and the Village Hotel. It was the birthplace of the County of Rensselaer on April 15, 1791, and served as a stagecoach stop for travelers going from Lansingburgh to Albany. In 1864, Zebina E. Fobes built the brick addition that runs on 116th Street to Alley.

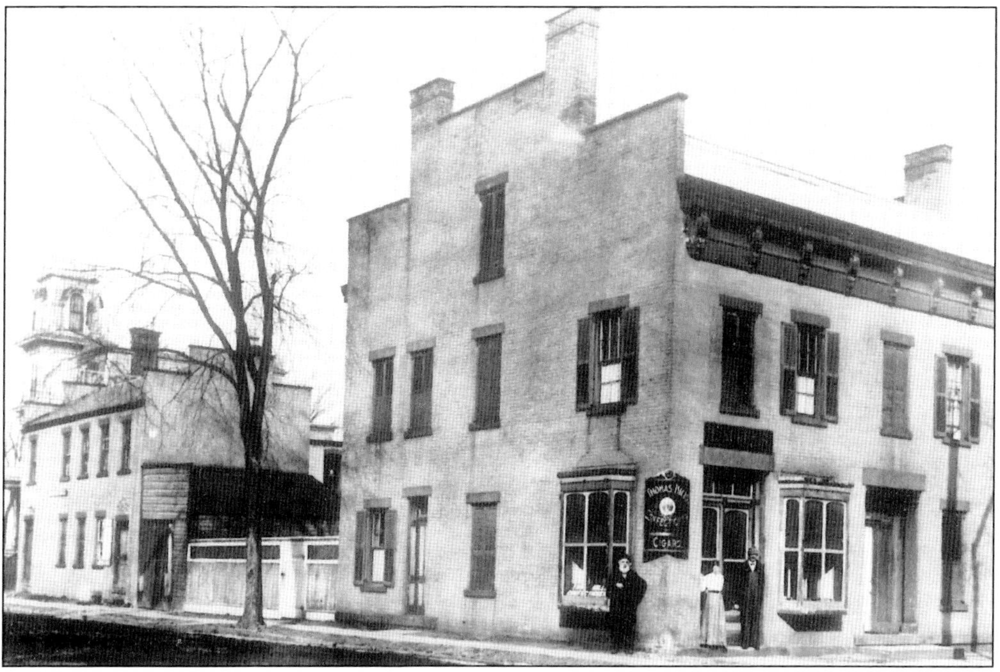

THOMAS MILLS, A CONFECTIONER AND CIGAR MANUFACTURER AT 662 SECOND AVENUE, THE NORTHEAST CORNER OF SECOND AVENUE AND 118TH STREET. Mills lived in the classic Federal-style building as well. The man with the white beard is John Davery, who died in 1915.

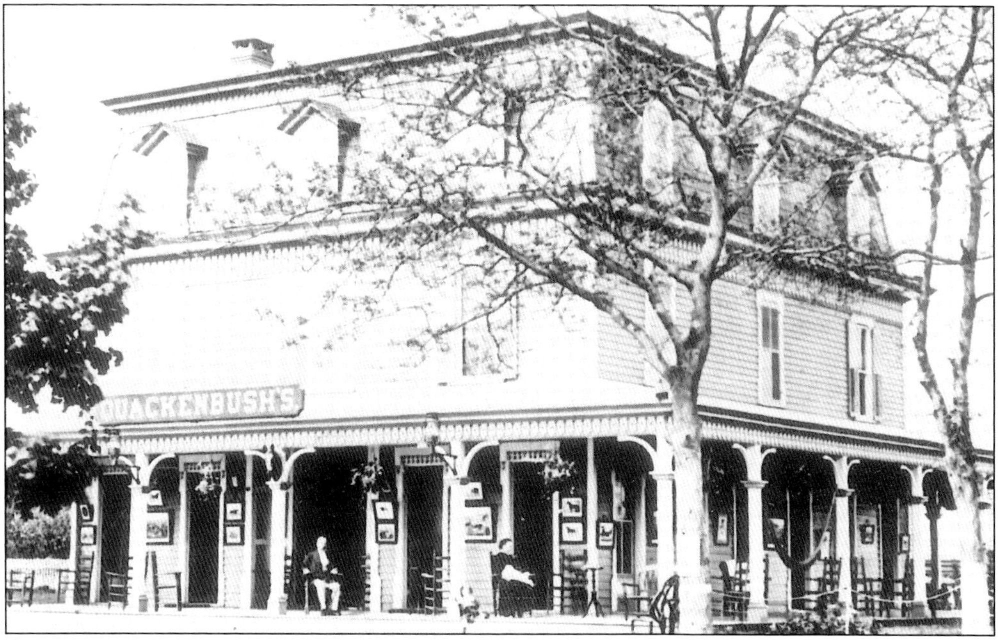

QUACKENBUSH'S, LOCATED AT THE SOUTHWEST CORNER OF 103RD STREET AND FIFTH AVENUE. This Fifth Avenue building was moved to the south side of 103rd, between Second and Fifth Avenues, where it was used as an apartment house. The pictures hanging on the outside walls are of horses.

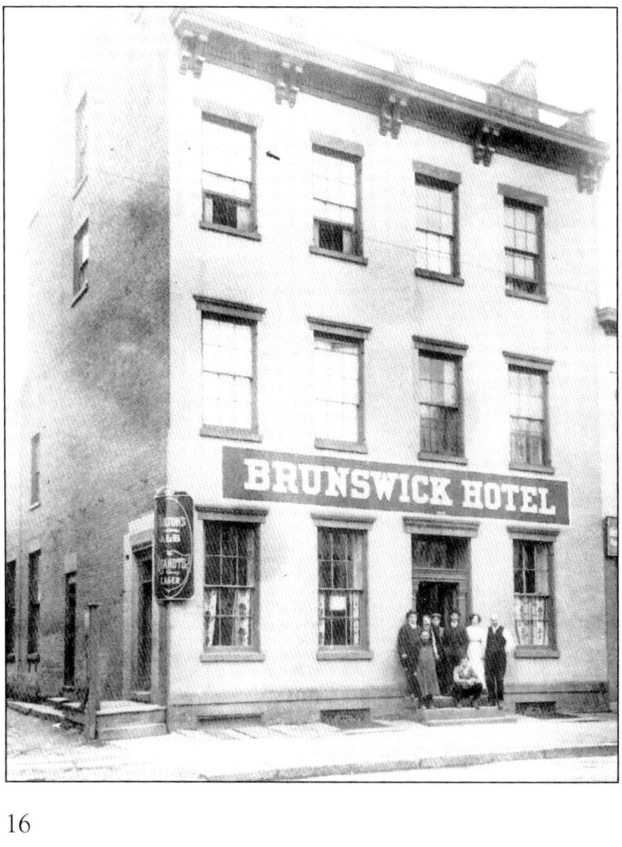

THE BRUNSWICK HOTEL, 596 SECOND AVENUE. This early-20th-century hotel was owned by John R. Fulton in 1939, and was later used as the Lansingburgh Boys Club. It was demolished in 1964. The Boys Club is still in Lansingburgh but is now the Boys and Girls Club. The Boys Club was originally created in the city of Troy in 1911 by George B. Cluett to help poor boys become good citizens.

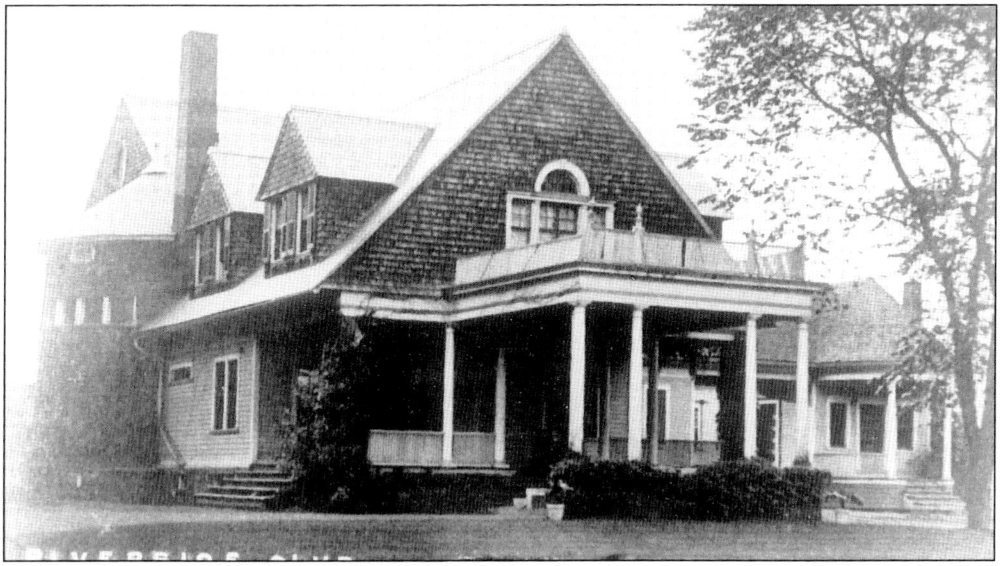

The Riverside Club on Second Avenue near the Waterford Bridge. Social affairs and bowling were normal pasttimes for the select members who belonged to this club. In 1925, the club had already been using this building for 25 years. It is now used by Friehofer's as offices.

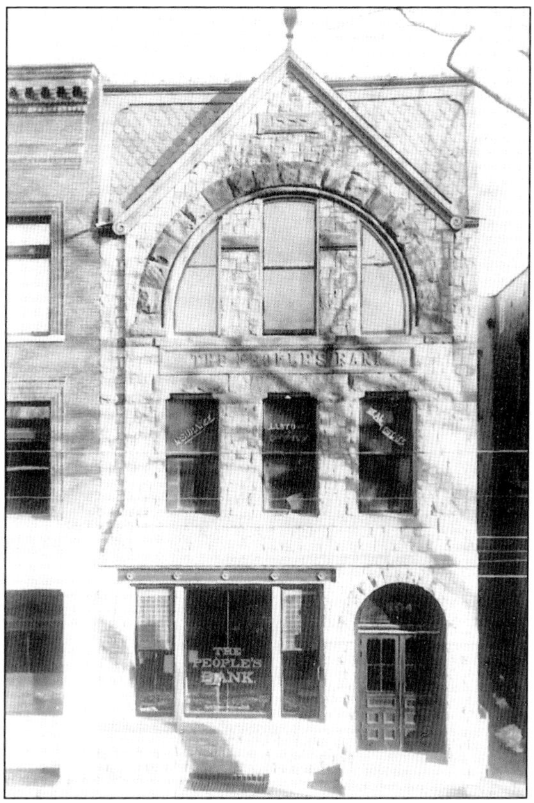

The People's Bank, located at 604 Second Avenue North of 116th Street. This financial institution was organized in 1888, with J.K.P. Pine as president, after the Bank of Lansingburgh closed. It opened in February 1890 and served until November 17, 1923, before being absorbed by the Manufacturer's National Bank of Troy. Pine also owned the Lion Factory and the Troy Carriage Works in Lansingburgh.

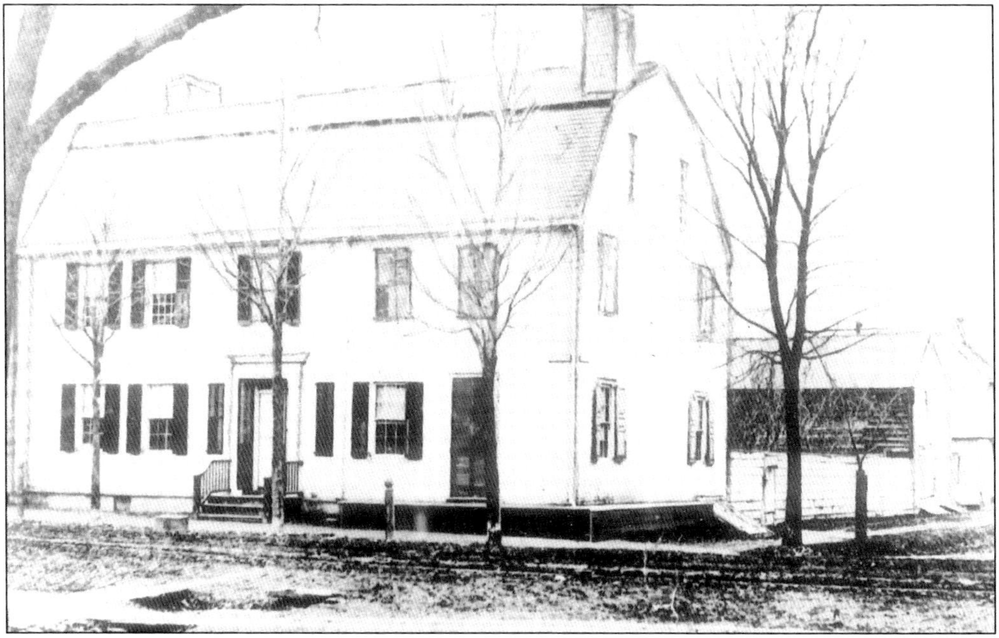

The Home of Augustus Filley, 499 Second Avenue and 113th Street. During the 1800s, famous Filley Tinware was made and decorated in this building, which was built *c.* 1770. Second Avenue was then called King Street and 113th Street was called Hoosick. It is one of the few Dutch-designed homes left in Lansingburgh.

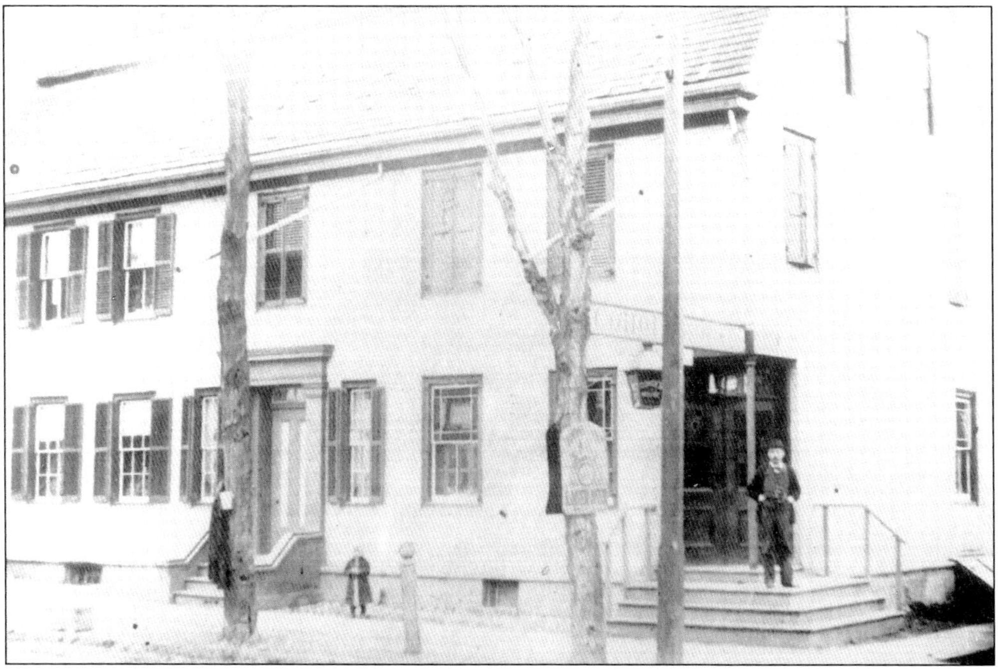

Another View of 499 Second Avenue, Known as the Cohoes House in 1900. Julius Saehrig is standing at the door. The building became Daley's Hotel in 1939 after James E. Daley. It is now known as the Old Daley Inn and offers fine dining. Note the placement of the doorway between the two pictures.

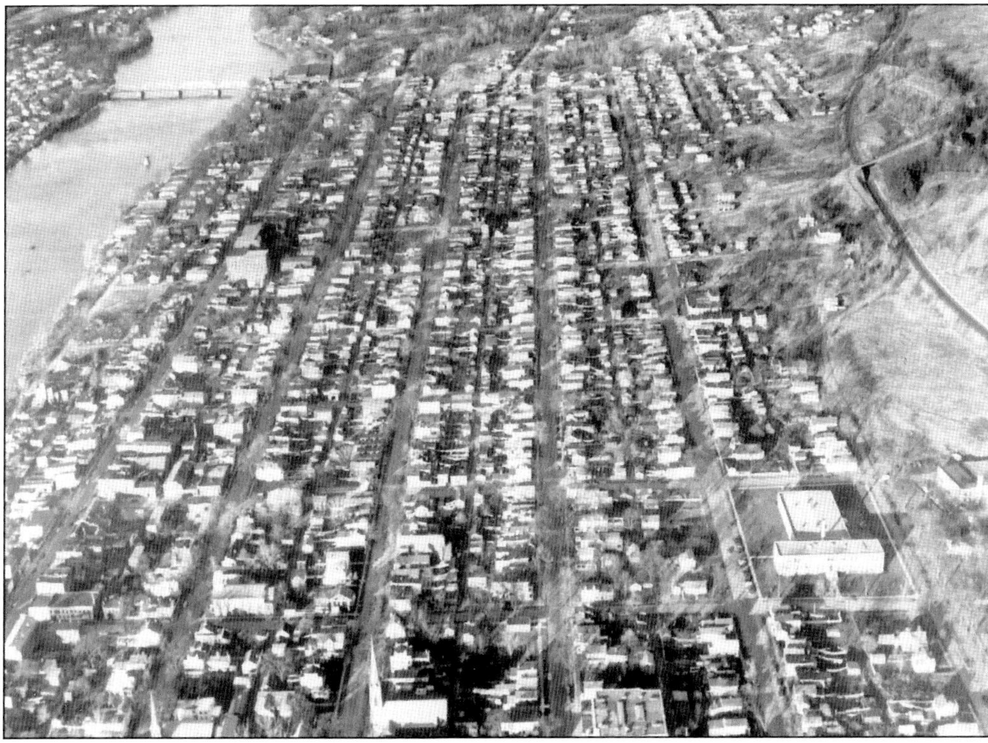

The Northern Part of Lansingburgh in the 1950s from about 112th Street, Looking North. Notice the well laid out streets and alleys, and the railroad track that hugs the hill. The Waterford Bridge can be seen at the top left. Lansing laid out his "city" in an orderly fashion.

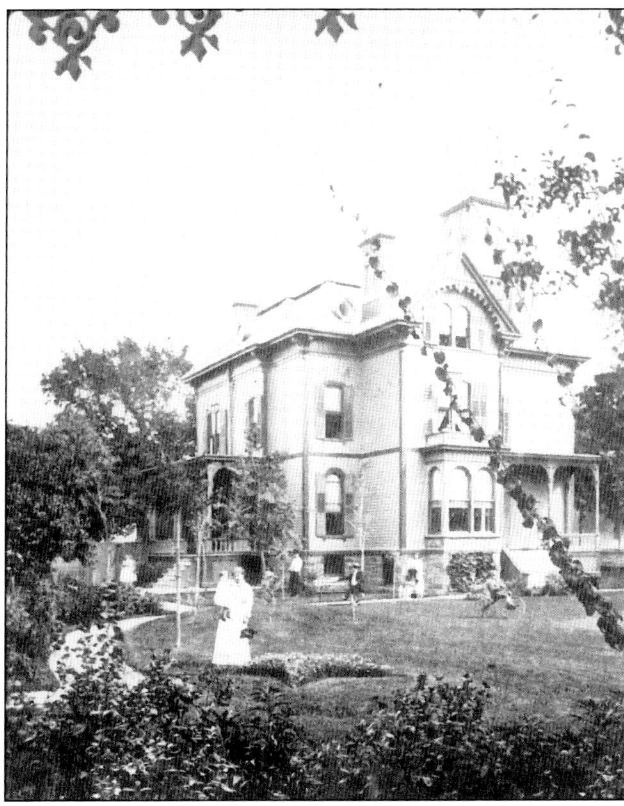

The South Side of the LeGrand Benedict Mansion. This expansive building originally cost $70,000 to build, with the octagonally shaped sidewalks costing an additional $6,000. It was also the home of Major-General Joseph Bradford Carr, a Civil War hero and New York's secretary of state in 1879. Carr is buried in Oakwood Cemetery.

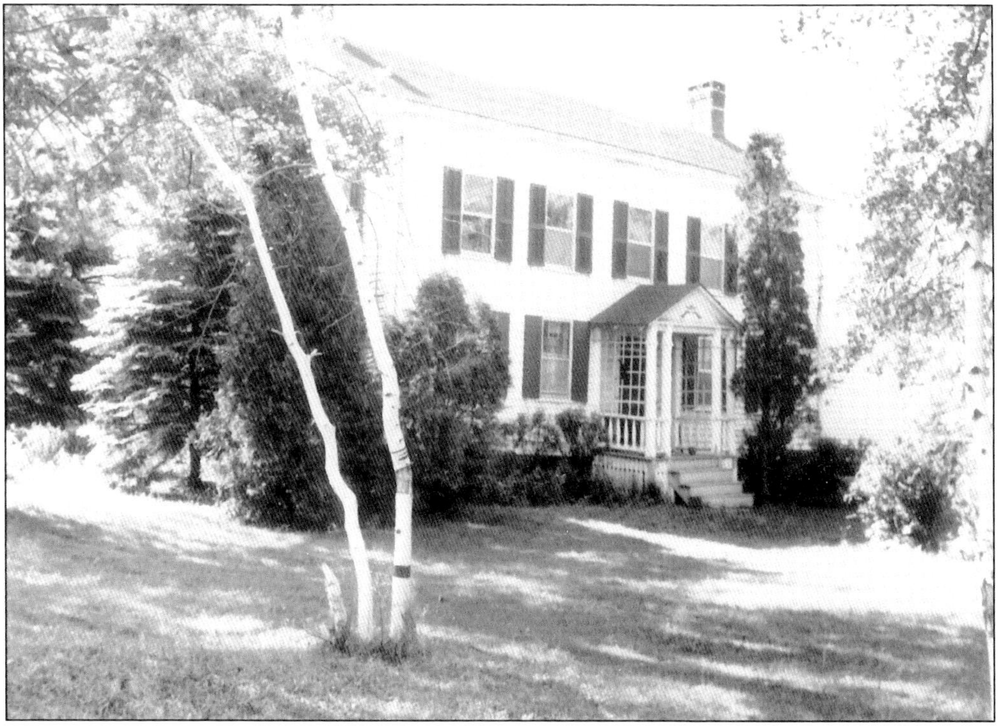

ABRAHAM JACOB LANSING'S FARMHOUSE, BUILT IN 1765 IN WHAT IS NOW PLEASANTDALE. The building is still standing on the River Road to Lansing or Halfmoon Ferry.

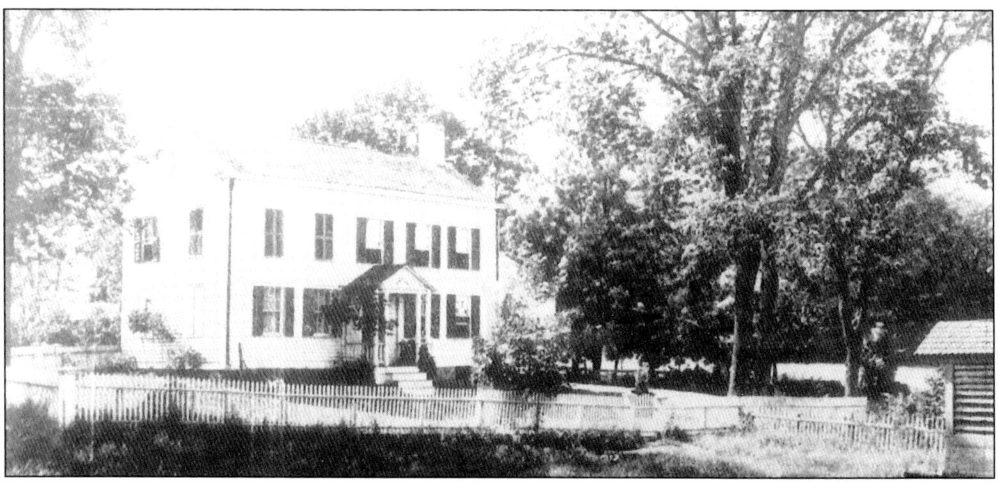

ANOTHER VIEW OF THE LANSING HOUSE, WITH THE HUDSON RIVER IN THE BACKGROUND. This home was just a short ride from Lansing's village home, which was destroyed for a supermarket in the 1960s.

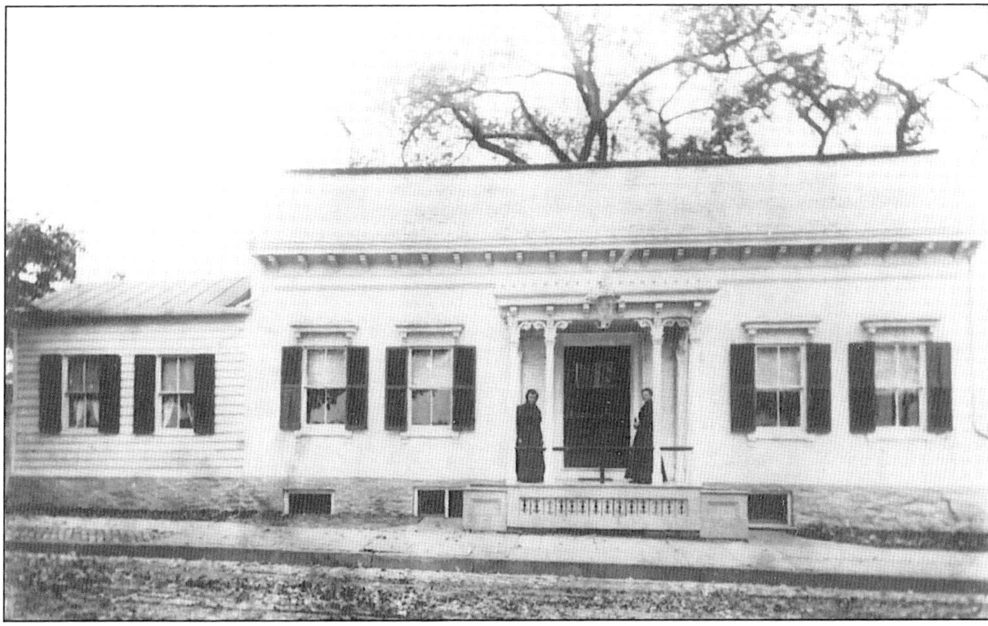

AN EARLY DUTCH HOUSE ON FIRST AVENUE, ANOTHER SURVIVING EXAMPLE OF DUTCH ARCHITECTURE IN LANSINGBURGH. This building faces west on the Hudson River. First Avenue is the thoroughfare that runs along the river and was the center of many a river-based business. The doctor's house at left was once the home of Dr. Aaron B. Hinman.

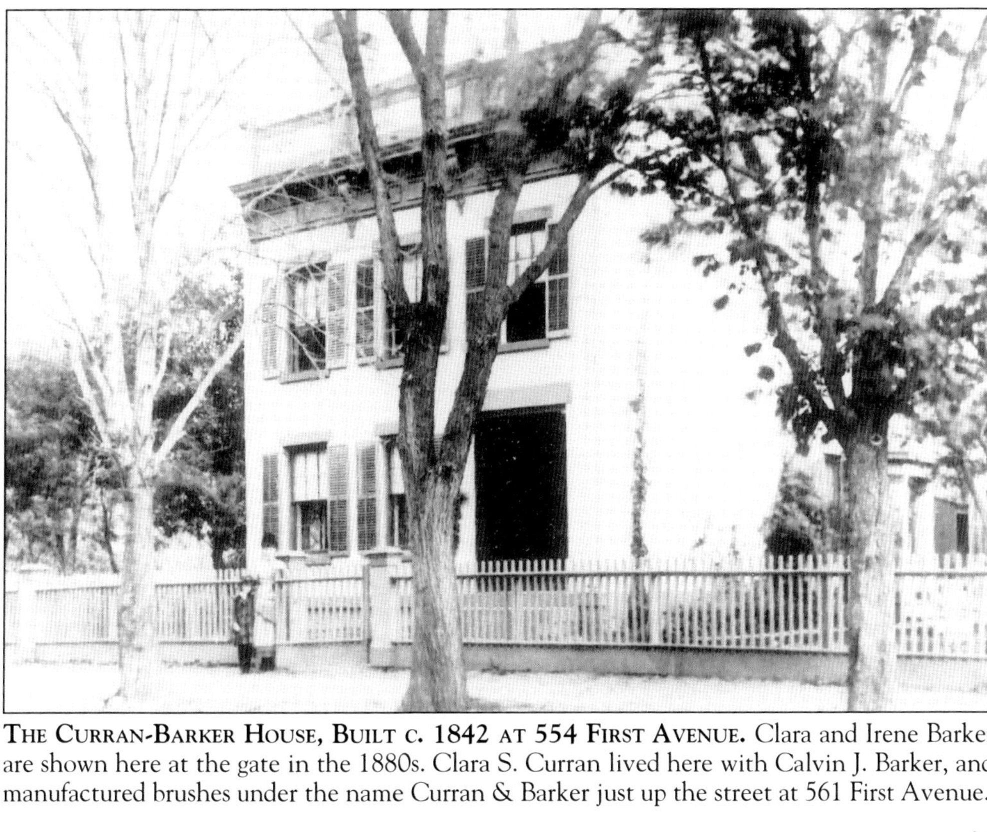

THE CURRAN-BARKER HOUSE, BUILT C. 1842 AT 554 FIRST AVENUE. Clara and Irene Barker are shown here at the gate in the 1880s. Clara S. Curran lived here with Calvin J. Barker, and manufactured brushes under the name Curran & Barker just up the street at 561 First Avenue.

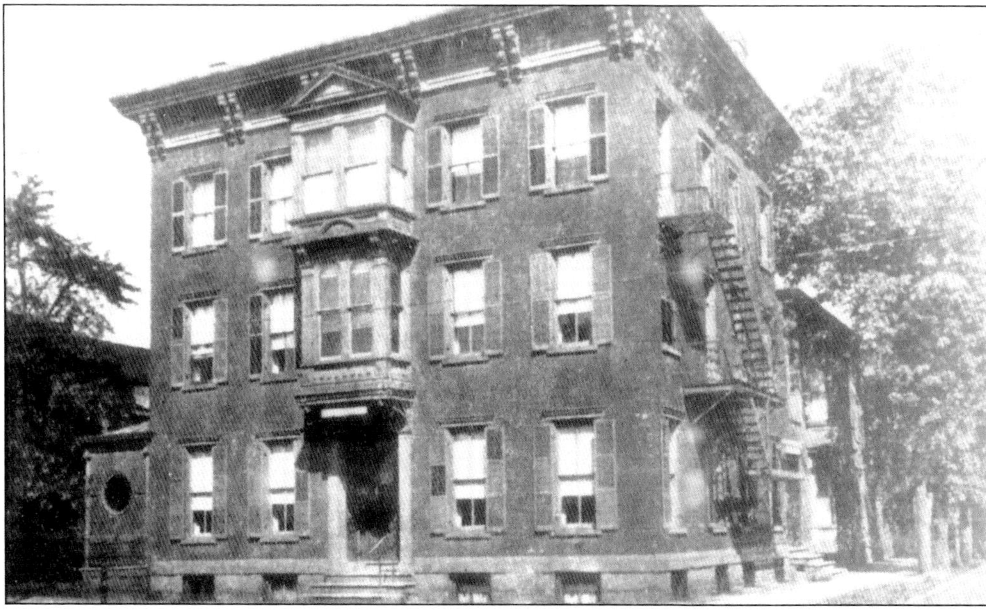

The Bethesda Home for Aged Women at 504 Second Avenue. The home, organized in April 1901 for homeless and friendless girls and women, left Lansingburgh and moved to Watervliet across the river on Third Avenue and 18th Street in 1909. In November 1920, they purchased this building, built by brushmaker John Ames in 1872, and moved back to Lansingburgh.

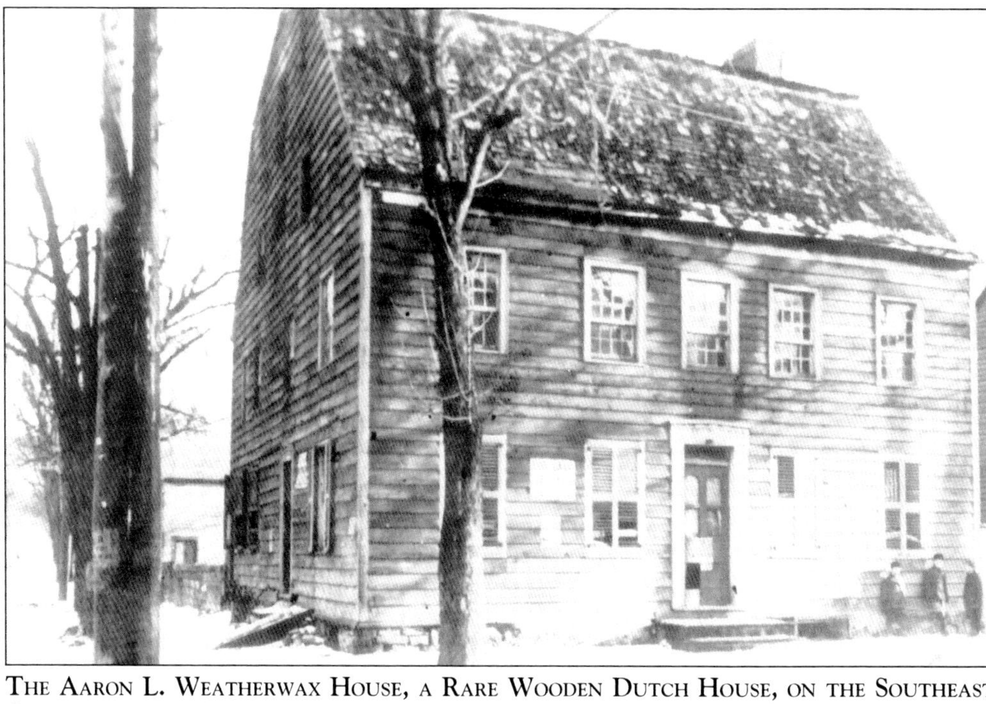

The Aaron L. Weatherwax House, a Rare Wooden Dutch House, on the Southeast Corner of 115th Street and 562 Second Avenue. This building was eventually demolished and a three-story brick house was erected on the site. Ironically, there is a "For Sale" on the front of the building. Weatherwax was a shoemaker.

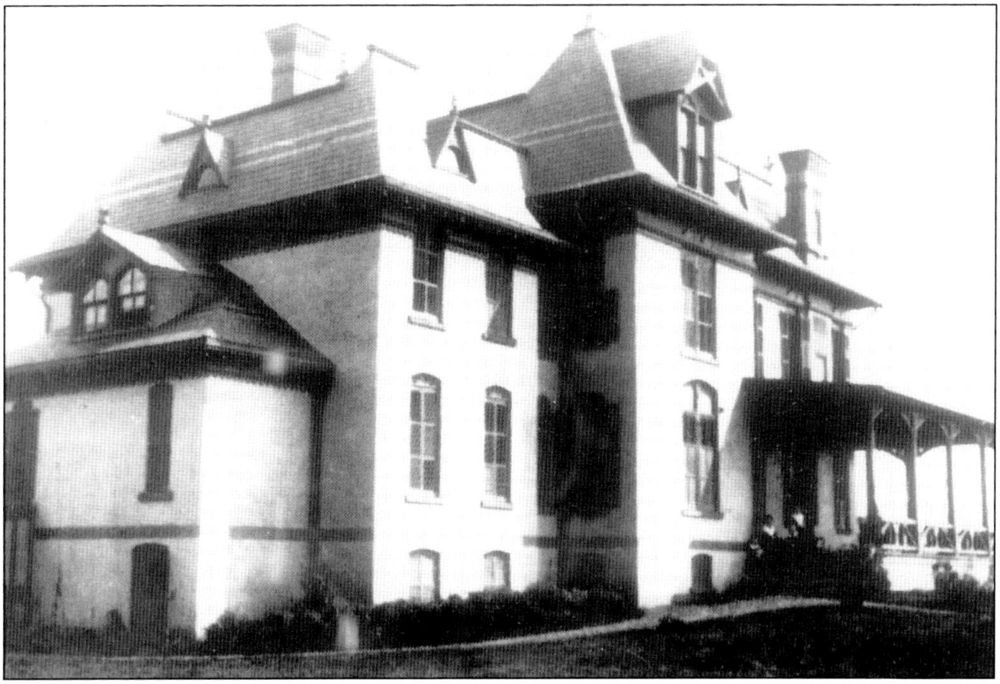

Cool Ridge Acres on Gurley Avenue, Built in 1879. Also known as the Paul Cook Mansion, the building was later used by the Garden Way Company. The site overlooks the Hudson River flood plain that the village of Lansingburgh sits upon.

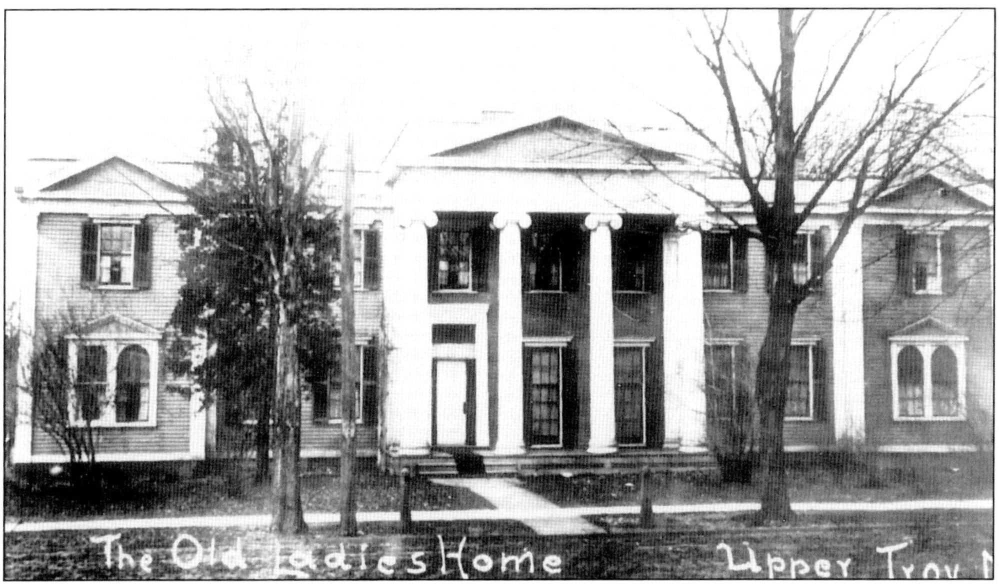

The Deborah Powers Home for Old Ladies. In 1882 at age 93, D. Powers devoted part of her property for the use of the less fortunate. This site on Third Avenue, 123rd Street, and Second Avenue was purchased on April 10, 1883. It was the former Daniel Davenport homestead, remodeled and with another story placed on both wings. Originally built in 1846, the homestead is on the National Register of Historic Places.

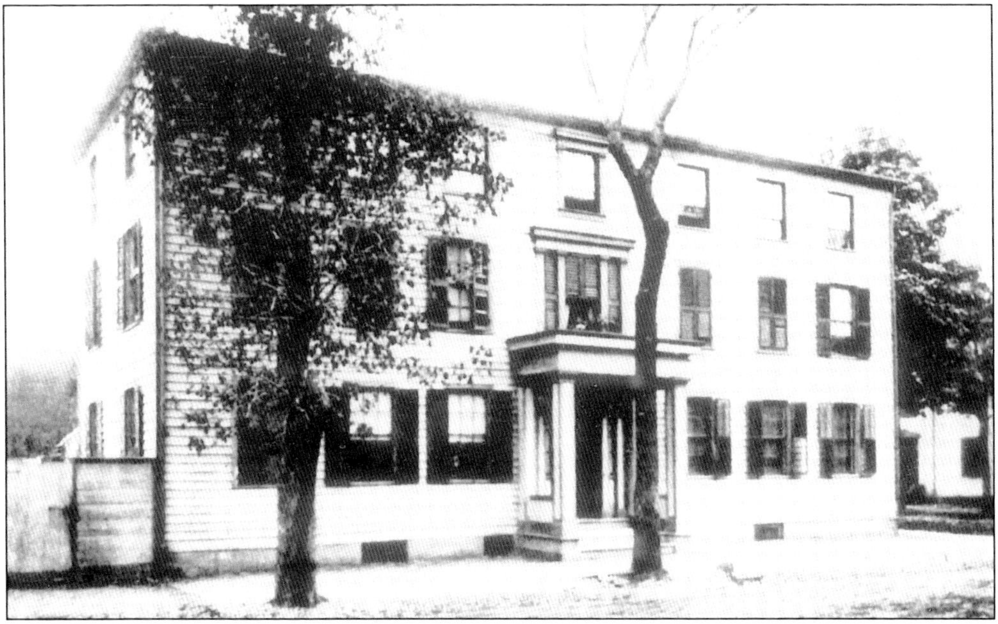

THE SOUTHEAST CORNER OF 113TH STREET AND SECOND AVENUE. Rev. Samuel Blatchford lived here from 1804 to 1828, although the house pre-dated 1804. General Lafayette entertained here during the day on July 1, 1825. Later in the day, he went to Troy and visited with Emma Willard. Lafayette was on a New England tour.

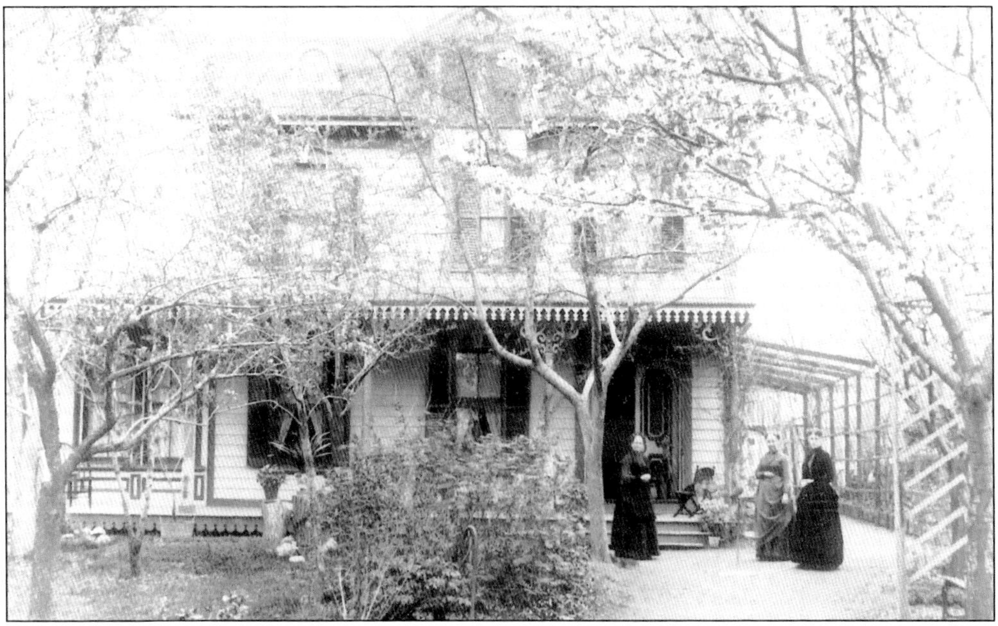

THE EAST SIDE OF THE IDA MUNN HOUSE, 102 SECOND AVENUE, NORTH OF 102ND STREET. Ida Munn inherited this house from her parents, Rufus S. and Elizabeth A. Munn. The Lansing family also owned the house in Lansingburgh's early years. The Rensselaer County Junior Museum used the building, which was remodelled in the 1870s, for many years. The museum took one area of the house and converted it to a log cabin. I spent many a day at the museum as a boy and later worked there as a college student.

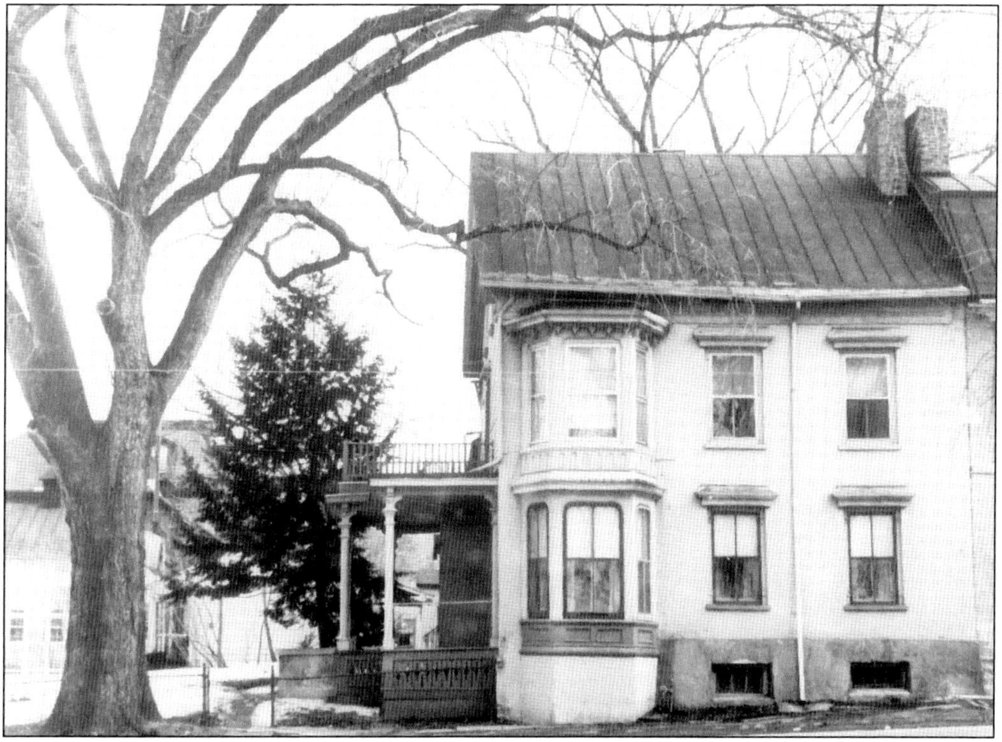

HERMAN MELVILLE'S HOME, FIRST AVENUE AND 114TH STREET. Famed novelist Herman Melville, best known for *Moby Dick*, spent his youth here and wrote his first two novels at this house. It is now the Lansingburgh Historical Society. The house is also interesting in that its entrance is not on First Avenue, like the other homes in the area.

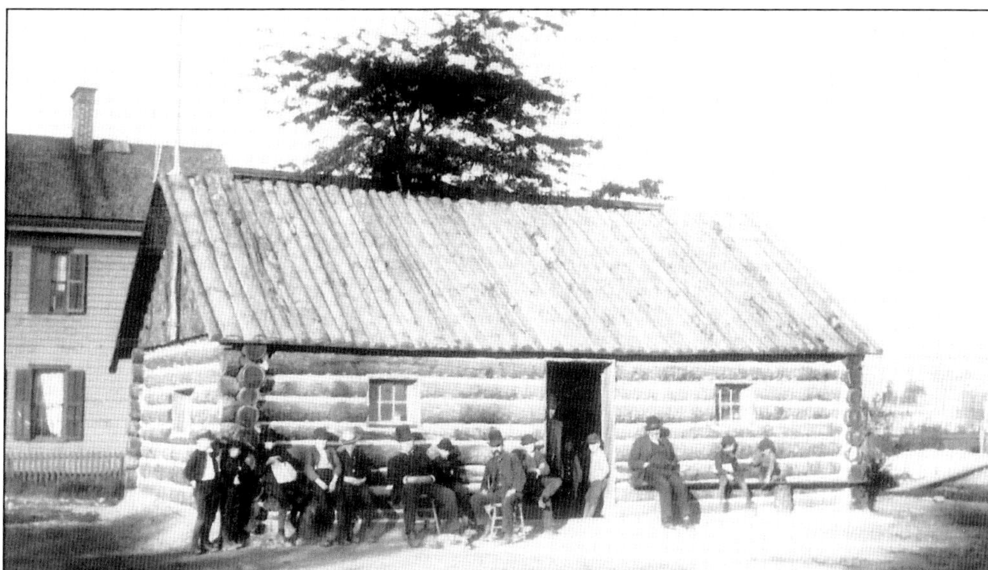

THE LOG CABIN BUILT IN 1876 AT FIRST AVENUE AND 122ND STREET FOR THE CENTENNIAL CELEBRATION. This appears to be a reenactment of an earlier way of life, although it is unlikely there were many log cabins in Lansingburgh.

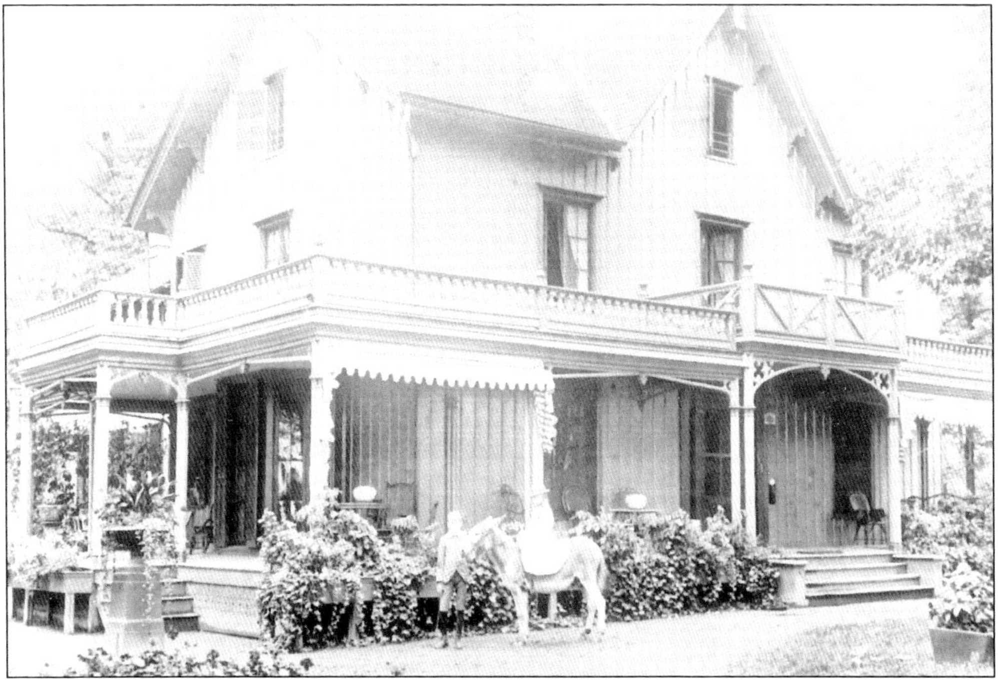

"Oaklands," Set back on Seventh Avenue just North of 103rd Street. This mansion, owned by George and Sarah Gould, remains standing. Each summer Sarah Gould invited all the children from the Troy Orphanage to spend a day at the estate enjoying pony rides and strawberries and cream. She died here in 1899.

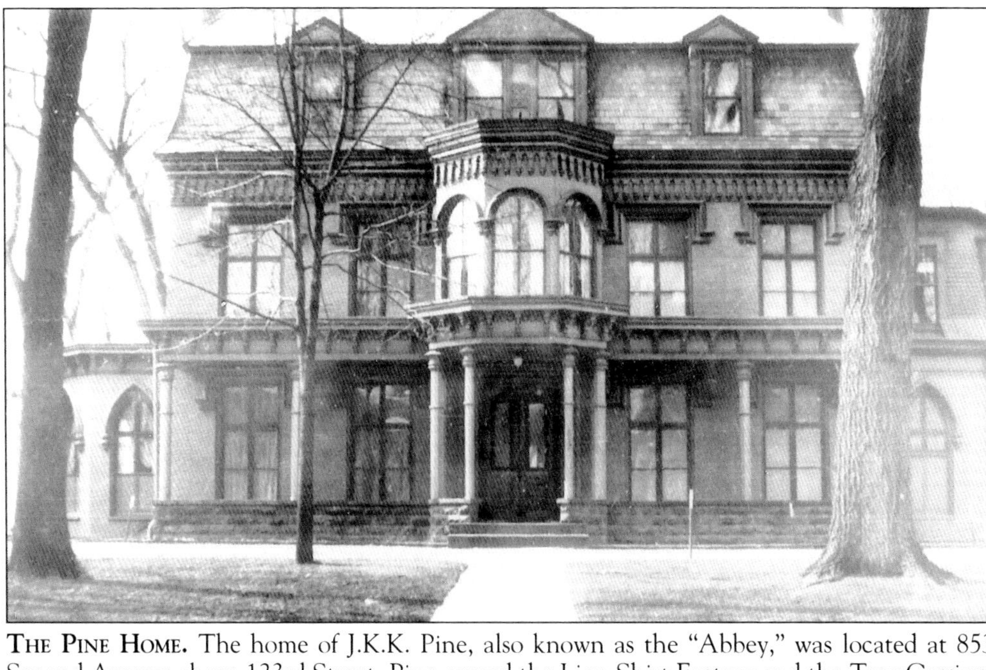

The Pine Home. The home of J.K.K. Pine, also known as the "Abbey," was located at 853 Second Avenue above 123rd Street. Pine owned the Lion Shirt Factory and the Troy Carriage Works, and was president of The People's Bank, all in Lansingburgh. This house is actually an earlier Dutch house, built by Abraham Jacob Lansing's son Cornelius.

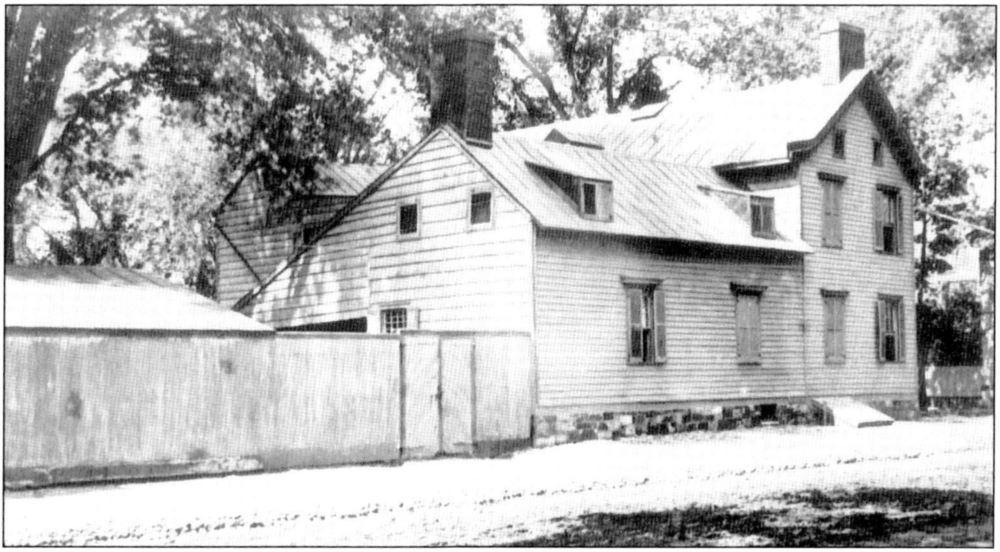

THE ANTHONY AUGUSTUS PEEBLES HOUSE AT THE SOUTHEAST CORNER OF 534 THIRD AVENUE AND 114TH STREET. Aaron Burr was supposedly hidden here for some time after his famous duel in 1804. Cadwallader Colden, a friend of Burr and the nephew of Governor of New York Morgan Lewis, owned the house at the time. Mary L. Parmelee (1834–1915), the wife of A.A. Peebles (1822–1905), was an author of note and wrote many books in Lansingburgh under the name of Lynde Palmer.

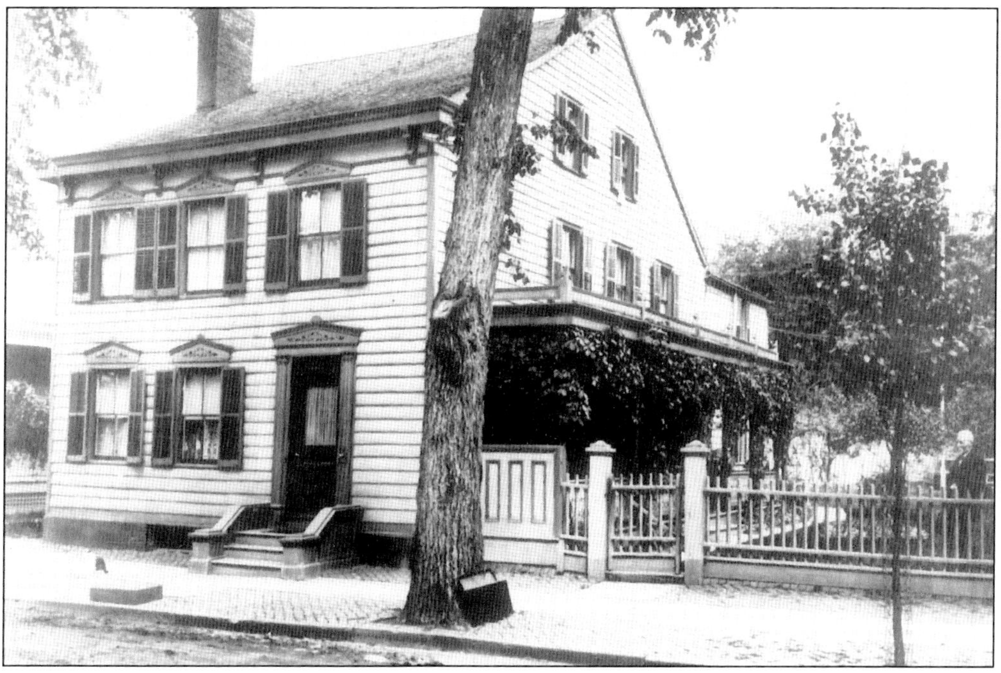

A C. 1912 PHOTOGRAPH OF 696 THIRD AVENUE. Painter George Henry Babcock (1838–1914) is in the yard. Notice the stone foot stool for getting out of carriages on the front curb. Homes often had wrought- or cast-iron boot scrapers to keep mud out, and hitching posts out front. A few of these relics survive around homes on First Avenue and Third Avenue. This house is still standing.

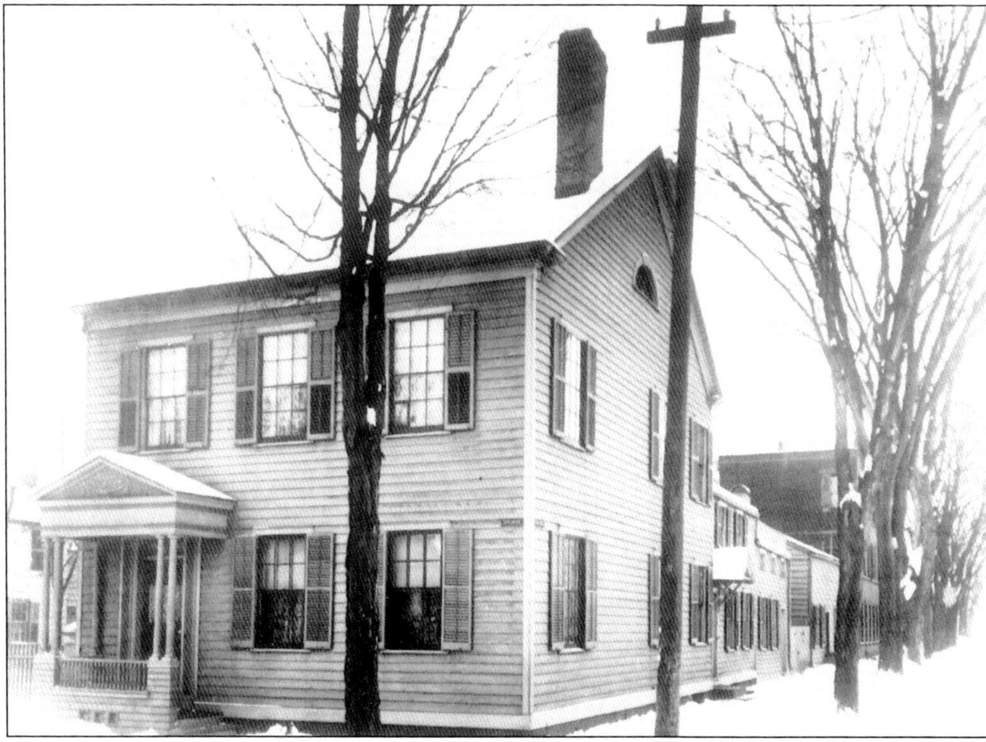

The House of Cabinetmaker Seth Seeyle at the Southwest Corner of Third Avenue and 116th Street. His shop was in the rear. The house was demolished for the Lansingburgh Methodist Church Hall.

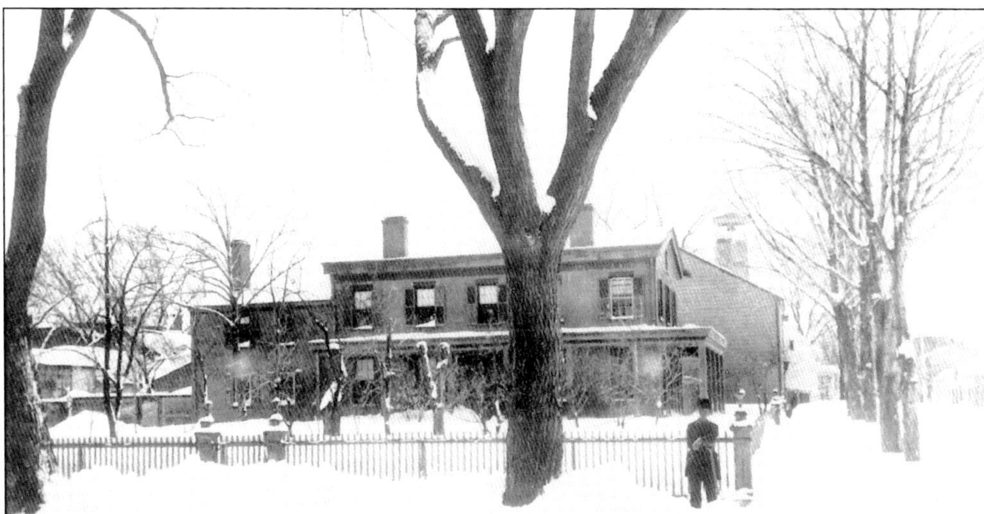

The Eliza Bates House at the Southeast Corner of First Avenue and No. 2 116th Street. This is the site of the present post office. The post office was housed in the Phoenix Hotel and Masonic Temple before it finally got its own building.

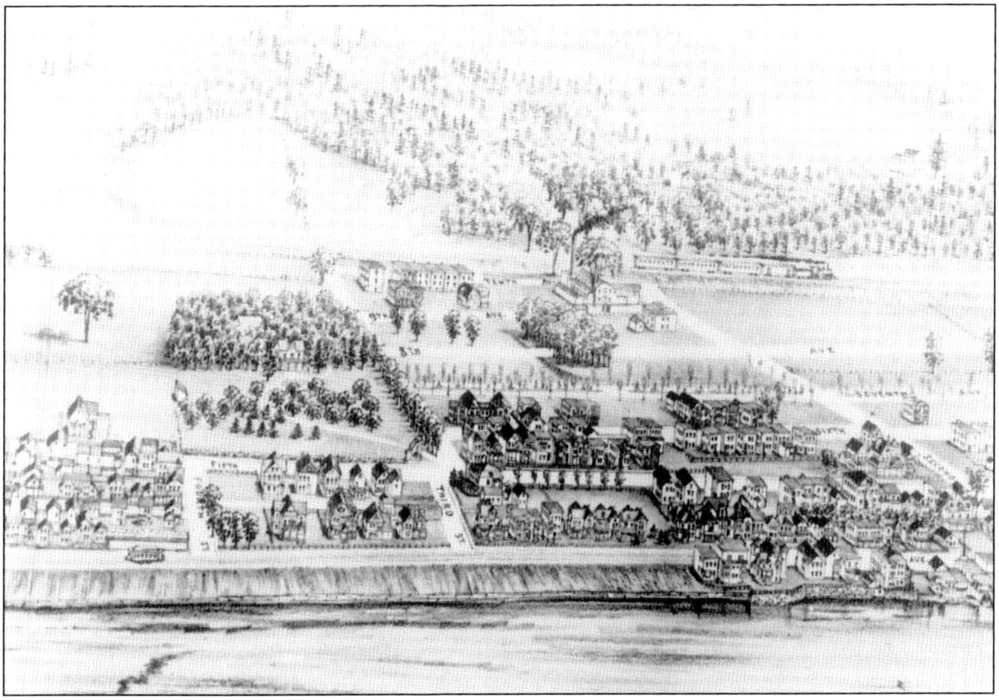

A Lithograph of Lansingburgh Showing the Gould Estate at 103rd Street in 1891. "Oaklands" was the name given to the (George and Sarah) Gould Mansion. The building is still standing. Each summer Sarah Gould invited all the children from the Troy Orphanage to spend a day at the estate.

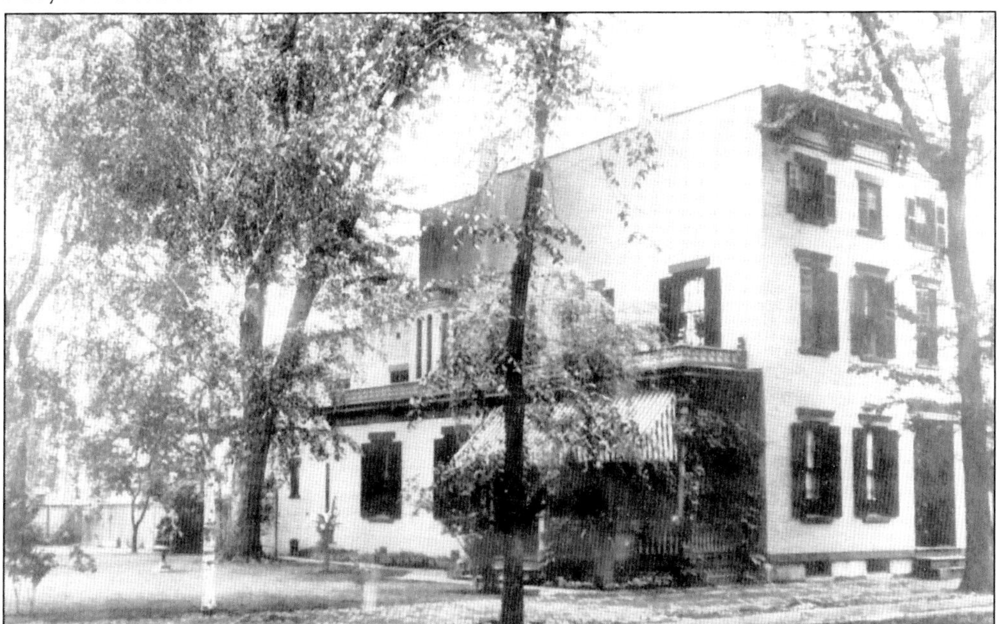

The Kellogg Family House at Third Avenue, the First Building North of 114th Street on the West Side. Salesman Frank P. Kellogg, who lived at 541 Third Avenue, probably owned this structure.

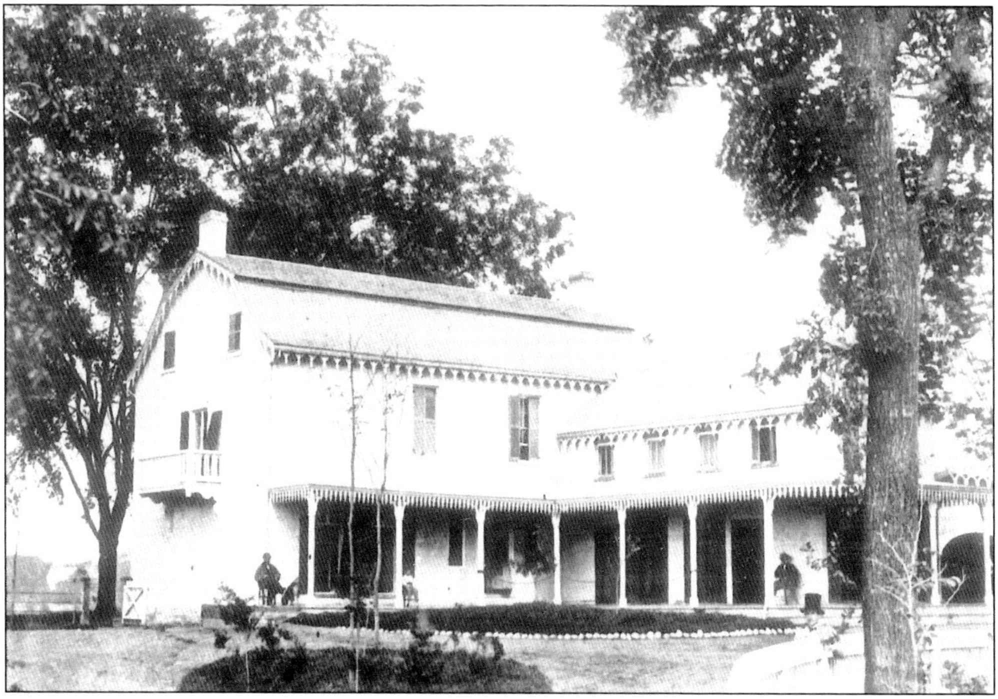

The Abbey, a Dutch House on the West Side of Second Avenue Built c. 1700s by Cornelius Lansing. Businessman J.K.P. Pine remodeled this house after purchasing it in the late 1800s.

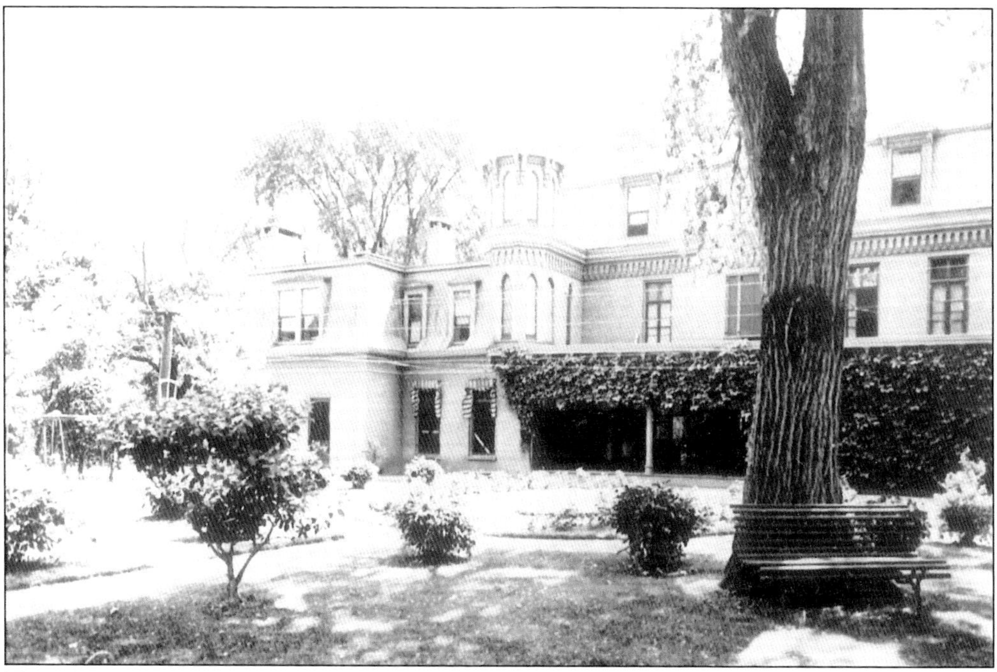

The Abbey after Being Remodelled. The original front, which faced the Hudson, was remodelled to become the back. The now-demolished building was on the west side of Second Avenue, north of 123rd Street.

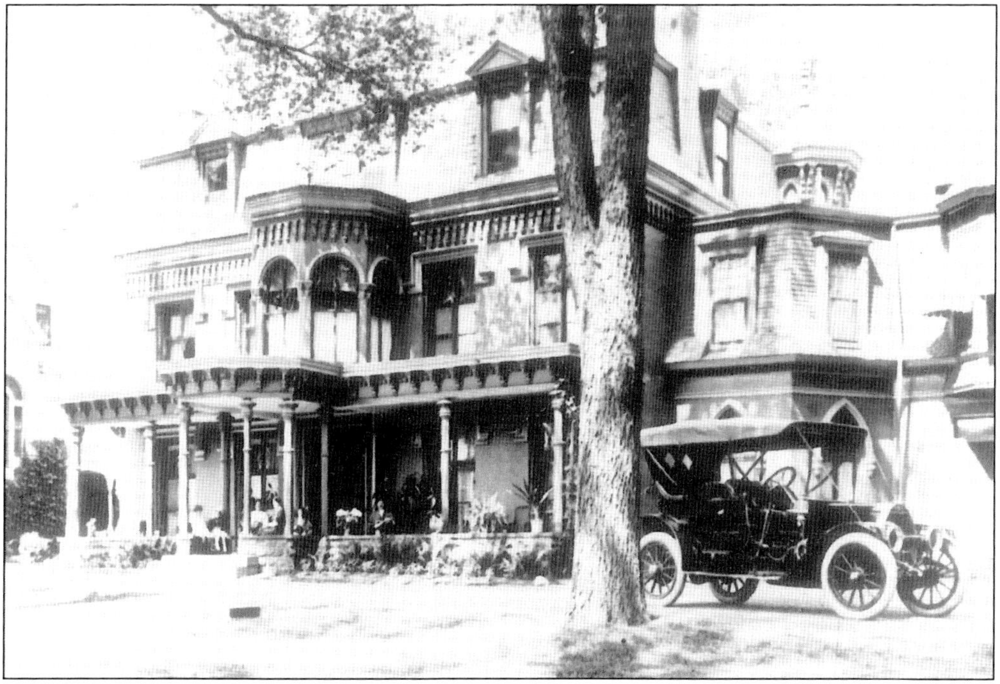

ANOTHER VIEW OF THE ABBEY AFTER BEING REMOLDED BY PINE. From this photograph, one would never guess the building was originally the Cornelius Lansing Dutch house of 1770.

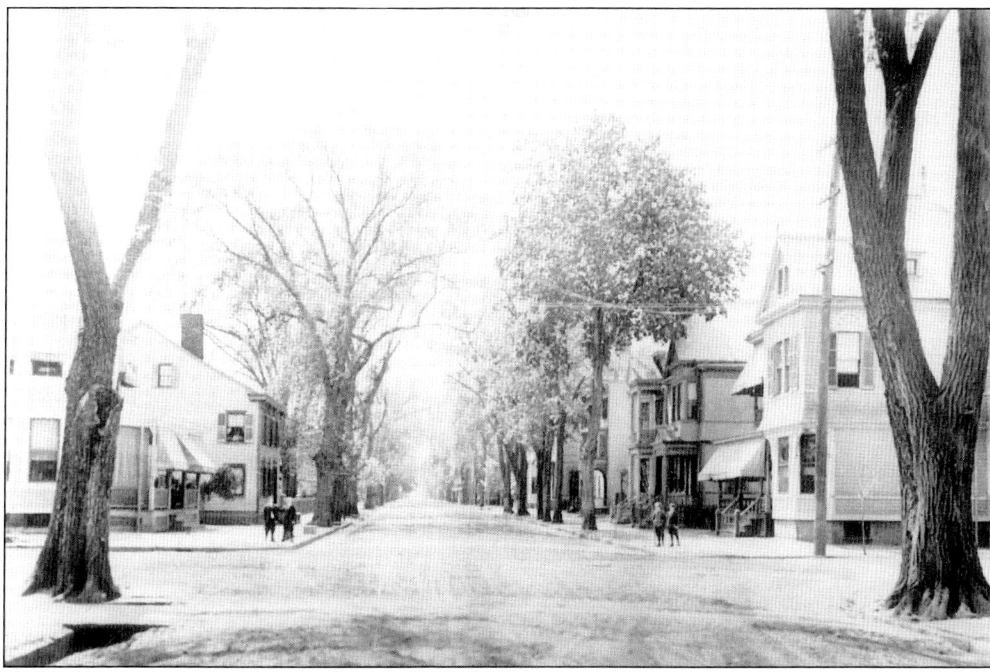

THE INTERSECTION OF THIRD AVENUE AND 115TH STREET, LOOKING SOUTH. Notice the unpaved roads and tree-lined streets devoid of the noise and pollution of automobiles. Certain parts of Lansingburgh still preserve this tranquil setting.

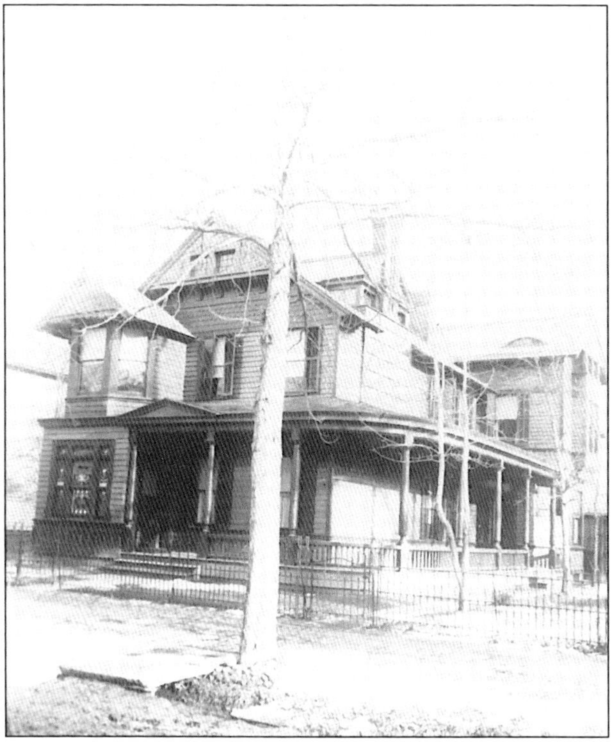

The Warren Todd Kellogg Residence on 450 Second Avenue. Todd was the manager of the Empire Forge Company at 464 Fourth Avenue. This sturdy home still stands.

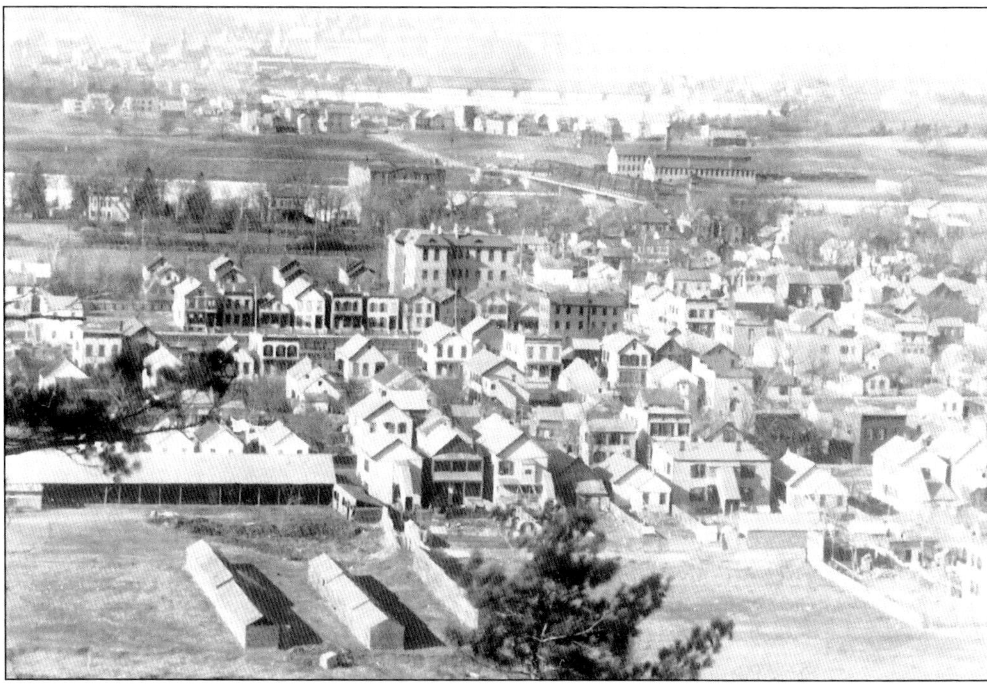

An Aerial View of Lansingburgh Looking West, Probably from the Oakwood Cemetery. Rensselaer Park is visible at the bottom of the image. Cohoes Bridge and mist of the Cohoes Falls can be seen in middle top, along with the Haskell Oilcloth Factory on the riverbank and the Powers School in the near background.

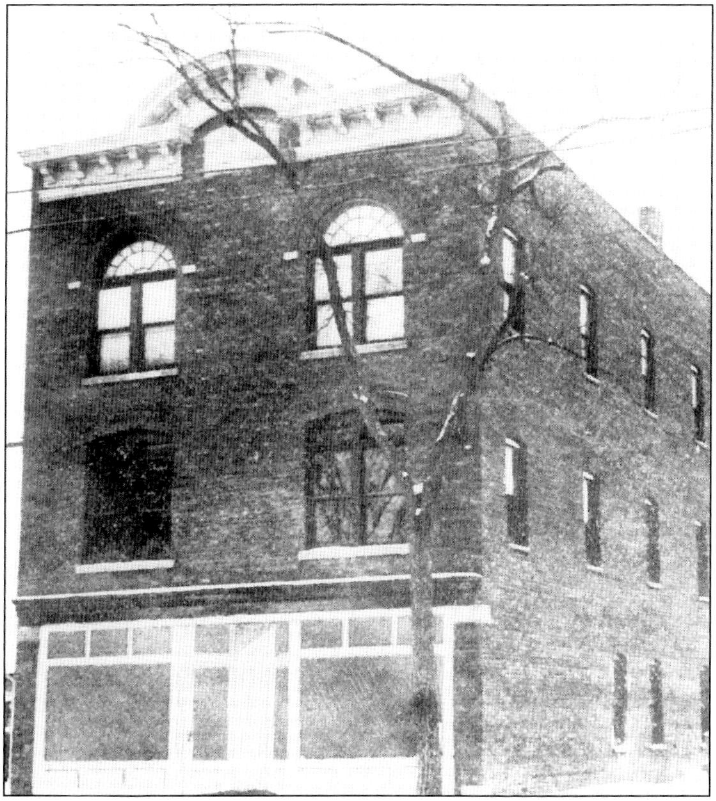

THE NEW ODD FELLOWS TEMPLE, BUILT IN 1909 ON 112TH STREET BETWEEN FOURTH AND FIFTH AVENUES. The Lansingburgh Rebekah Lodge met here. The first Odd Fellows group in Lansingburgh was the Star Lodge No. 20. Created after 1841, it was forced to give up its charter in 1861 because most of its members were fighting in the Civil War.

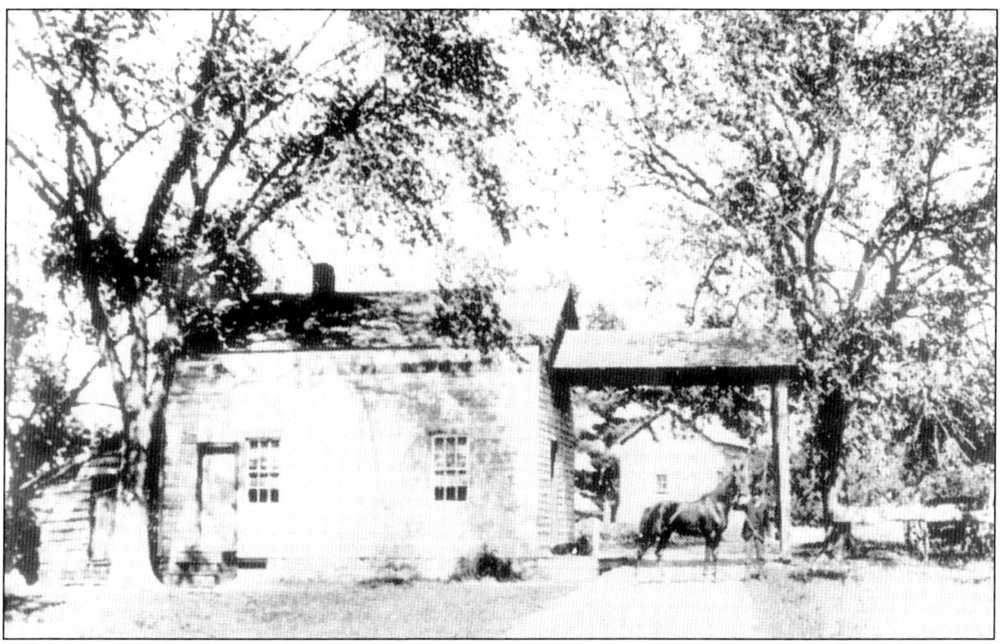

THE OLD TOLL GATE IN PLEASANTDALE ON THE HUDSON RIVER TURNPIKE. This road that connected Lansingburgh to Schaghticoke is now called River Road. Portions of Fifth Avenue were planked and had tolls as well.

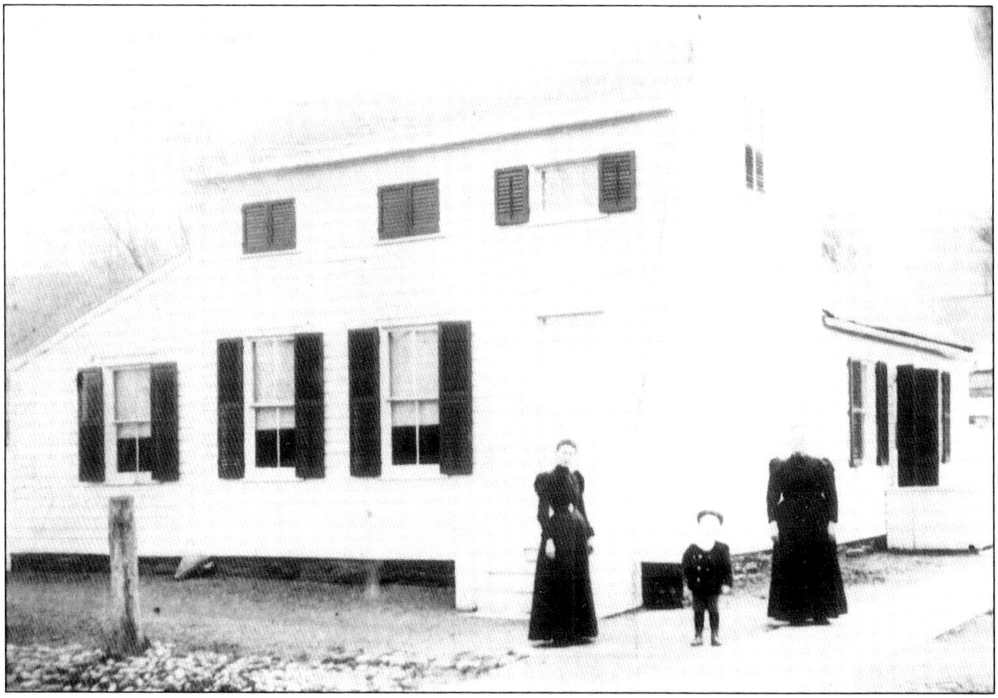

No. 632 Sixth Avenue. Home of Morris Kirkpatrick, captain of Lansingburgh Police Precint. Woman standing on left is Mrs. Ella Groesbeck, his sister. The little boy is William Groesbeck, her son, and woman to right is Mrs. Agnus Kirkpatrick, mother of Ella.

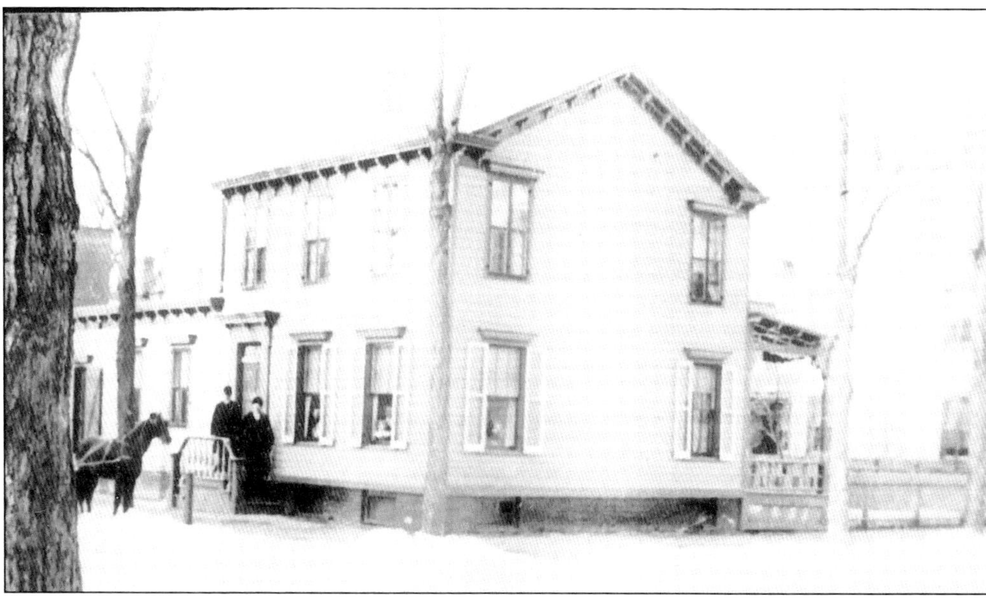

The George A. Flack Home at No. 15 116th Street, c. 1890. George Flack owned Flack & Co., wholesale grocers and flour dealers, at 375 River Street in Troy. The company supplied tea, coffee, sugar, molasses, rice, and advertised that feed seeds were their speciality. Isaac G. Flack and Charles I. Flack were partners.

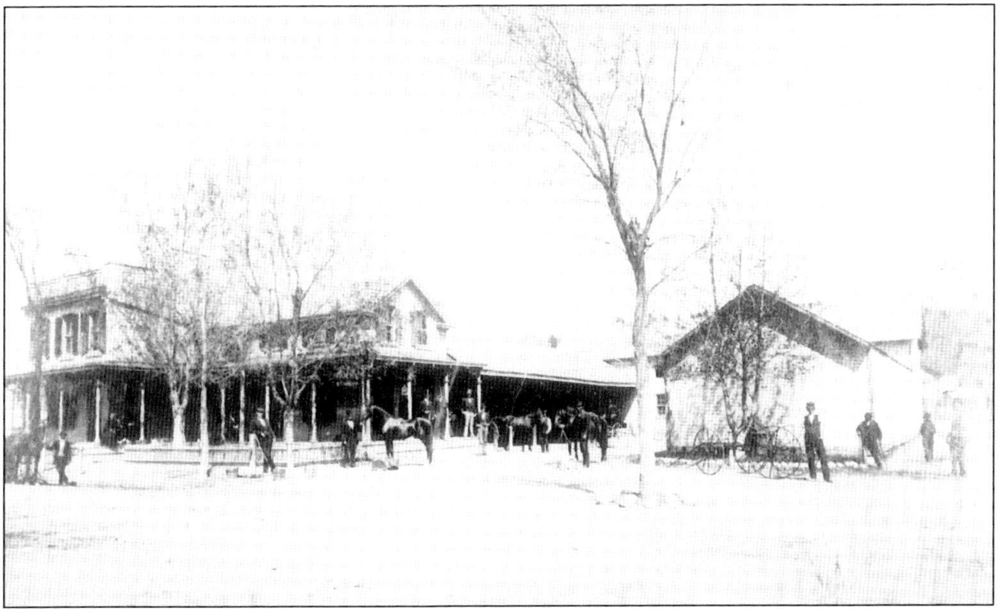

THE PARK HOTEL AT THE NORTHEAST CORNER OF FIFTH AVENUE AND 112TH STREET. Owned by W.F. Armstrong, this view looks more like the Wild West with no sidewalks and ample space for horses to roam. It is amazing how an area can be transformed. Stand on this corner today and try to imagine the site only 80 years ago.

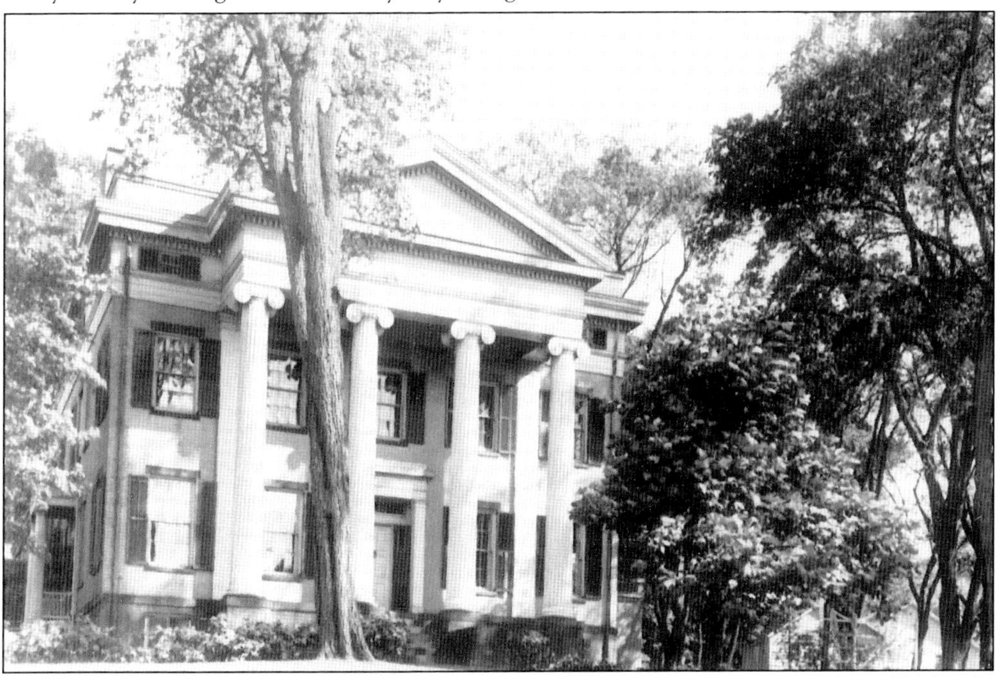

"GLENWOOD," THE TITUS EDDY HOME, LOCATED OFF OAKWOOD AVENUE. The Eddy family entertained the Burgh's gentry in this home, which was actually located in Troy, just over the border of Lansingburgh. The structure now serves as offices for the Troy Housing Authority. The Eddy family made a fortune by providing the secret ink that was used for printing all American paper currency until World War I.

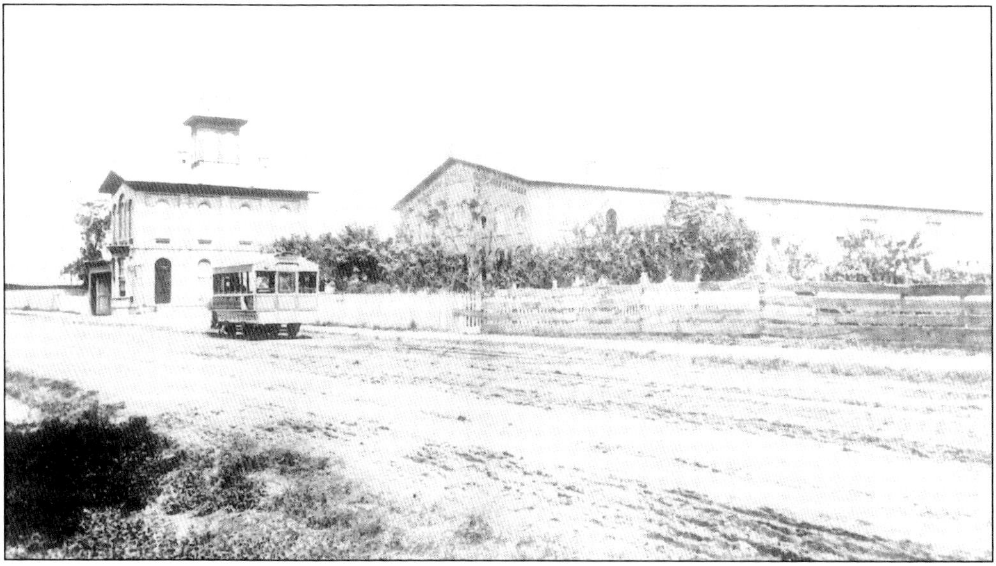

Early Car Barns for the Troy and Lansingburgh Horse Railway on Second Avenue near 102nd Street. This site later became the home of Ludlow Valve. Now a residential area, it is hard to imagine the area as a commercial enterprise. Ludlow Valve became world famous for their products.

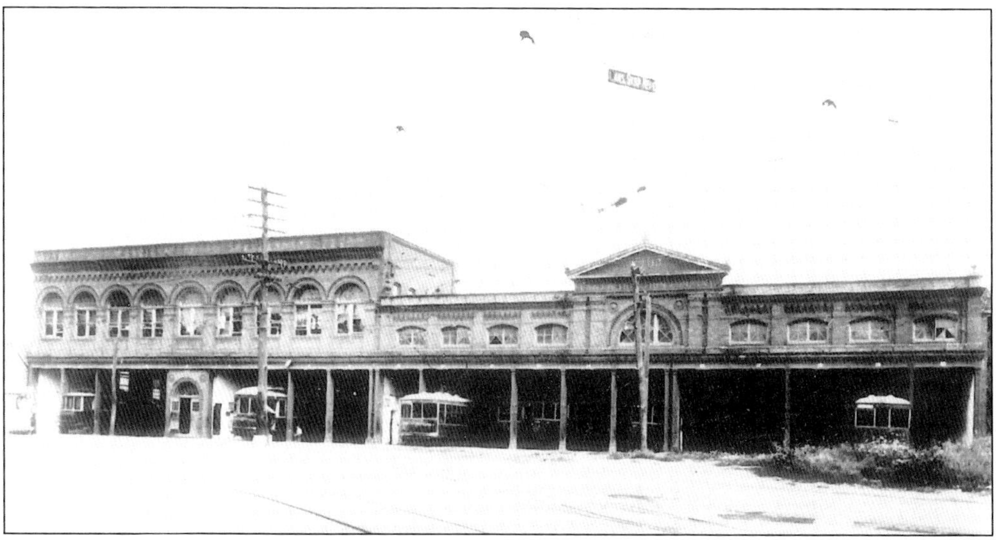

Trolley Barns of the United Traction Company. After the car barns in the image at the top of the page were taken over by Ludlow, this trolley barn was built near the northern limits of the village. All trolleys became electrified by 1924. They were stored here near the Waterford Bridge, as were the earlier horse-drawn cars. The first electric cars ran from 101st Street to the Waterford Bridge using the Sprague electric, single overhead trolley-wire system in 1889.

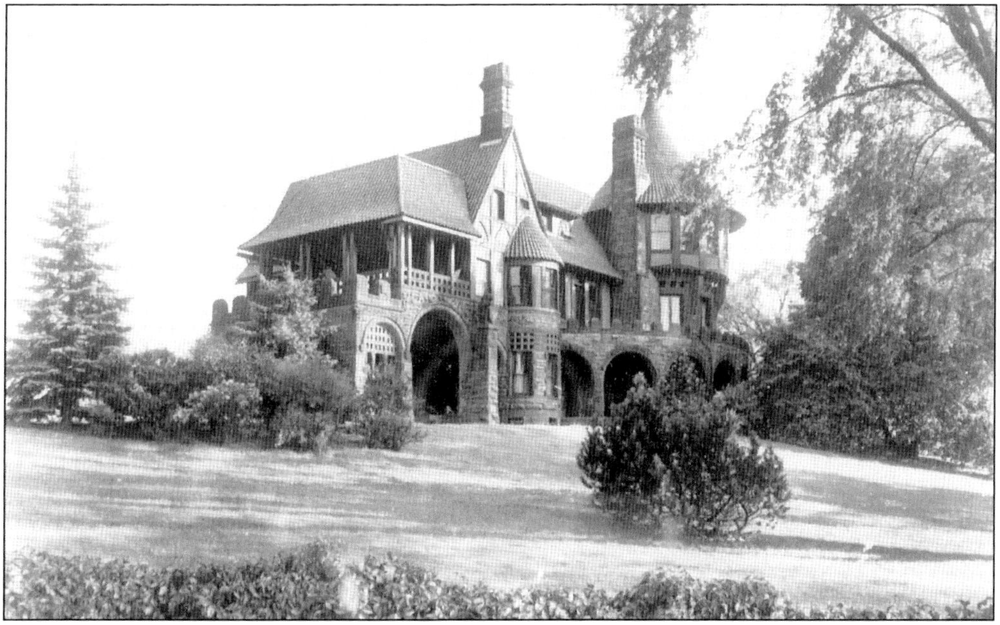

BORADAILE, THE ESTATE OF THE DAWES FAMILY NEAR DIAMOND ROCK. Formerly one of the most impressive homes in the village, it later was turned into a restaurant and then a kennel. Sadly, it burned to the ground while under restoration. It is rumored that local gangster Legs Diamond hid here while he was on the lamb. Diamond was finally killed at a boardinghouse in Albany.

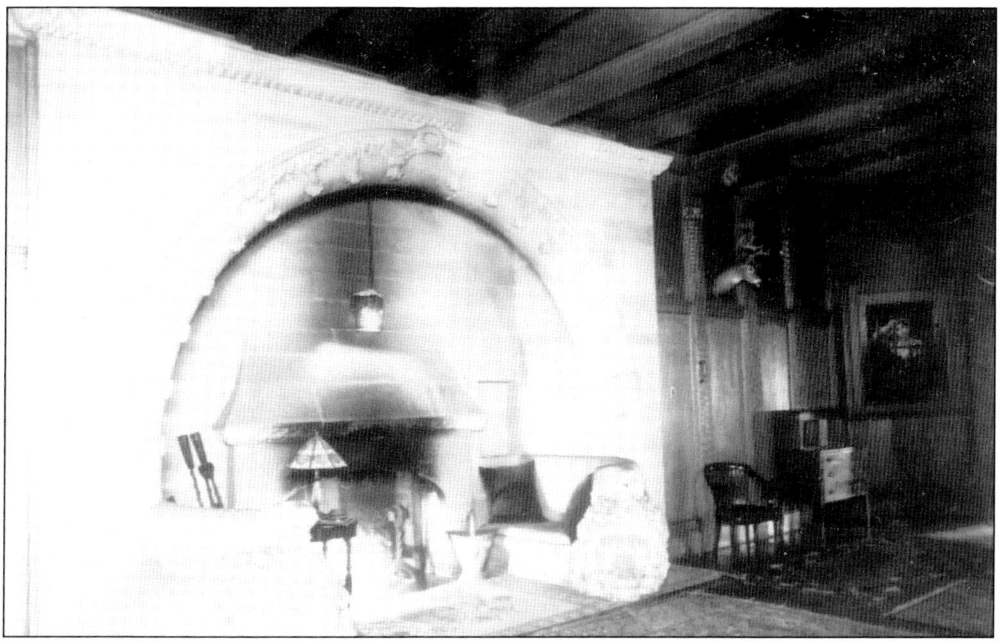

THE FIREPLACE OF BORADAILE. You could sit right in the built-in seats to keep warm. This house had one of the most beautiful interiors in the world. So many one-of-a-kind homes in the village are now gone due to fire, neglect, or being torn down for "progress." It is truly tragic that so much of our history has been wiped out for the benefit of a few.

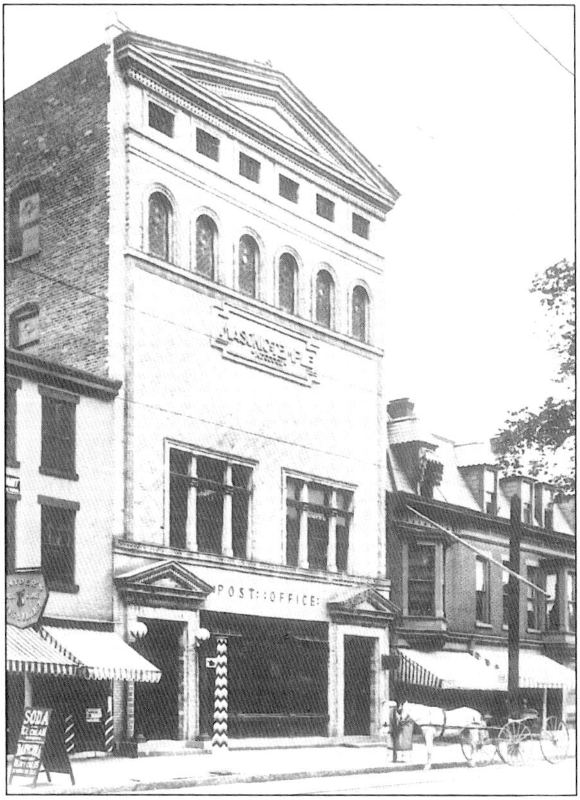

THE MASONIC TEMPLE OR HALL, 635 SECOND AVENUE. This building, constructed *c.* 1902–1903 to house several of the Troy lodges, was built by the Lansingburgh Masonic Temple Association, Inc. The post office used part of the building for years. The building still stands tall and is in use.

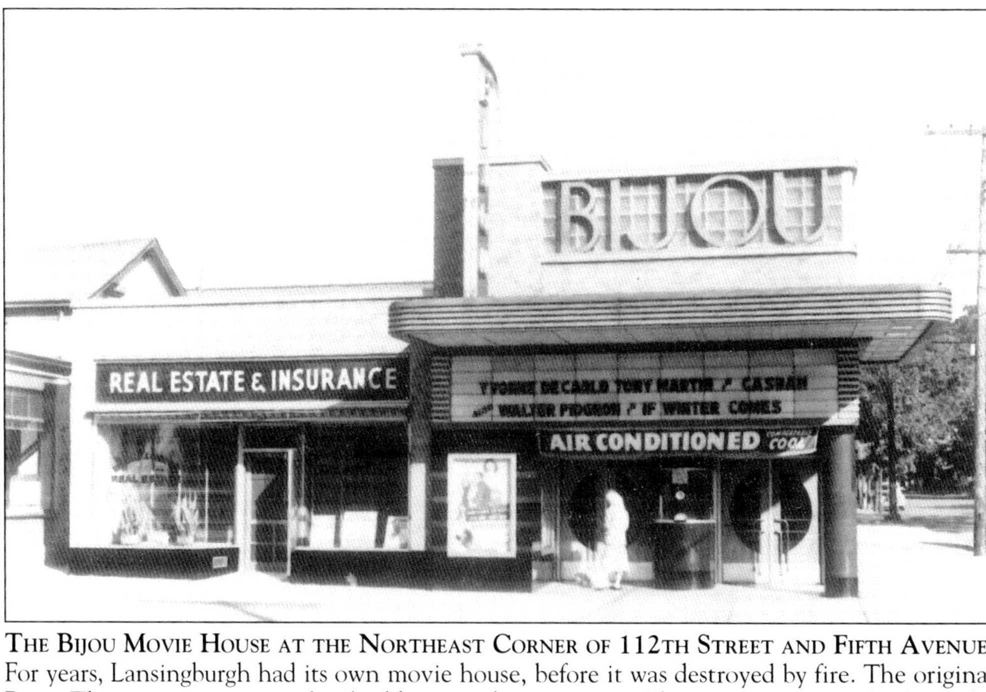

THE BIJOU MOVIE HOUSE AT THE NORTHEAST CORNER OF 112TH STREET AND FIFTH AVENUE. For years, Lansingburgh had its own movie house, before it was destroyed by fire. The original Bijou Theater was in a wooden building on the same site. This newer one was built in the 1930s. There are no movie houses anywhere in Lansingburgh today.

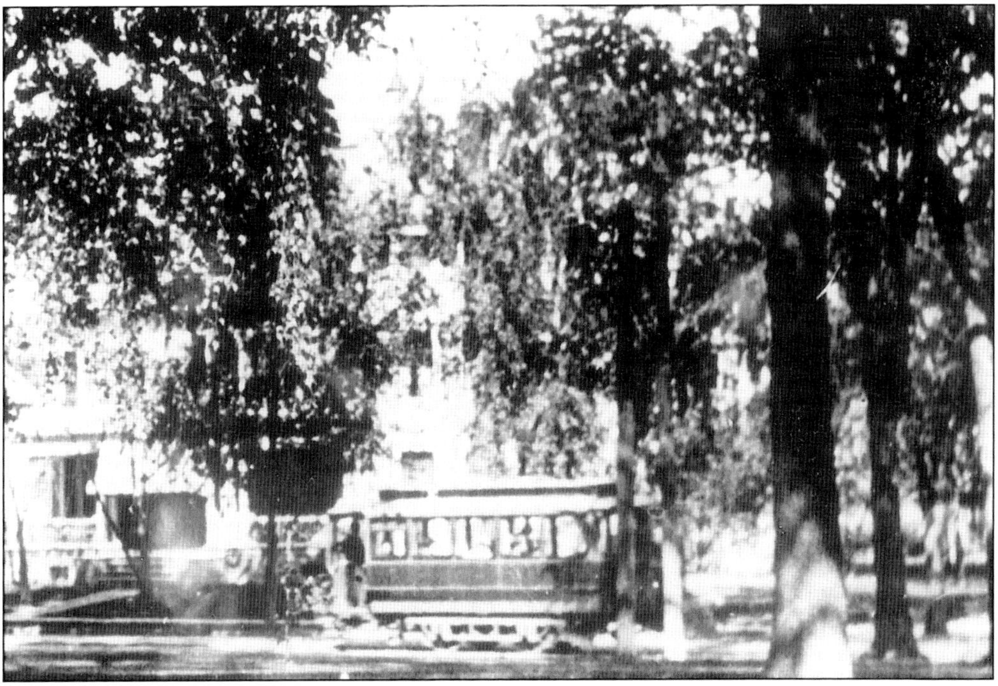

A Trolley Moving Down a Tree-lined Second Avenue. Listening to the clanking of the wheels going over the tracks or the whirring of the engines was probably less intrusive than the sounds of modern automobiles whizzing down the street. The pace of life was not as fast during these times.

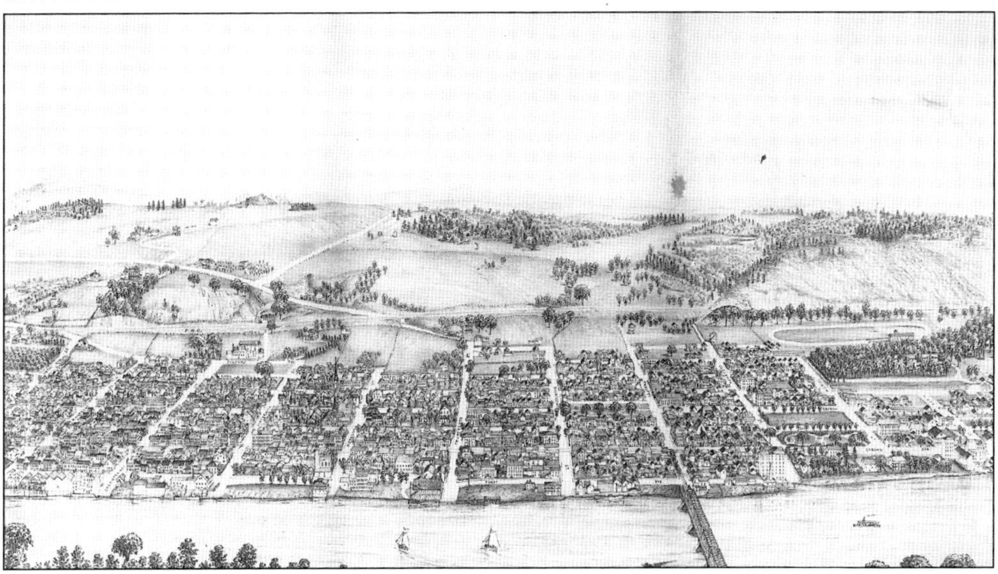

A Burleigh Lithograph of the First and Second Wards. Rensselaer Park is visible to the upper right in this photograph. Notice the half-mile racing track and the lake within it to the right. The grove of trees in front housed the amusement section. The Cohoes Bridge crossed the Hudson. Lucien R. Burleigh had the offices of the Burleigh Lithographing Company on Fulton Street in Troy, but lived at 350 Second Avenue. His lithographs of Lansingburgh are outstanding.

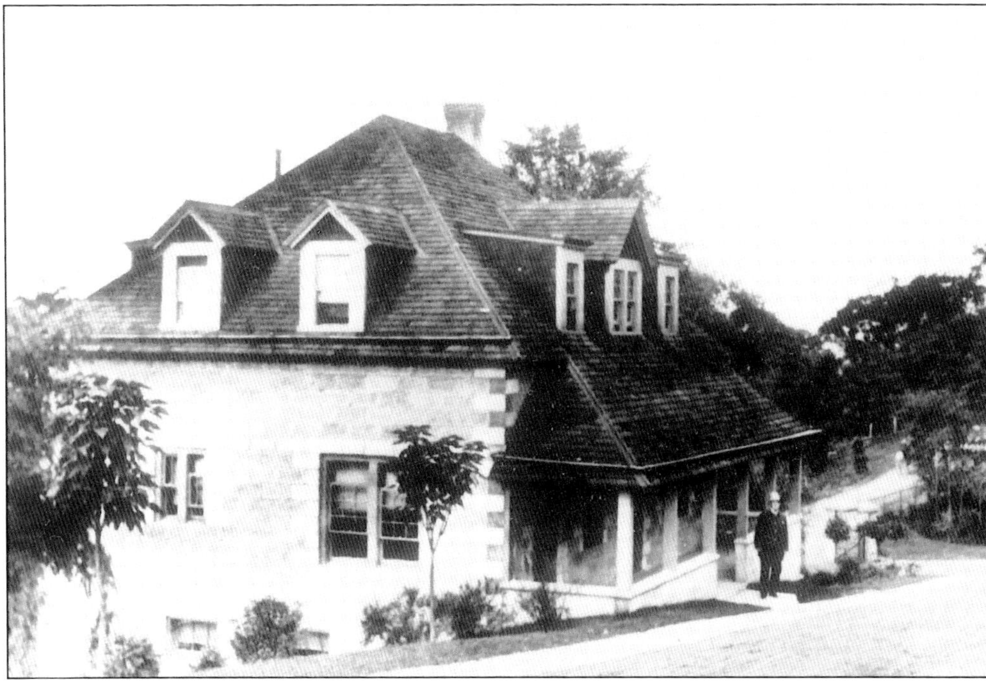

THE NO-LONGER-EXTANT GATEHOUSE AT OAKWOOD CEMETERY AT 114TH STREET. There were a few gatehouses and various entrances for the cemetery. Some entrances had closed and the cemetery was falling into disrepair when a volunteer organization of local citizens recently began the process of restoring it to its original splendor.

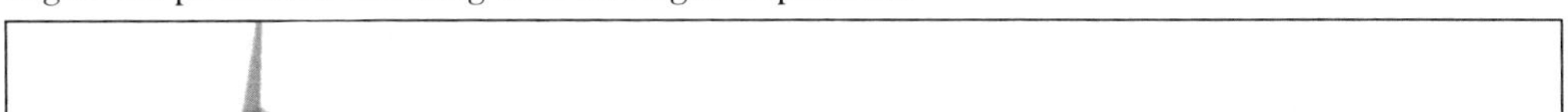

OAKWOOD CEMETERY. When the Troy Cemetery Association purchased 150 acres between Oakwood Avenue and the land overlooking Lansingburgh in 1848, Oakwood Cemetery was organized. It was designed by J.C. Sidney, a landscape engineer, and dedicated on October 16, 1850. This beautiful cemetery is on the National Register of Historic Places. Many notable figures are buried here, including "Uncle Sam" Wilson.

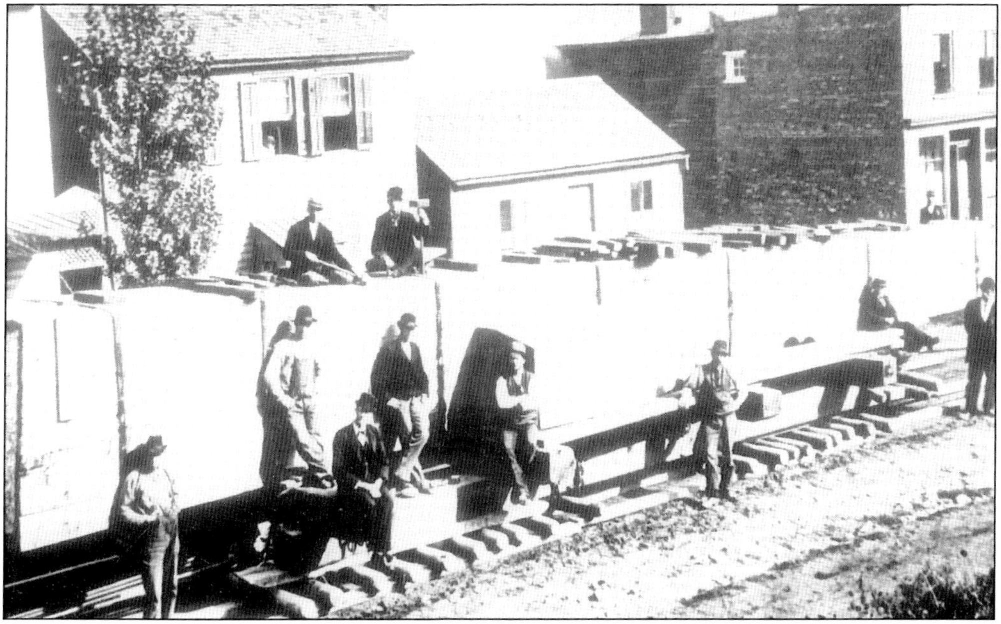

General Wool's Monument Being Towed up Hoosick Street in Troy. General John Ellis Wool served in the War of 1812, the Mexican War of 1848, and the Civil War. He died in Troy on November 10, 1869, and was buried with military honors. This monument, which is 75 feet high, is perhaps the tallest in Rensselaer County. It overlooks Lansingburgh at Oakwood Cemetery.

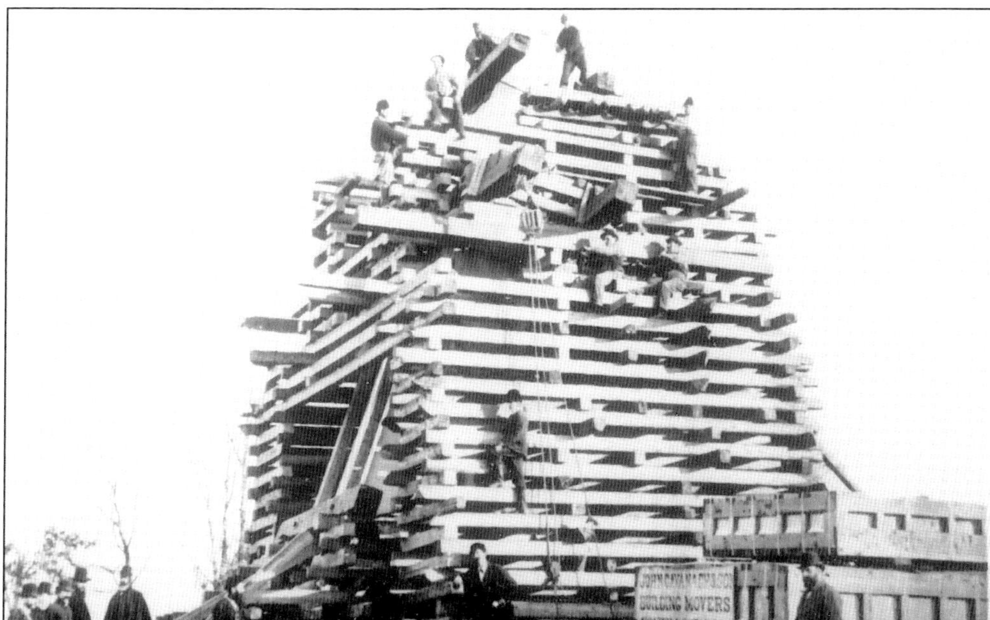

The Wool Monument, Erected by John Cavanaugh & Son, Building Movers from South Boston, Massachusetts. It is remarkable that something this high could be erected by moving timbers back and forth. These folks had a good knowledge of working physics. There were no cranes in those days.

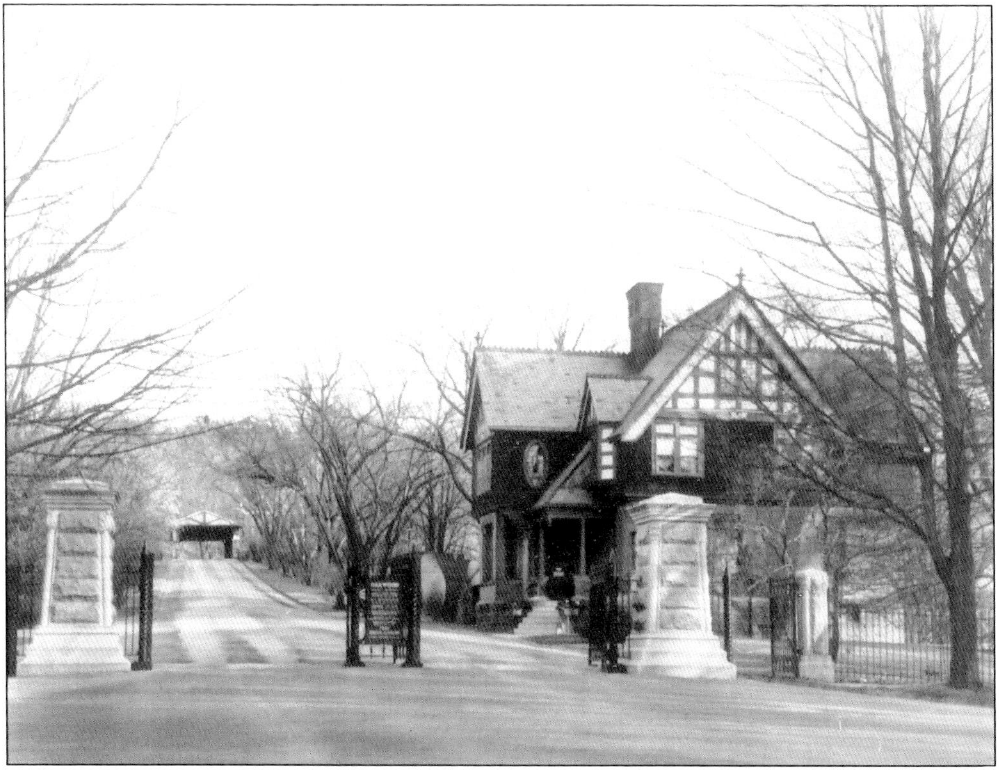

THE 101ST STREET GATEHOUSE TO OAKWOOD CEMETERY. This entrance to the cemetery, and one on Oakwood Avenue, are the main entrances. The keeper's house is still in use. The covered bridge over the railroad tracks is also visible here.

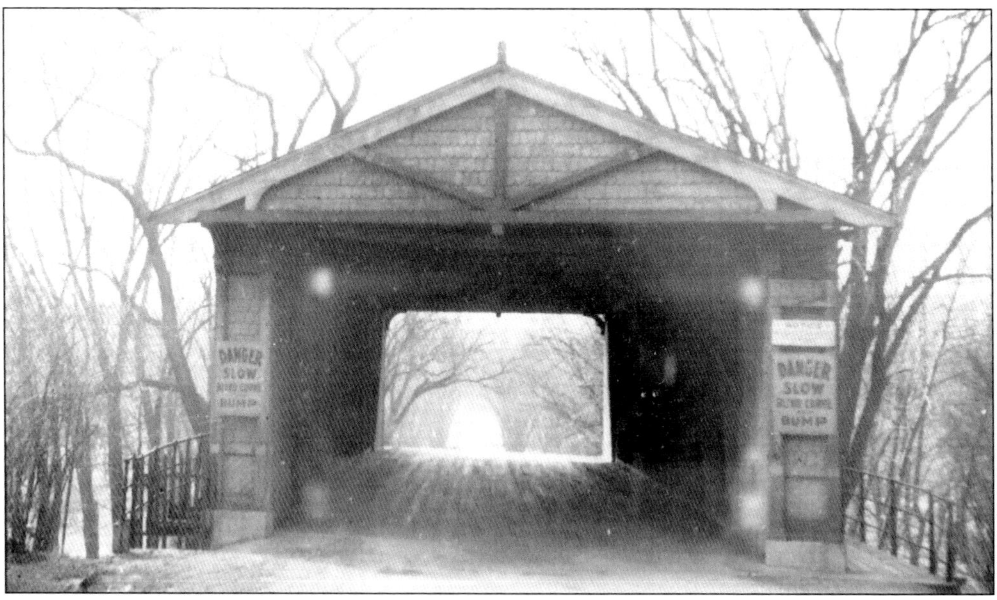

A CLOSEUP OF THE COVERED BRIDGE THAT BURNED ON JULY 14, 1963, PROBABLY AS THE RESULT OF ARSON. Rensselaer County had a number of covered bridges, most of which are now gone.

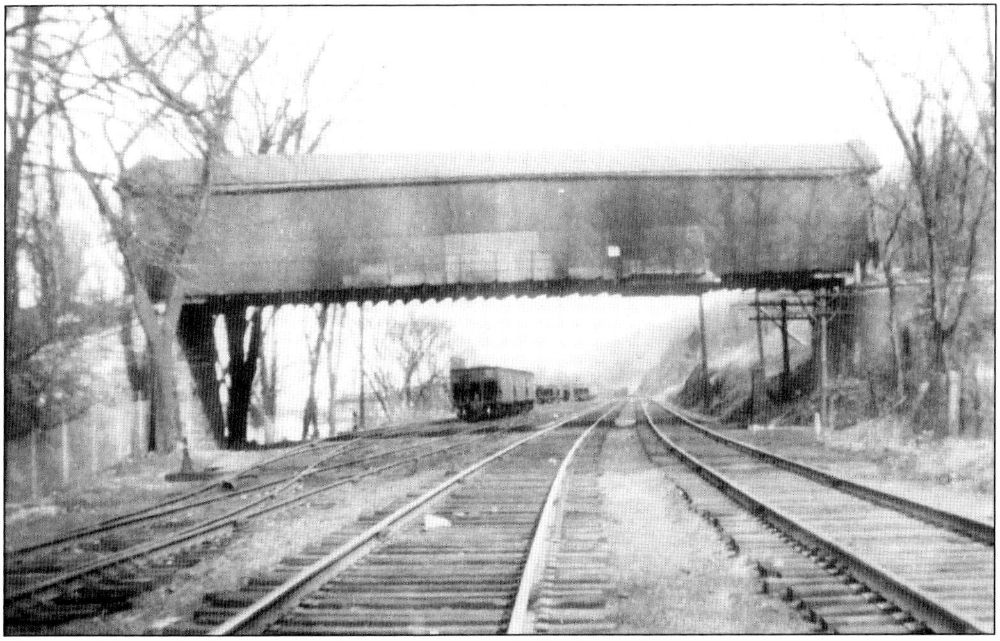

Another View of the Bridge over the Train Tracks. If you were going over the bridge when a steam locomotive sped by, chances are you would have received a good dose of smoke and water vapor. These tracks belonged to the Boston & Maine, which absorbed the previous Fitchburg Railroad in 1905. The Fitchburg consolidated with the Troy & Boston Railroad (T&B) in 1887. The T&B built the famous Hoosac Tunnel.

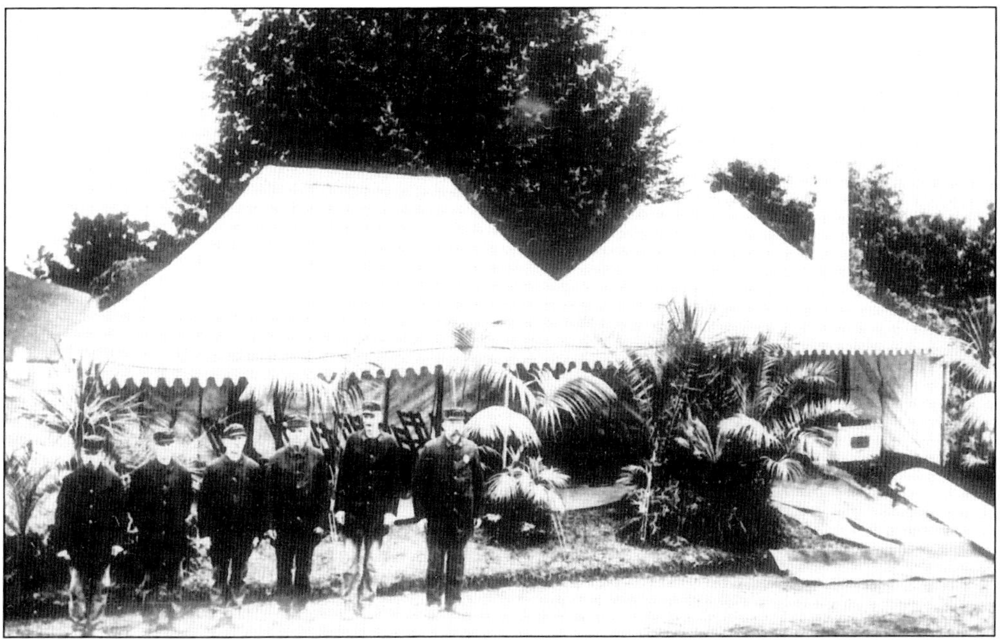

A Funeral at Oakwood Cemetery. Note the uniformed attendants, folding chairs, and palms. Many of the memorial stones at Oakwood are hand-crafted statues or stones and are works of art, in addition to being memorials to the deceased. Cemeteries such as this one were favorite picnic places during the 19th century.

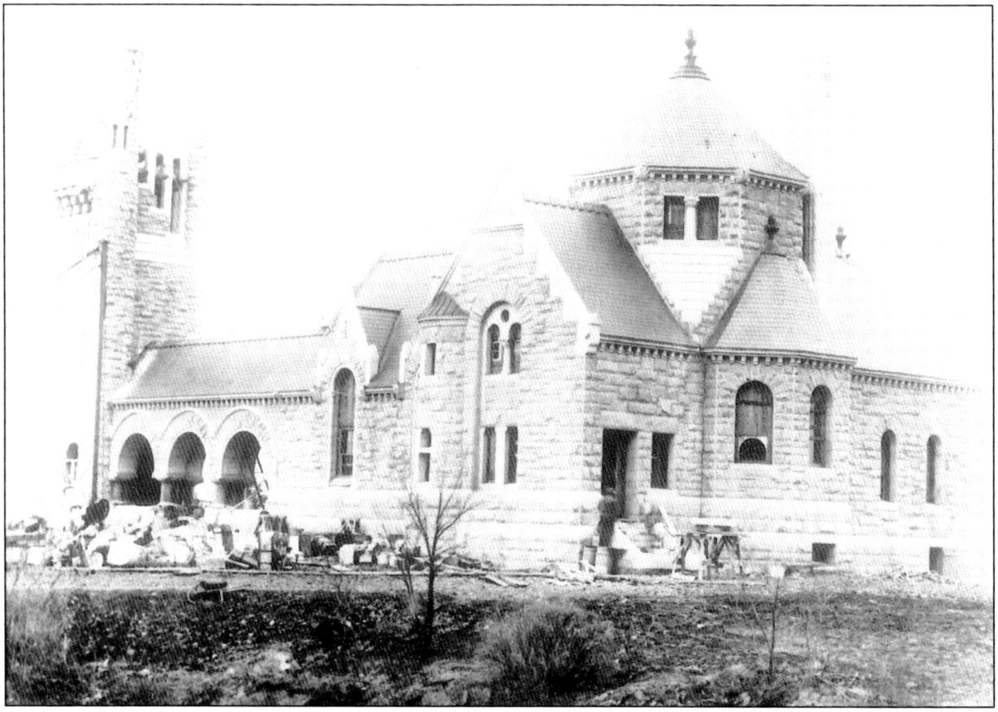

The Building of the Earl Crematorium at Oakwood Cemetery. William S. and Hannah M. Earl built this Romanesque Structure in 1888–89, in memory of their only son Gardner, who died in 1887. Designed by Fuller and Wheeler, the crematorium is still in use today. Earl (Earl & Wilson) was a famous collar manufacturer in Troy.

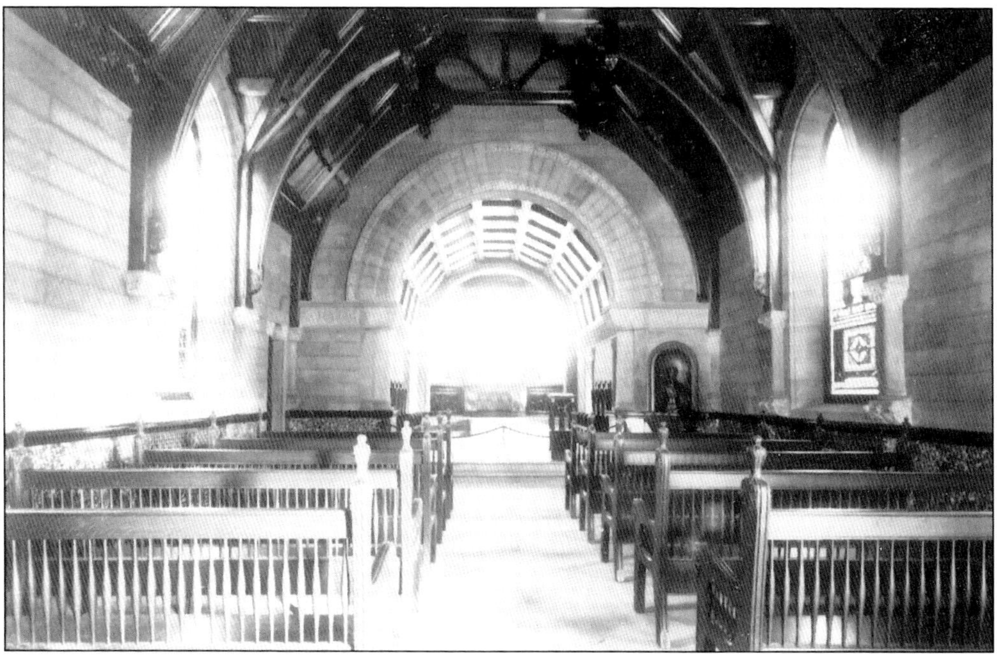

The Interior Chapel of the Crematorium. The Earl Crematorium is on the National Register of Historic Places and is one of the finest in the country.

Two

MERCHANTS AND INDUSTRY

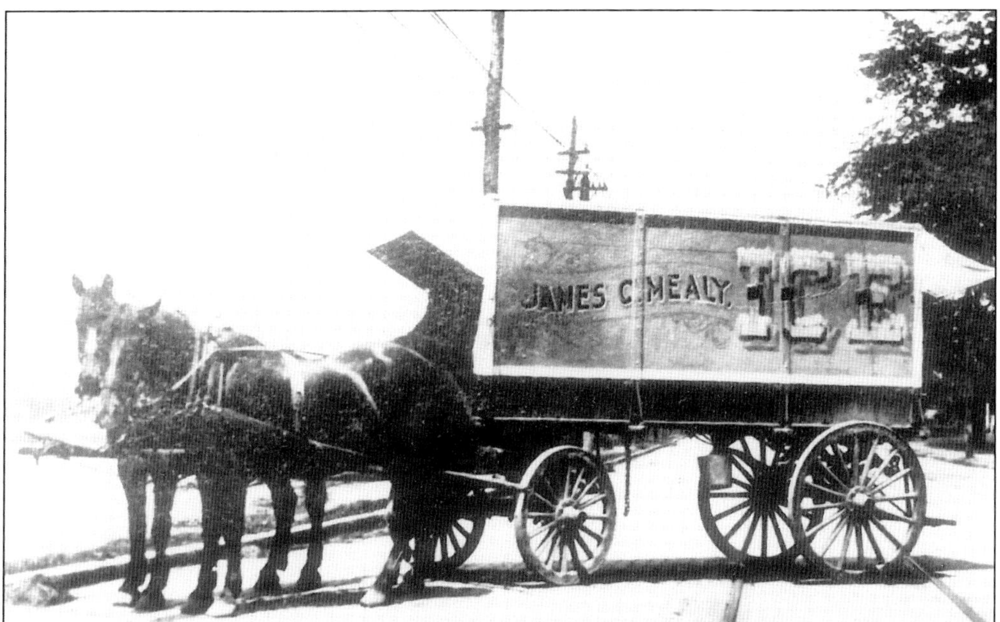

JAMES C. MEALY'S ICE TRUCK, SECOND AVENUE AND 105TH STREET. Mealy lived in Troy at 907 River Street. The ice business was lucrative before the invention of the refrigerator. Icehouses were built to store ice taken from the river. Mealy was one of 19 ice dealers in 1899.

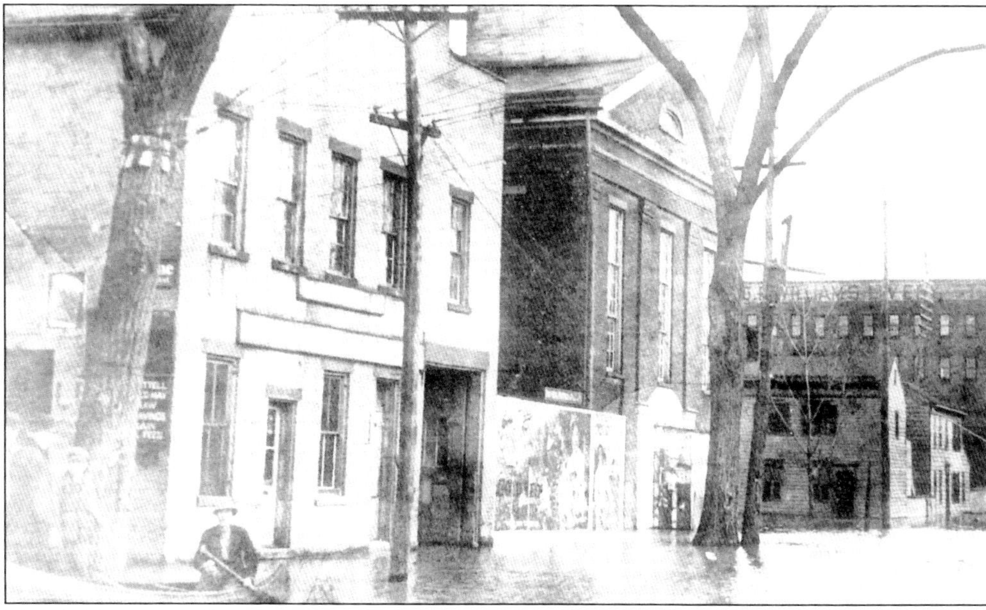

THE MCMURRAY BRUSH COMPANY IN THE BACKGROUND ON 117TH STREET AND THIRD AVENUE. William McMurray was the first to make brushes in Lansingburgh, starting in October 1818 on King Street. The building in foreground is the Olympic Saloon; next to it was a church and later the Powers Opera House, both of which are still standing. This photograph was taken during the 1913 flood.

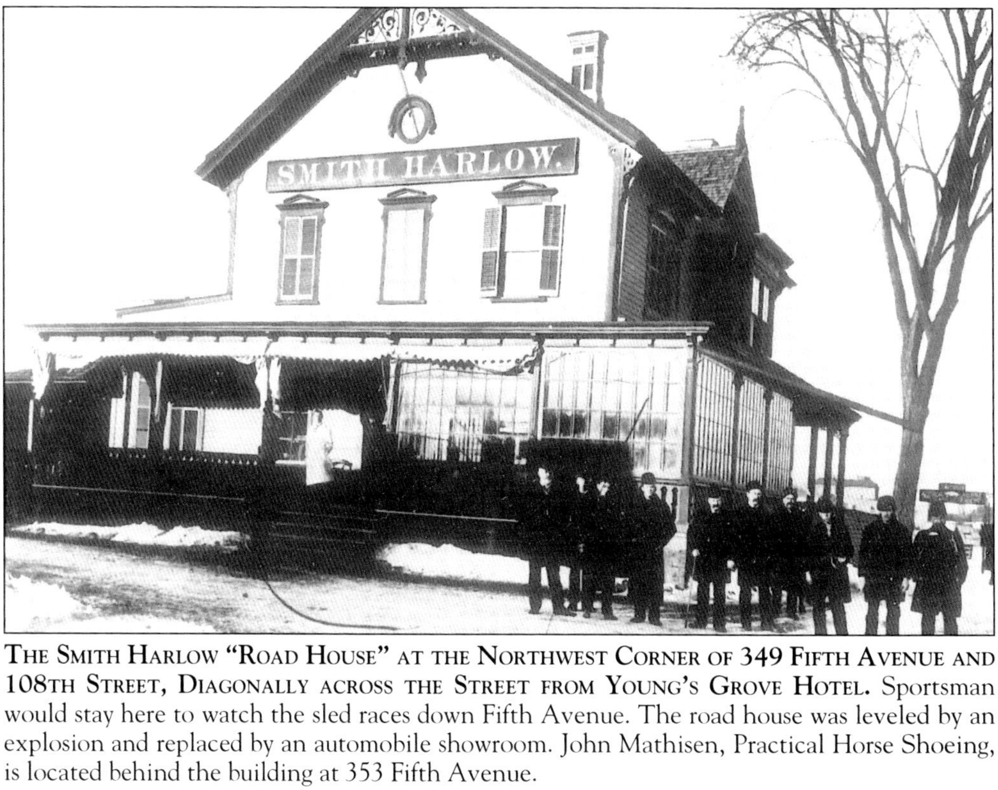

THE SMITH HARLOW "ROAD HOUSE" AT THE NORTHWEST CORNER OF 349 FIFTH AVENUE AND 108TH STREET, DIAGONALLY ACROSS THE STREET FROM YOUNG'S GROVE HOTEL. Sportsman would stay here to watch the sled races down Fifth Avenue. The road house was leveled by an explosion and replaced by an automobile showroom. John Mathisen, Practical Horse Shoeing, is located behind the building at 353 Fifth Avenue.

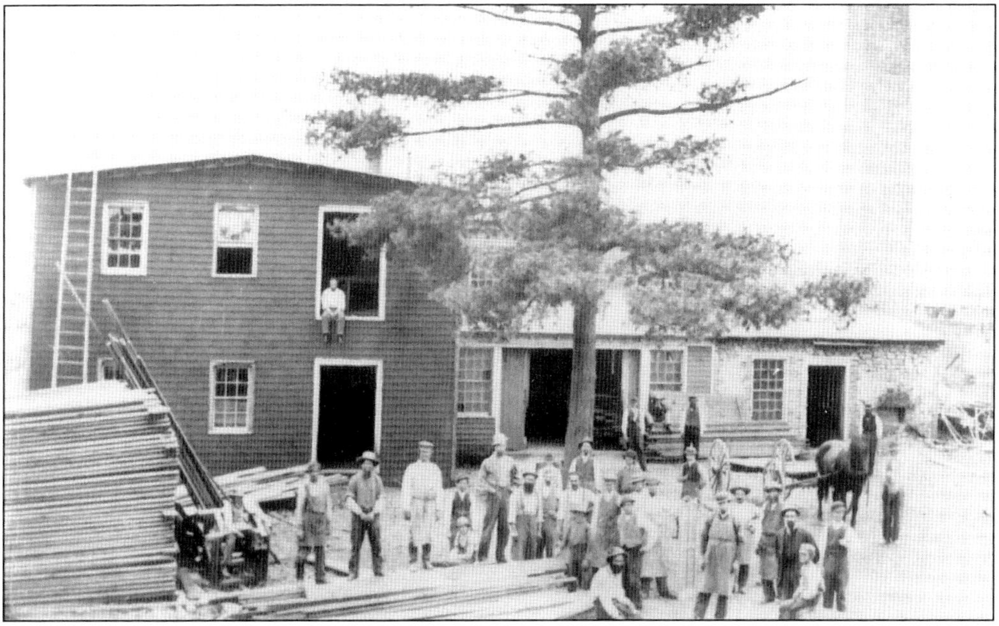

Jacob White's Sash and Blind Manufacturing, 102nd Street and Ninth Avenue. The present-day Garden Way Company property is located on this building's former site. White lived at 146 Second Avenue. One other blind-maker, J.B. Madden & Company, operated out of Lansingburgh.

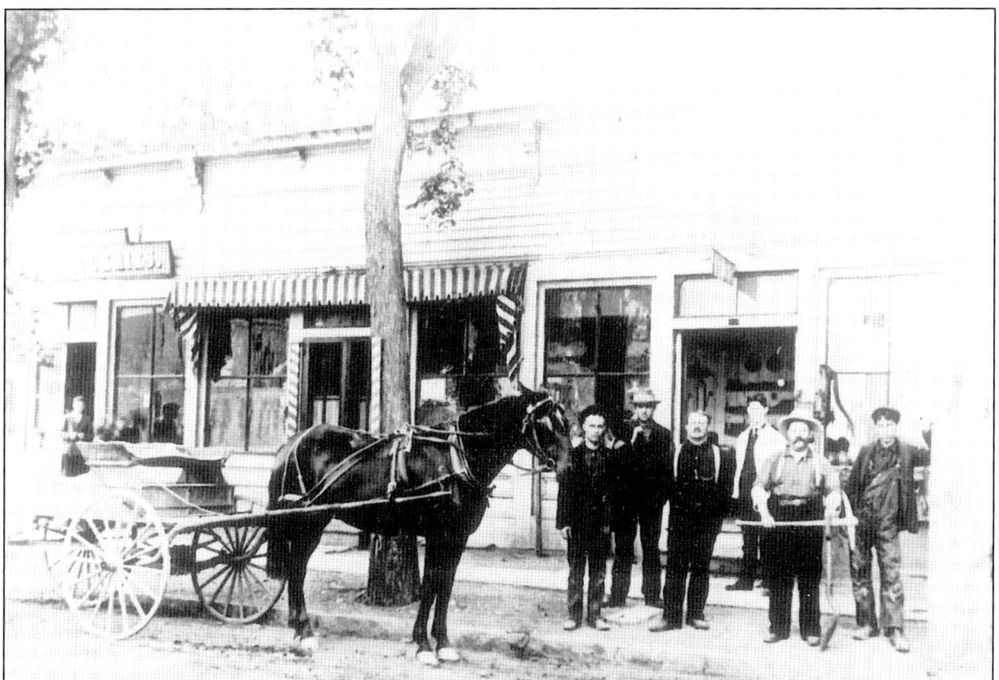

The Bensen Building, Located on the South Side of 112th Street between Fourth and Fifth Avenues. Howard Groceries is located in the Bensen Building. Notice the fellow standing with a pick in his hand.

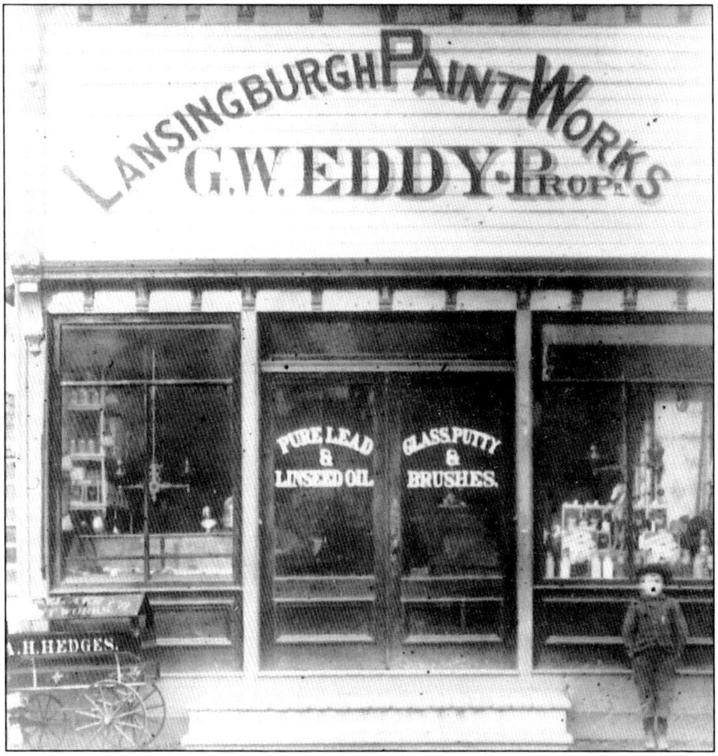

THE LANSINGBURGH PAINT WORKS, OWNED BY G. WALTON EDDY. You could buy "pure lead" and linseed oil at the Lansingburgh Paint Works, located on the north side of 119th Street between Second and Third Avenues near Second Avenue. Eddy lived at No. 13 119th Street. It wasn't until recent times that lead paint was linked to health problems in children under the age of 6. If you still live in a building that has old paint you should check it for lead content.

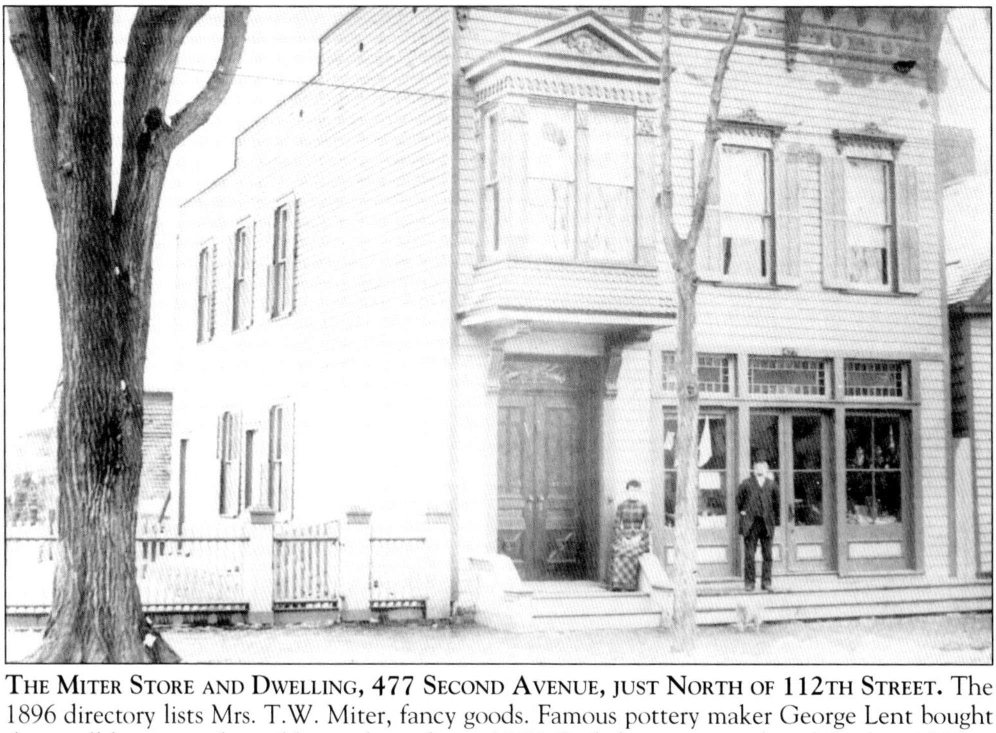

THE MITER STORE AND DWELLING, 477 SECOND AVENUE, JUST NORTH OF 112TH STREET. The 1896 directory lists Mrs. T.W. Miter, fancy goods. Famous pottery maker George Lent bought the small house partly visible on the right in 1825. Both houses were demolished in 1966 to allow the construction of a gas station.

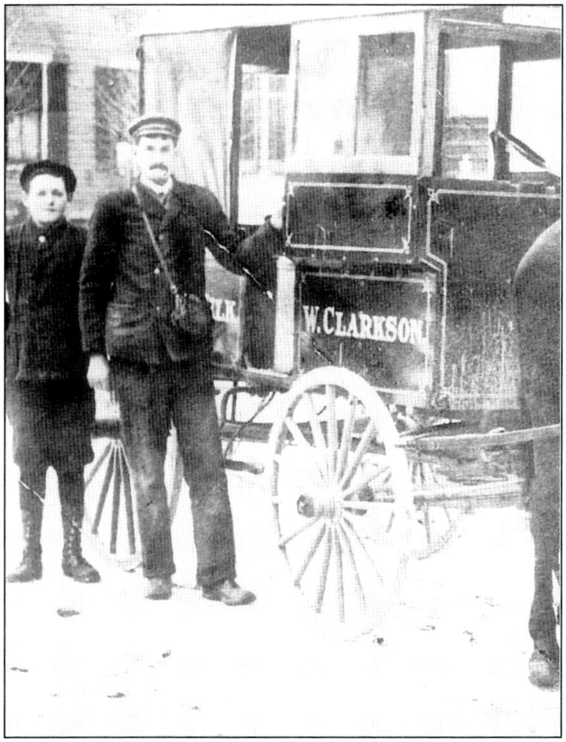

William C. Clarkson, the Milkman. Many things we buy at the supermarket, such as ice, milk, and bakery products, were delivered to the door. This kind of horse-drawn delivery took place right up to the 1960s.

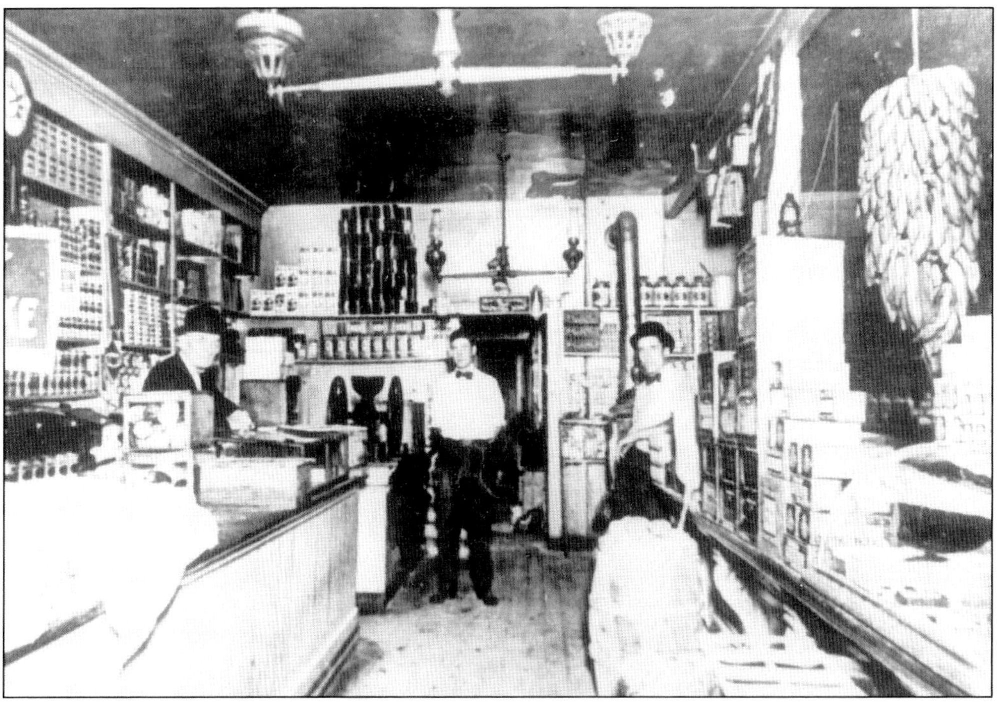

D&A (Douglas & Argyle) Smith's Grocery Store at the Southeast Corner of 502 Fifth Avenue and 119th Street. Notice the bunch of bananas hanging from the ceiling and the gas chandelier for lighting. The structure was later converted to a dwelling.

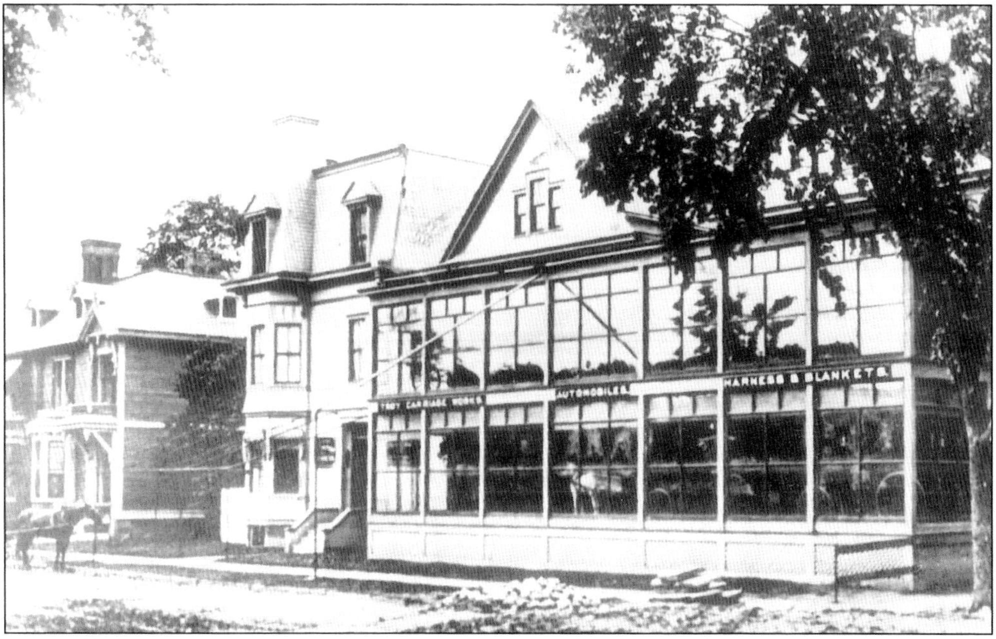

The Troy Carriage Works at 745 Third Avenue, on the West Side near 121st Street, c. 1895. The front of the structure was removed; it is now used as two dwelling houses. James K.P. Pine owned this works, the Lion Factory, and was president of The People's Bank.

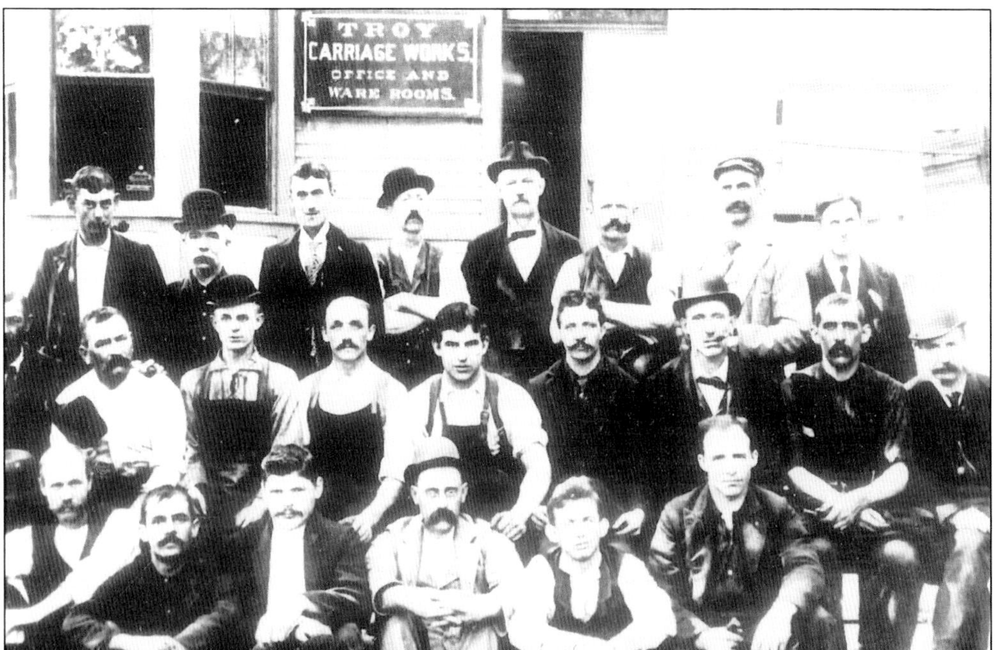

Another View of the Troy Carriage Works. Here is a group shot of workers posing in front of the office. It appears that mustaches were popular with this group. The carriage company was established in 1882 and incorporated in 1894. The structure remains standing.

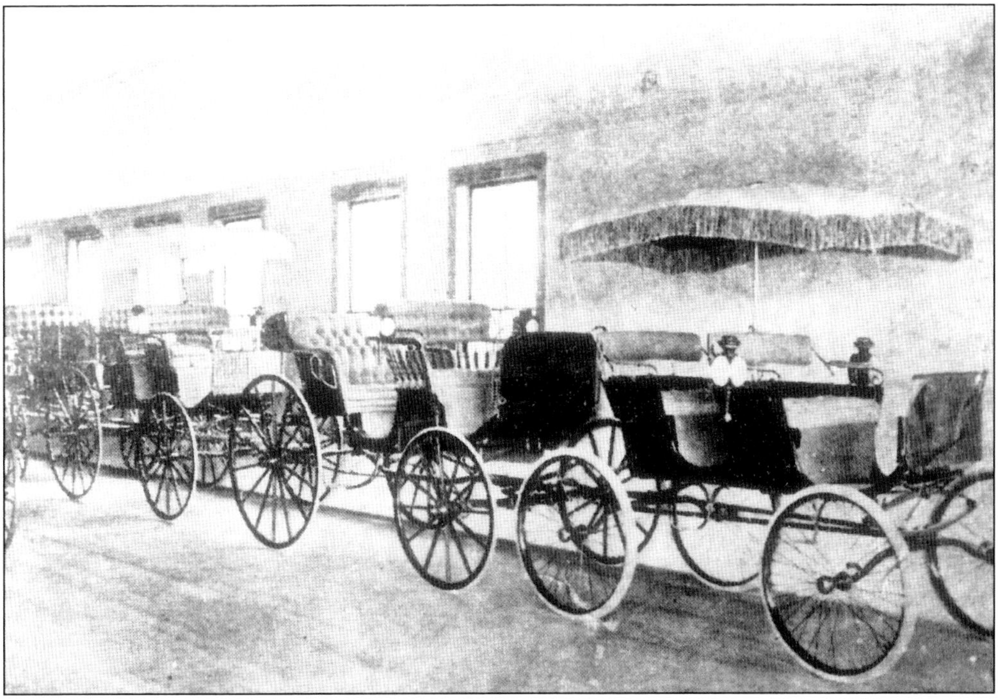

THE INTERIOR OF PINE'S CARRIAGE FACTORY ON THIRD AVENUE. Carriages, buckboards, and sleighs were made at Pine's Carriage Factory. They also had a repair shop and could fix any kind of carriage.

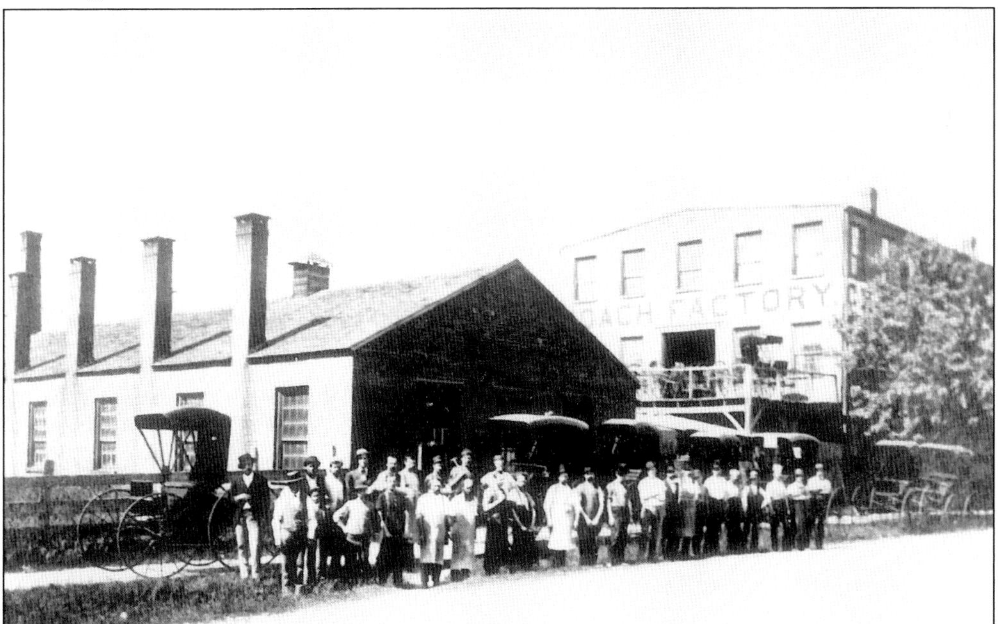

CHAMBERLAIN'S CARRIAGE FACTORY, BUILT IN 1858 AT THE SOUTHEAST CORNER OF 101ST STREET AND SECOND AVENUE. The taller building, seen in this view from 101st Street, burned in 1969. Edwin Chamberlain and his son Lee were early Lansingburgh carriage makers. John O. Merriam was the other partner.

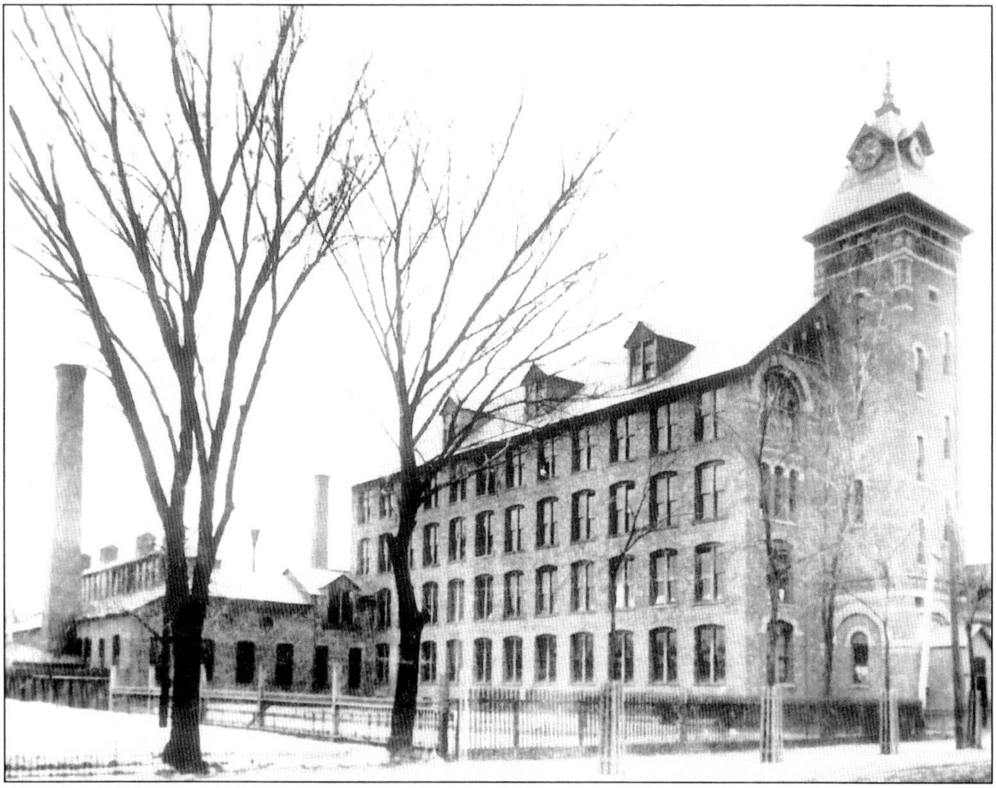

THE AETNA MILL AT 80 SECOND AVENUE, JUST SOUTH OF 102ND STREET. Owner William A. Harder lived at 65 Second Avenue. The Aetna Mill manufactured knit goods.

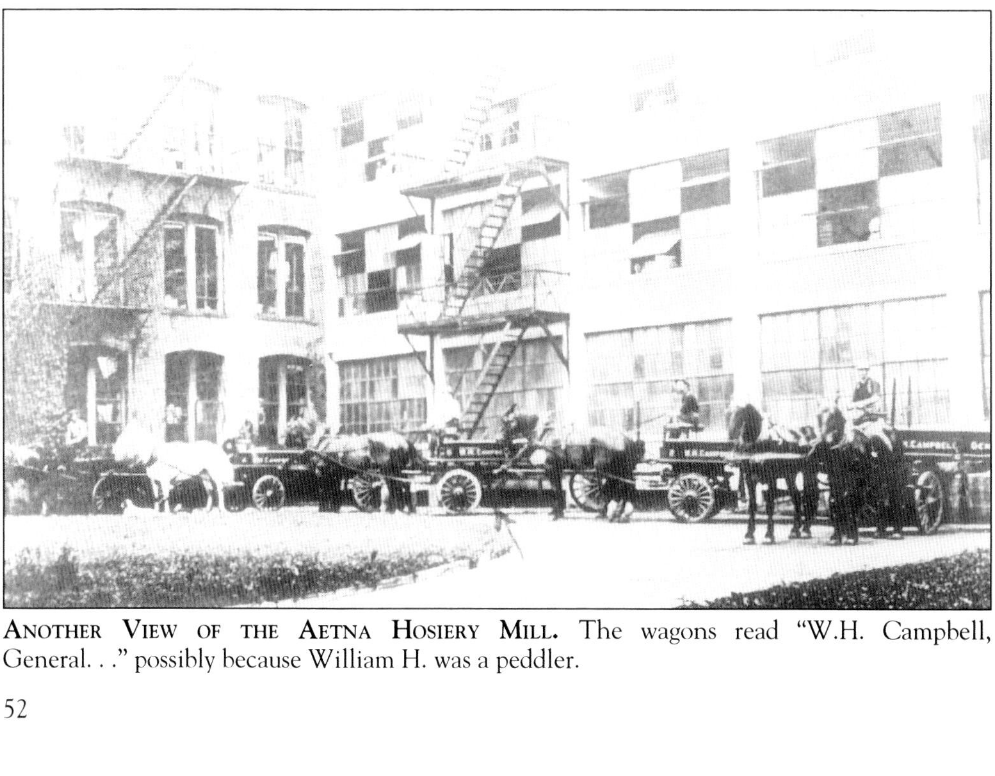

ANOTHER VIEW OF THE AETNA HOSIERY MILL. The wagons read "W.H. Campbell, General. . ." possibly because William H. was a peddler.

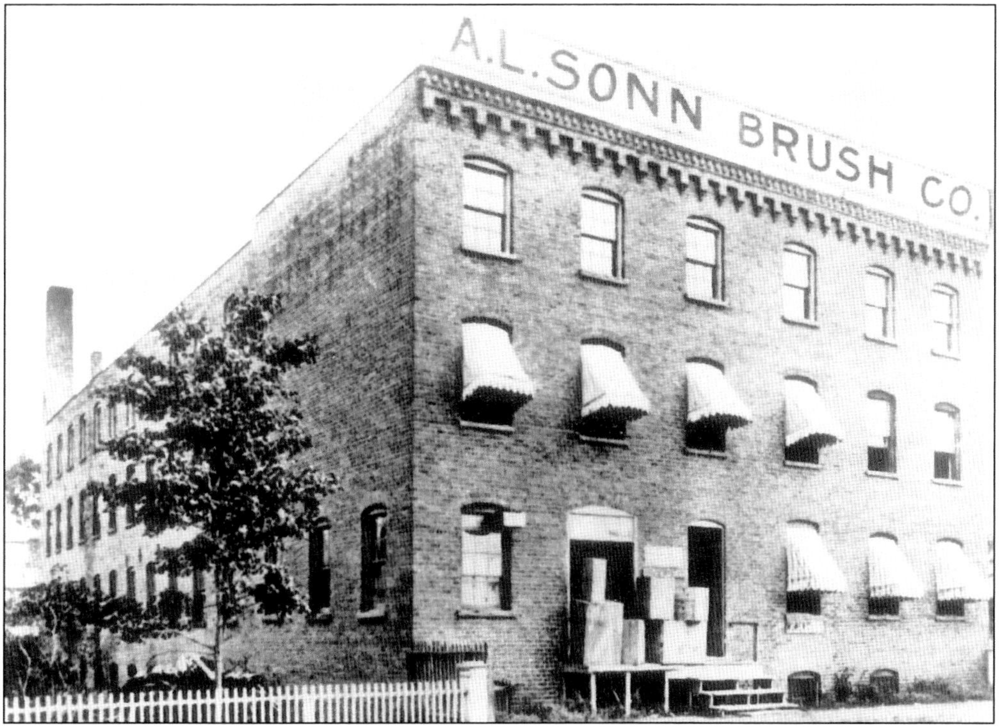

The Anson L. Sonn Brush Co., built in 1869 at 518 First Avenue, on the East Side between 113th and 114th Streets. E. Water's & Sons Paper Boats were made in the same building. By 1924, most of the 16 brush companies in Greater Troy were located in Lansingburgh.

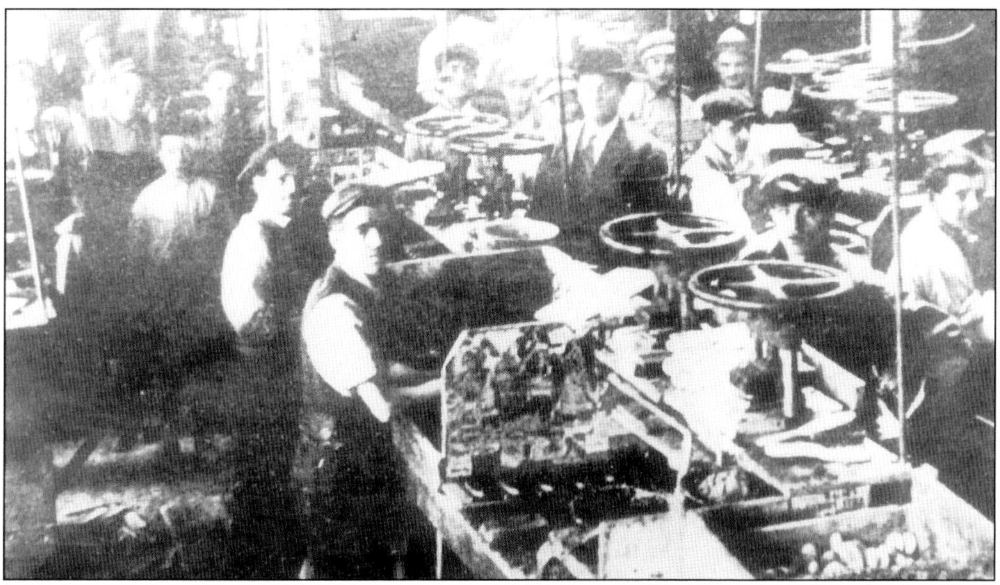

The Monarch Brush Company, 653 Third Avenue. Here you can see the brush filling operation. Lansingburgh was the chief center of brush making in Rensselaer County. In 1924, brush making was the third largest grosser of manufacturing dollars, nearly totalling a million dollars. At the time, the Monarch Brush Company employed more than 500 people.

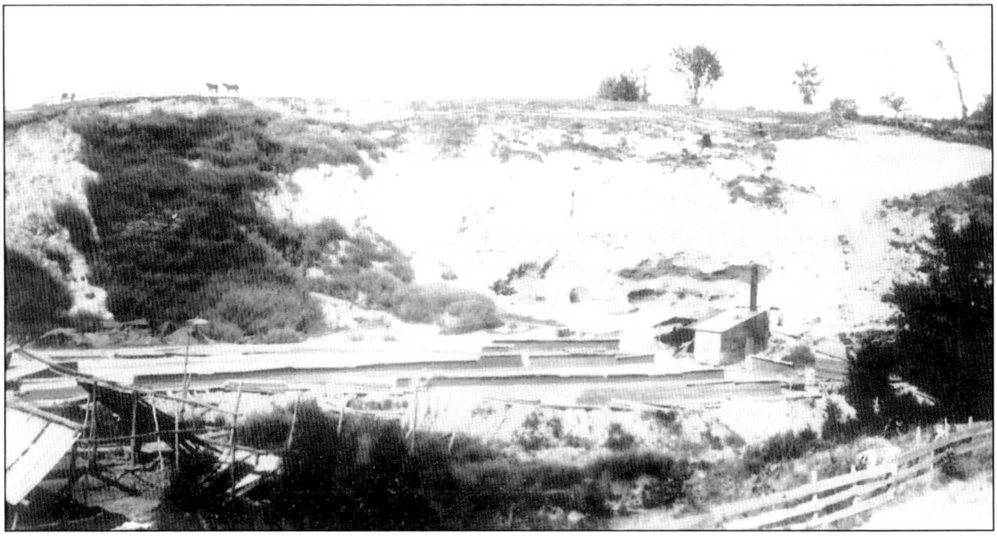

Thomas F. Morrissey's Brick Yards on Oil Mill Hill Road. Morrissey lived here as well. The city directory listed him as Spall & Morrissey, coal and brick makers. The silts laid down in the pre-glacial Hudson River Valley over the last 15,000 years provided plenty of clay for making bricks.

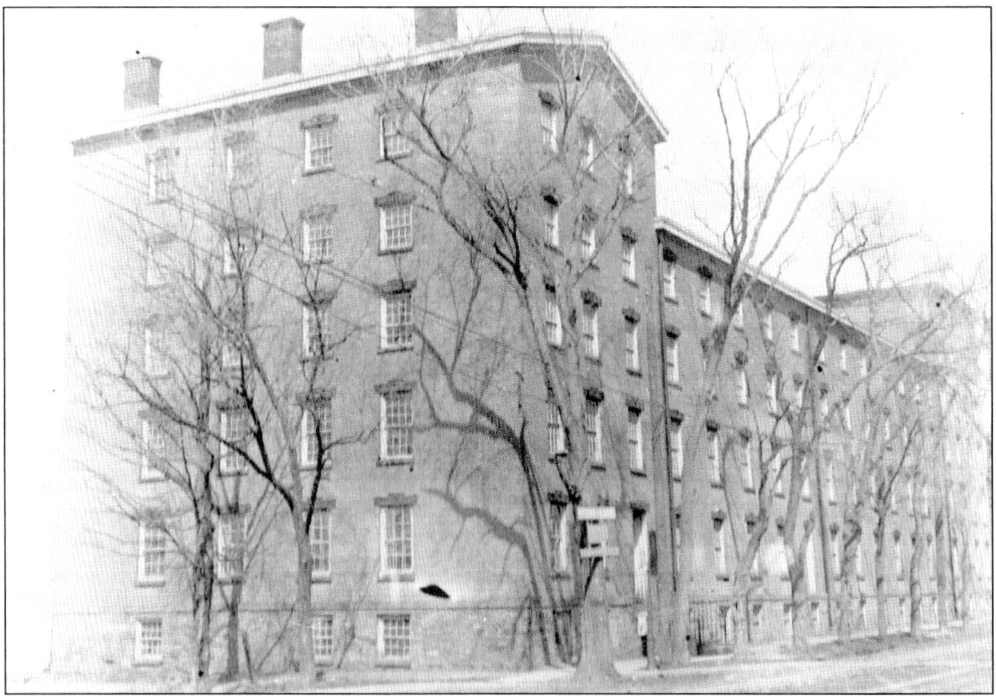

The Powers Oilcloth Factory at 375 Second Avenue. William Powers, a former schoolteacher, started this company in 1817. His widow, Deborah, and their sons carried on the business and were influential in many aspects of the village. They owned a bank and an opera house, and had a park, a school, and an old ladies home named after them.

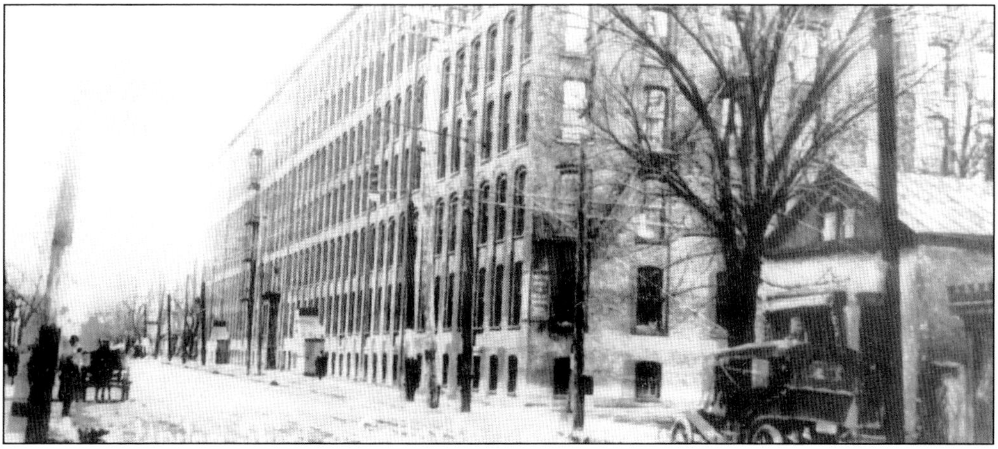

The United Shirt & Collar Company, or Pine Factory, between 120th and 121st Streets on Second Avenue. Known as the Lion Factory in 1884, owner James K.P. Pine consolidated five businesses into the United Shirt & Collar Company on May 7, 1890. After joining S.A. House's Sons, James K.P. Pine, Sanford & Robinson, Beiermeister & Spicer, and Marshall & Briggs, J.K.P Pine became president. The United Shirt & Collar Company had offices at the northeast corner of Fifth Avenue and Broadway, at an "Anchor Factory" at 509–513 River Street in Troy, and at the Lion Factory location in Lansingburgh. Standard Manufacturing, the present owner, makes sports jackets and other specialized items.

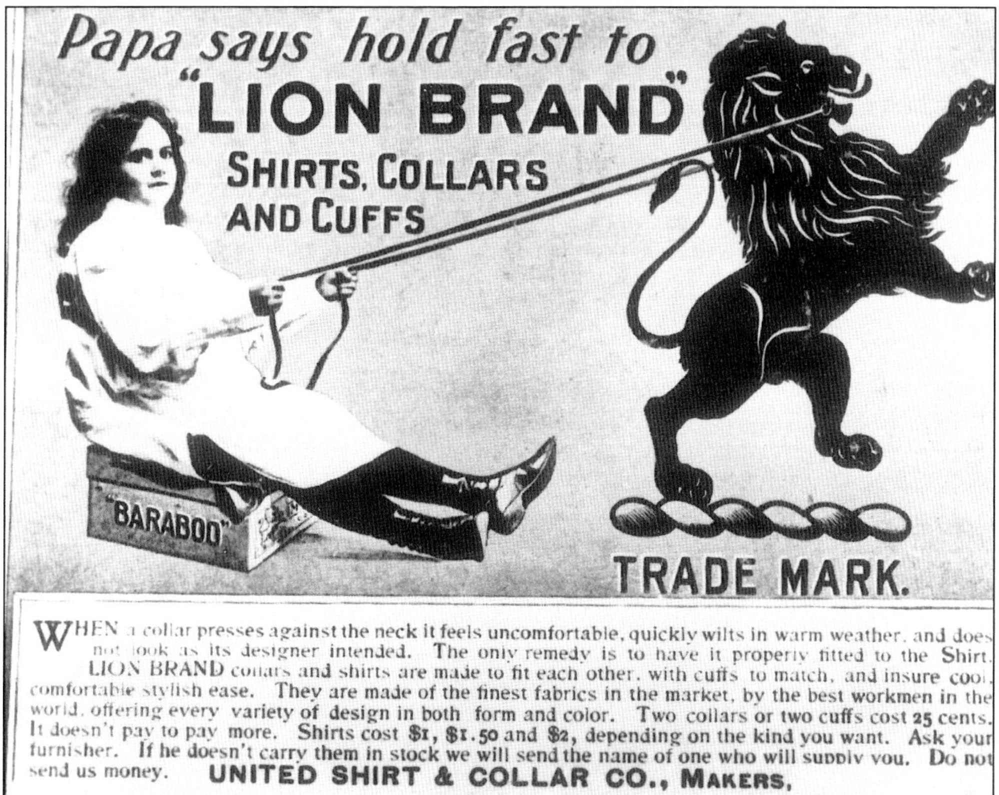

A Lion Brand Ad from Pine's United Shirt & Collar Company. Lion Brand and most of the textile manufacturers in the area were known the world over for their quality.

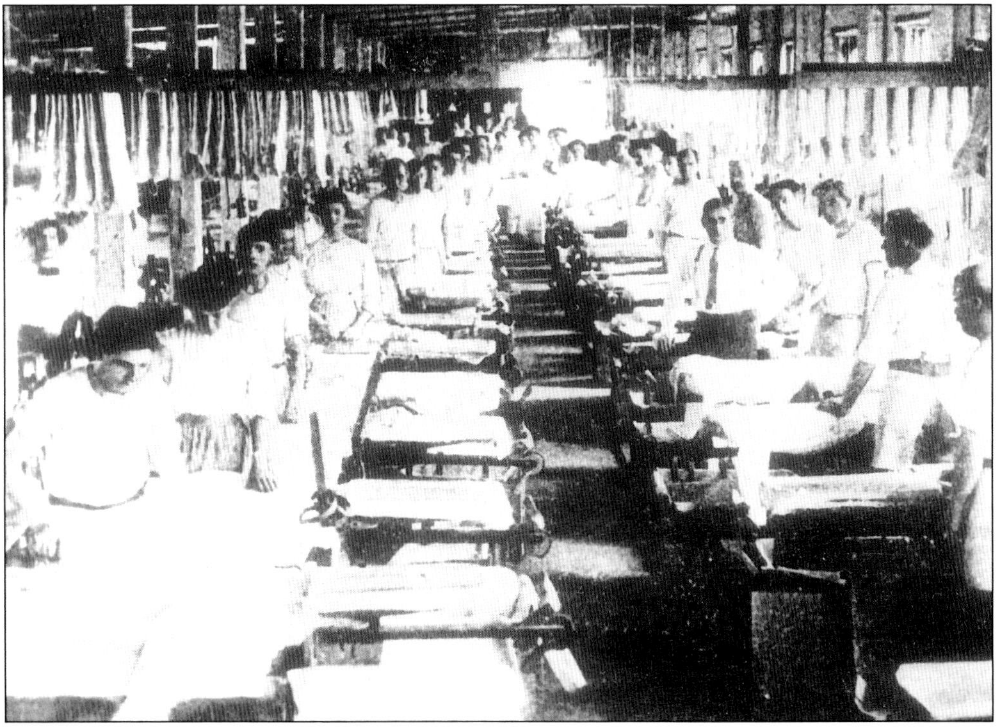

The United Shirt & Collar Company Ironer Department. Hundreds of local women had jobs here doing a variety of chores.

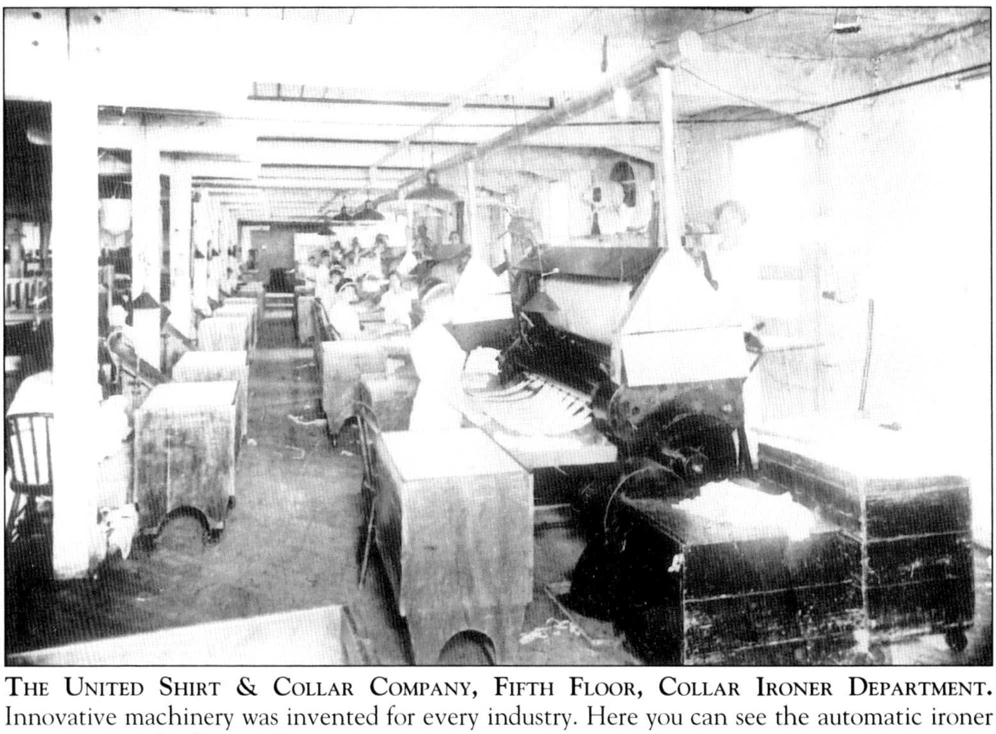

The United Shirt & Collar Company, Fifth Floor, Collar Ironer Department. Innovative machinery was invented for every industry. Here you can see the automatic ironer pressing several collars at the same time.

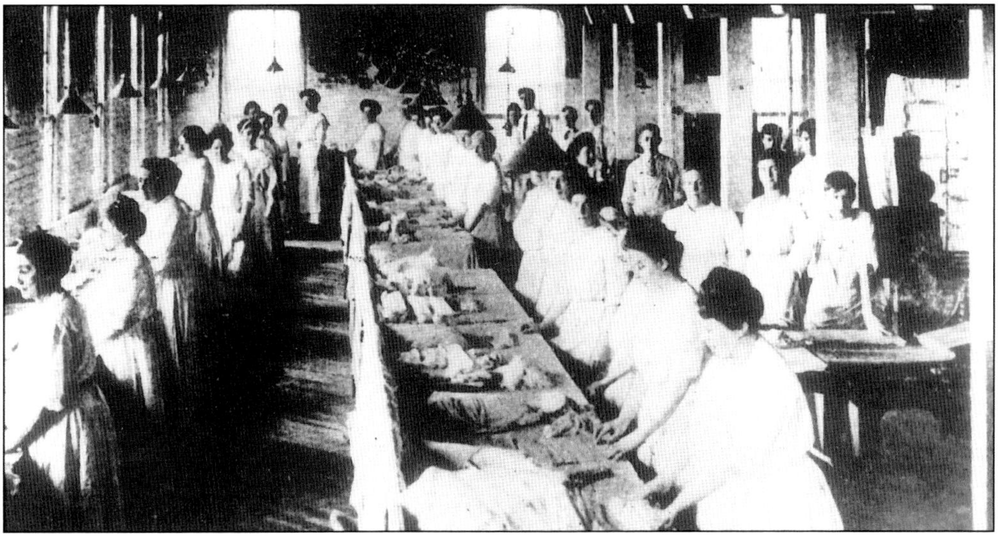

The United Shirt & Collar Company Folding Room. Here it looks like women are folding shirts. Some chores, like folding, had to be done by hand.

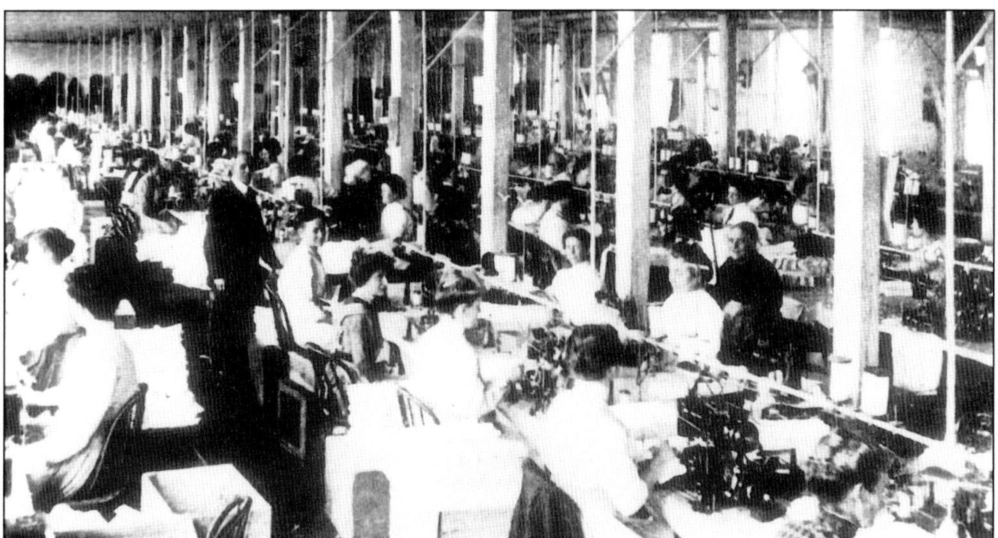

The United Shirt & Collar Company Collar Stitching Department. The Wheeler and Wilson Manufacturing Company from Troy invented a sewing machine that became the standard for the shirt, collar, and cuff industry.

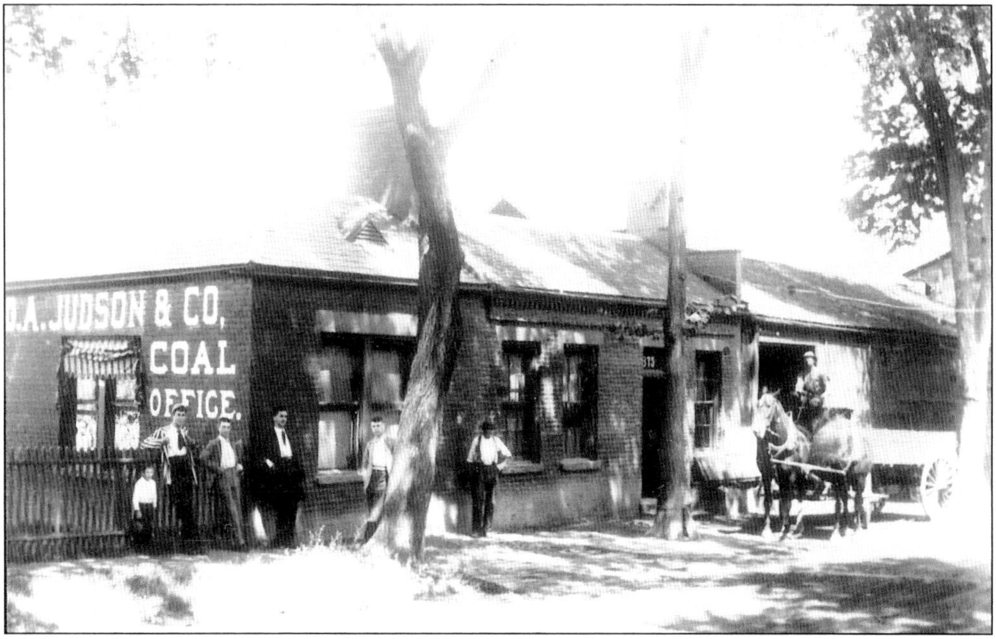

THE DAVID A. JUDSON COAL COMPANY, 125 RIVER (FIRST) AVENUE. Judson lived in Lansingburgh, and his wife was known for being kind to orphans. The coal company had a site in Troy as well.

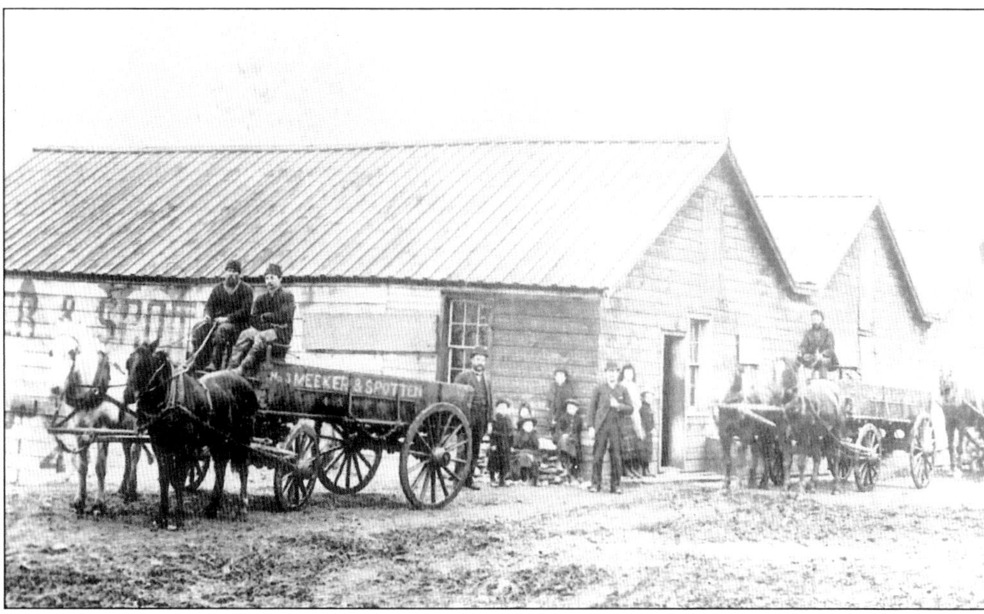

THE MEEKER & JAMES A. SPOTTEN COAL YARD ON 485–499 FIRST AVENUE. Coal was used to fuel industry and keep homes warm during the wintertime. Nearby Troy was world famous for making cast-iron stoves.

THE TROY STANDARD PRESS, 628–630 SECOND AVENUE. In 1787 the *Northern Centinel* and *Lansingburgh Advertiser* became the first newspaper published in Lansingburgh. In 1912, the *Daily Troy Press* merged with the *Evening Standard* to become the *Standard-Press*, which stopped printing on February 1, 1915. The people shown here are reading about rumors concerning an attempt to assassinate President Taft at the White House. Note the paper boy, who is more interested in the photographer than the news of the day.

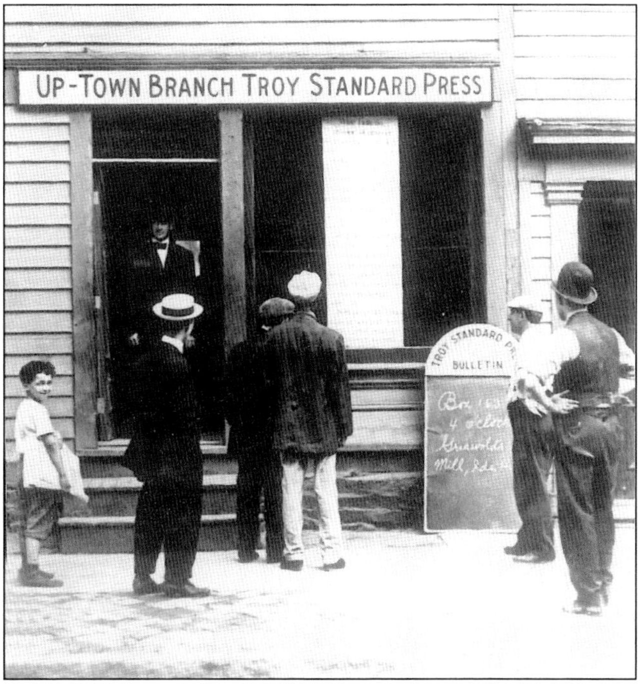

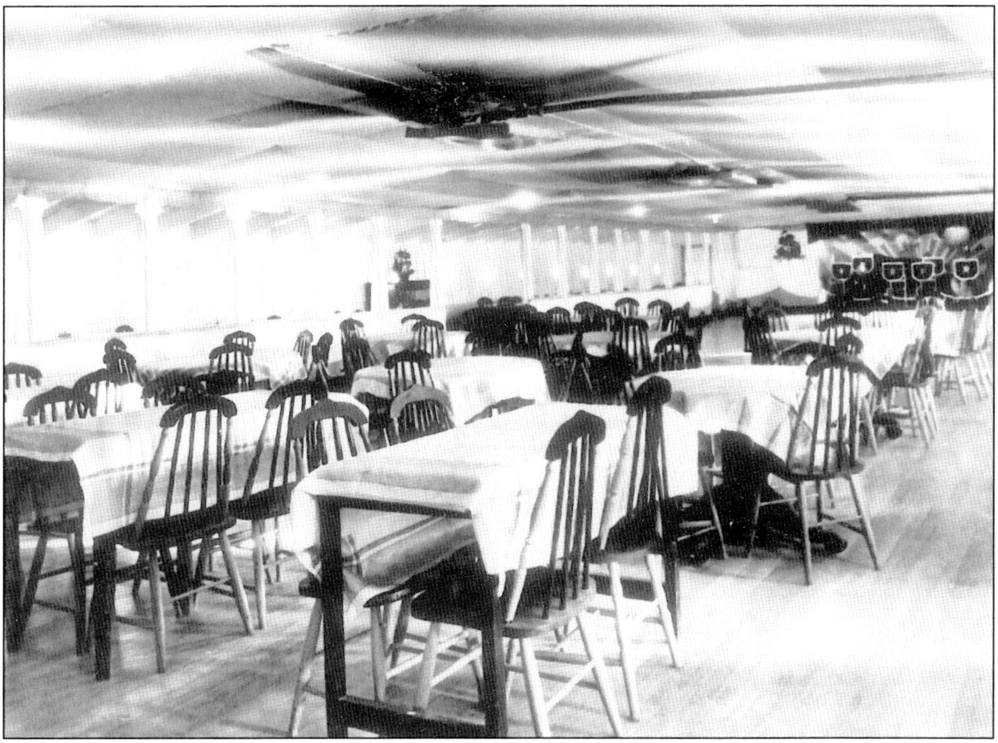

THE FLOATING NIGHTCLUB MADE FROM A BARGE, LOCATED AT THE END OF 109TH STREET. Owned by bandleader Charles Randall, this floating nightclub opened in 1931. It sank in the spring of 1935 after floating ice punched a hole in it. The *Paradise*, another vessel that docked in Troy, was a gambling boat; it sank in the flood of 1936.

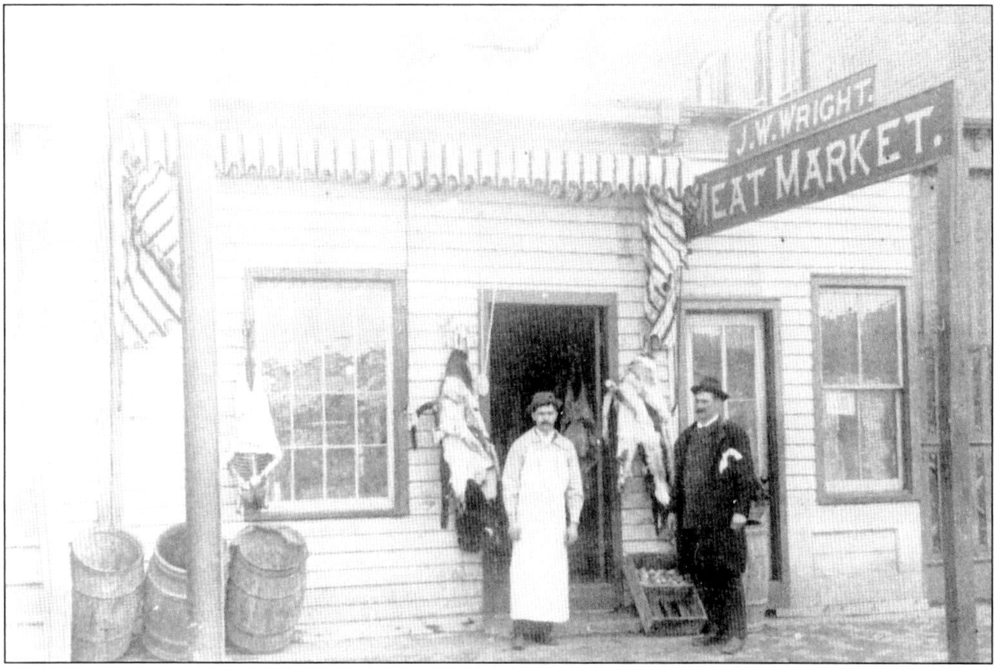

The John W. Wright Meat Market, No. 2 Fifth Avenue (at 105th Street). Modern health codes would not let you hang meat out in the front of a store, as shown in this photograph.

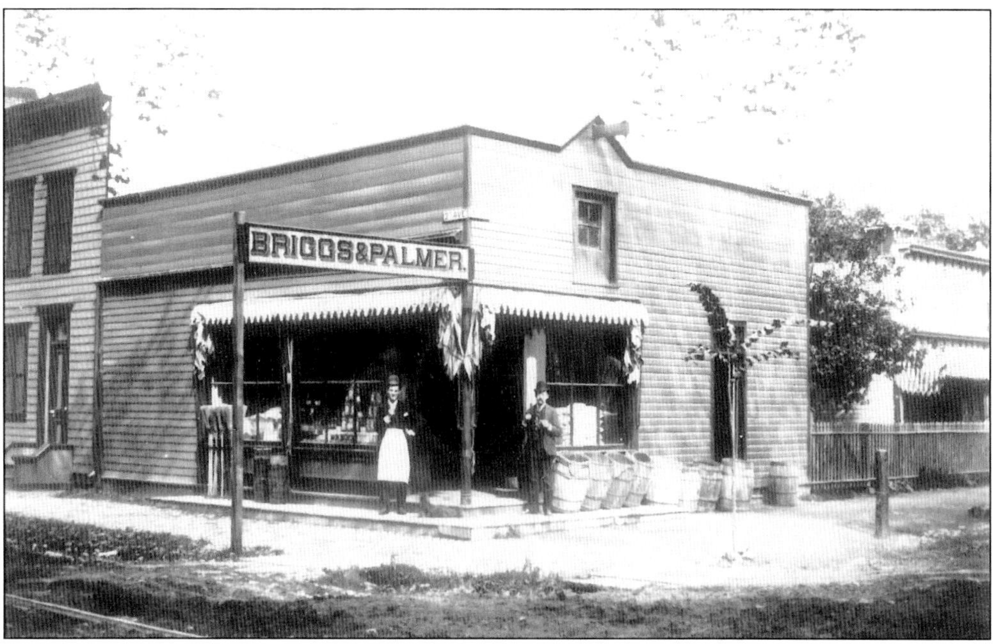

Briggs and Palmer, Grocers, Second Avenue and 119th Street. Notice the way they advertised their store by erecting a sign over the sidewalk; this was a common practice in those days. The building is still standing. Unlike today's supermarkets, villages like Lansingburgh had many neighborhood corner grocery stores where you could buy your food supplies.

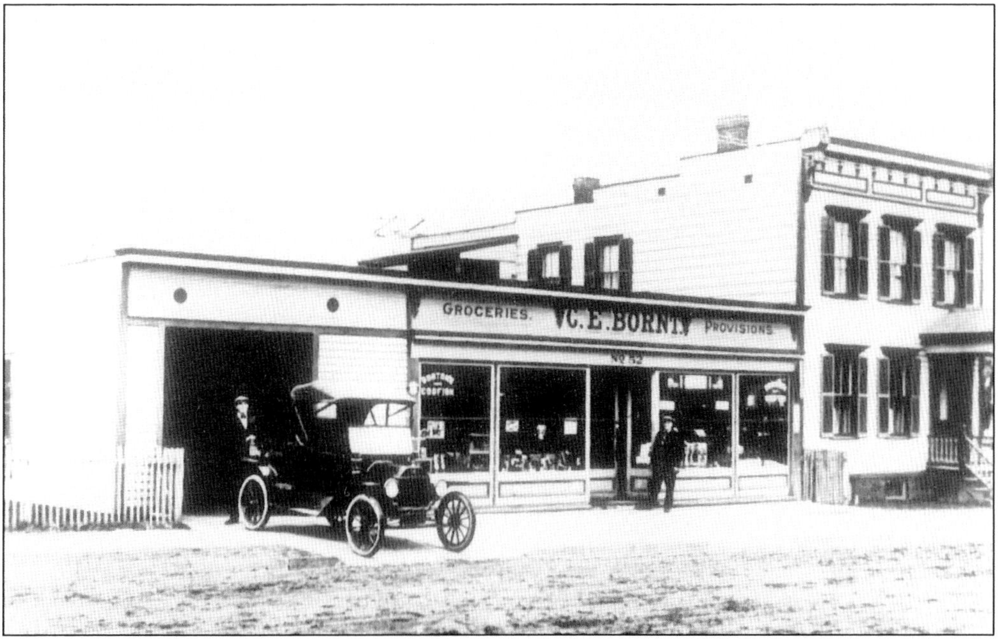

CLIFFORD L. BORNT'S STORE AT NO. 52 114TH STREET BETWEEN SEVENTH AND EIGHTH AVENUES. The garage was the location of the original store. At some point, the business moved from this location. A 1939 directory has the address listed at 661 Second Avenue.

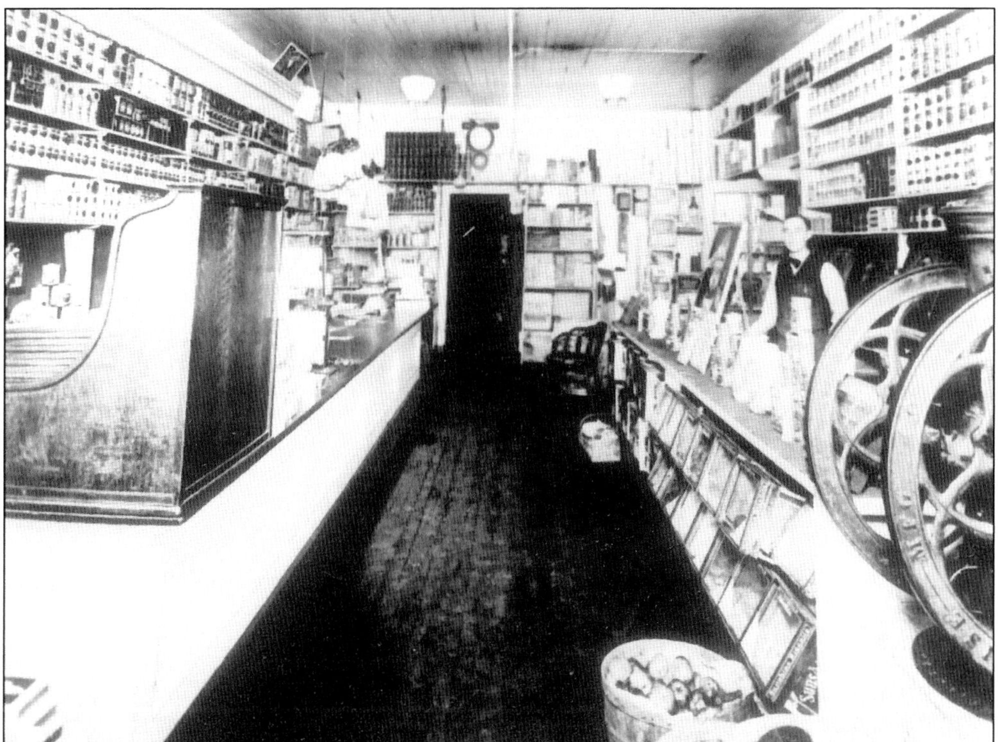

THE INTERIOR OF BORNT'S STORE. Notice how neatly items are stacked on the shelves and how clean the interior is. I've been in big supermarkets that are not this neat.

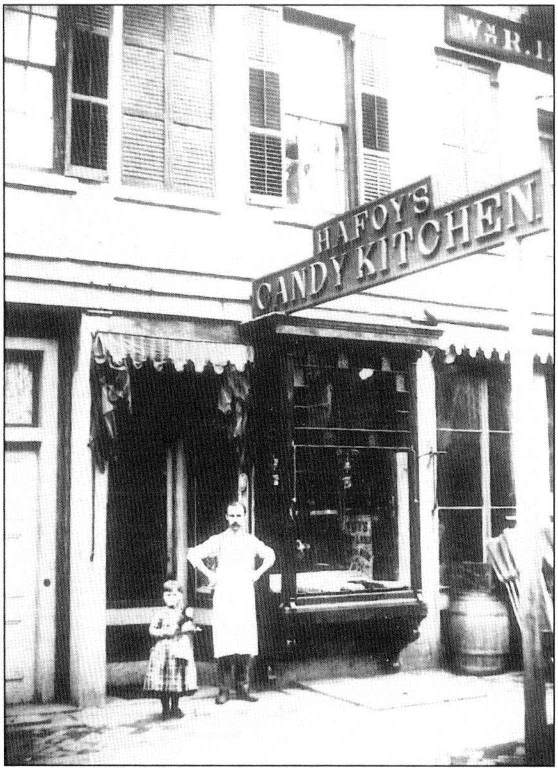

HENRY A FOY'S CANDY KITCHEN, 610 SECOND AVENUE. Foy made candy on one floor and lived in the rest of the house. The structure can still be found at its original location.

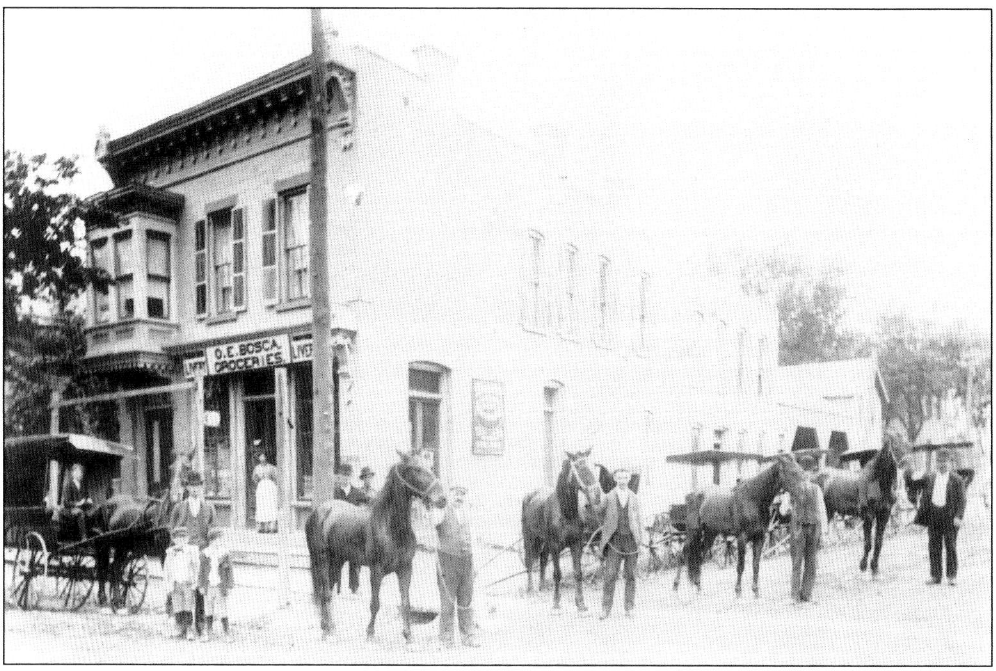

ORVILLE E. BOSCA'S GROCERY AND LIVERY ON THE CORNER OF 757 FIFTH AVENUE AND 121ST STREET. The Bosca delivery wagon, other livery wagons, and drivers are lined up in this photograph. The building is now a private residence.

A.H. Hedges' Rensselaer County Paint and Color Works on Fifth Avenue. I'm not sure if the sleds in front were for sale or just recently painted, using Rensselaer Co. paint no doubt.

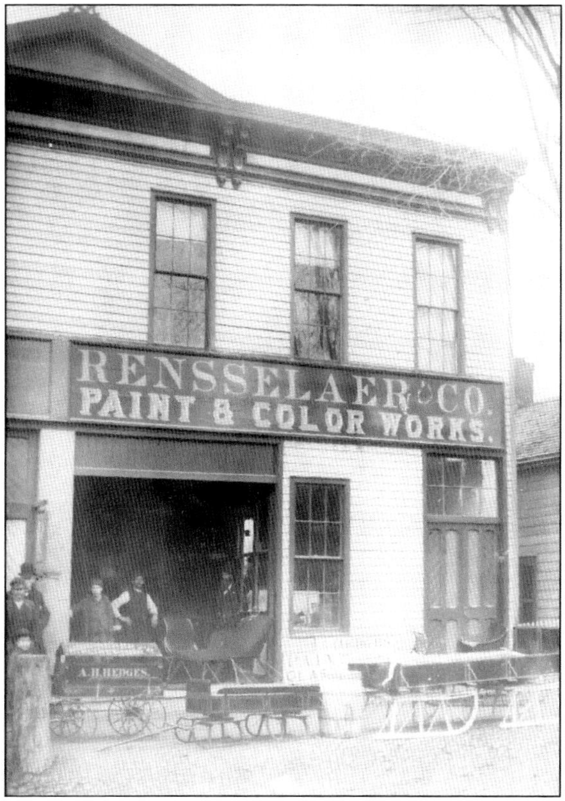

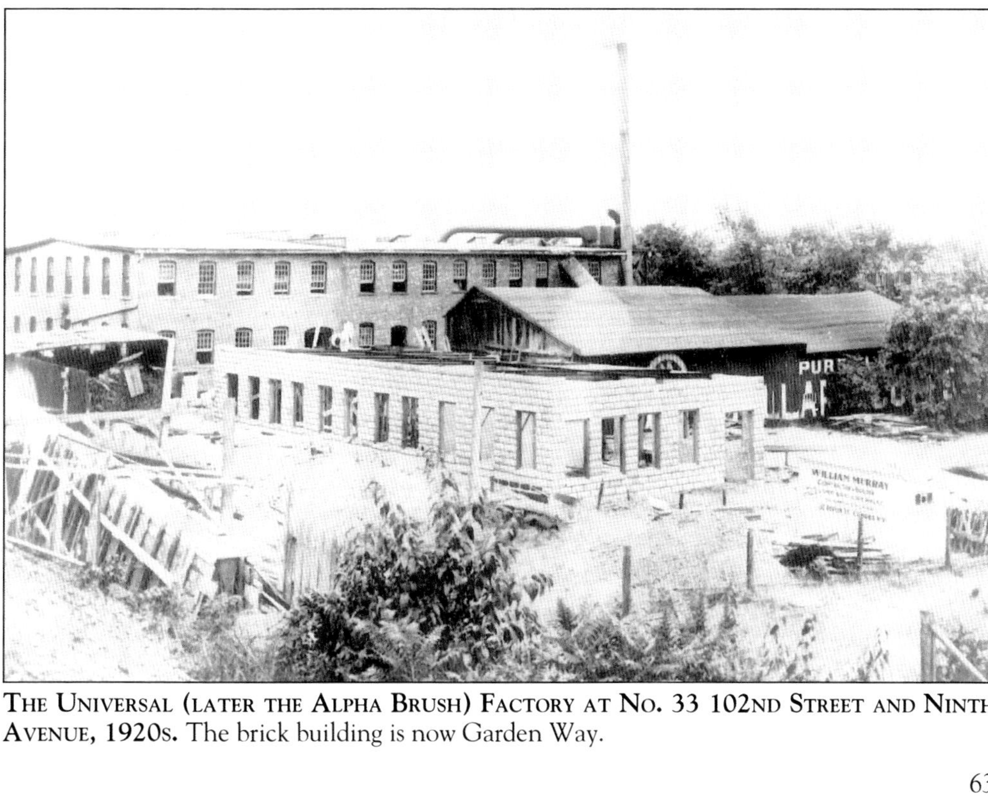

The Universal (later the Alpha Brush) Factory at No. 33 102nd Street and Ninth Avenue, 1920s. The brick building is now Garden Way.

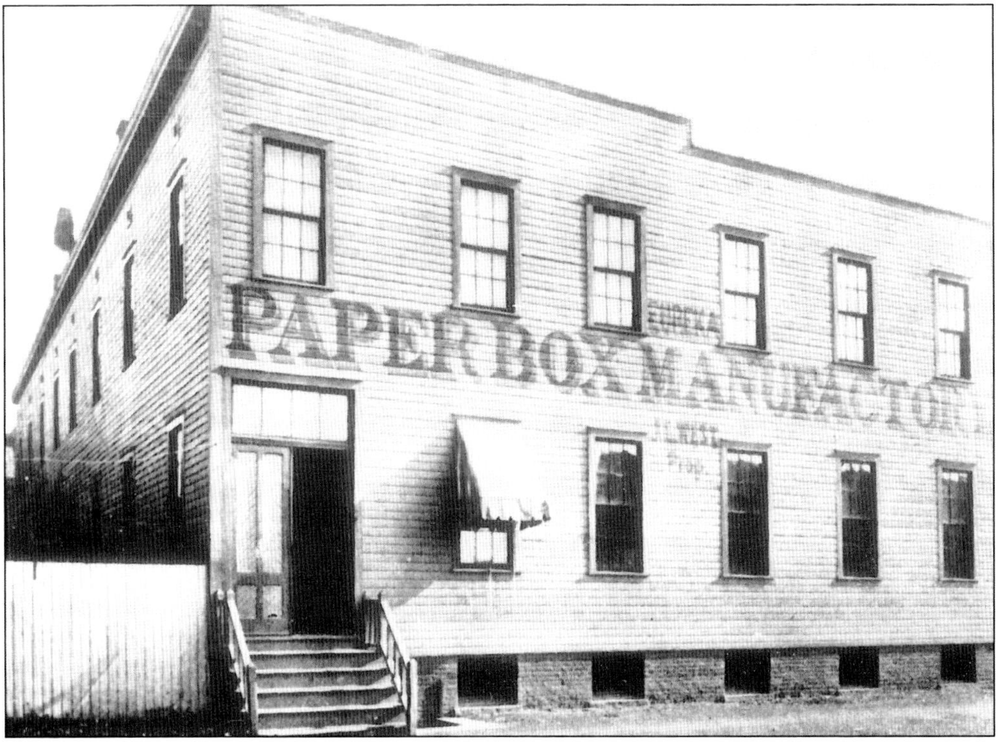

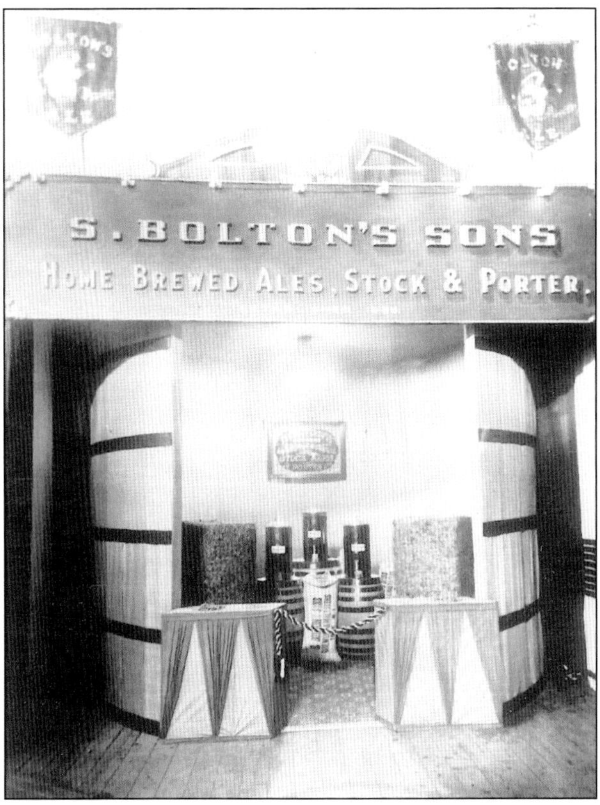

THE JOSIAH WEST PAPER BOX FACTORY AT 548 FIRST AVENUE, ON THE EAST SIDE, NORTH OF 114TH STREET. The company was called the Eureka Paper Box Factory when it was located at No. 13 and 14 Banker Block. In 1899, you could call them to order at their telephone, number 4120. The building is still standing today on First Avenue.

THE SAMUEL BOLTON'S SONS BREWERY, ESTABLISHED IN 1865 ON THE WEST SIDE OF SECOND AVENUE, BETWEEN 107TH AND 108TH STREETS. Bolton's Sons beer won a medal at the 1876 Philadelphia Centennial Exposition. After 1900, Bolton's had large land holdings in the village. They made home-brewed ale, stock, and porter. The business was also known as the Eagle Brewery.

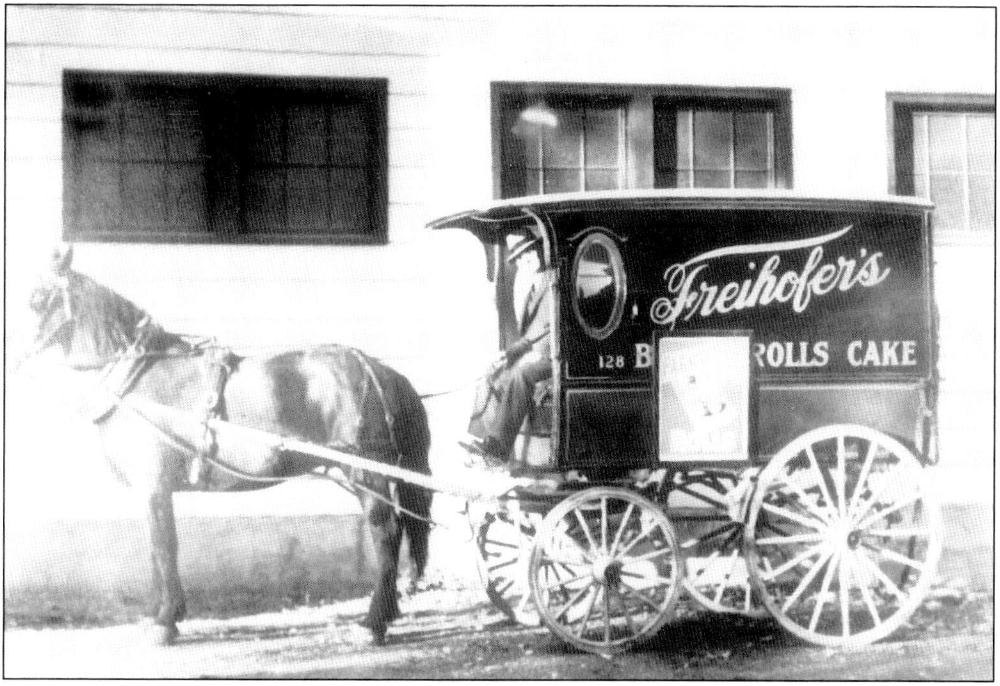

CHARLES F. FREIHOFER'S BAKERY, LOCATED NEAR THE WATERFORD BRIDGE. Freihofer's was started in 1913 by Charles C., Edwin, and Frank Freihofer. They delivered fresh bread, cookies, and baked goods by horse and buggy until the 1960s. The company is still in business, though it is owned by a national company. They make the best chocolate chip cookies in the world.

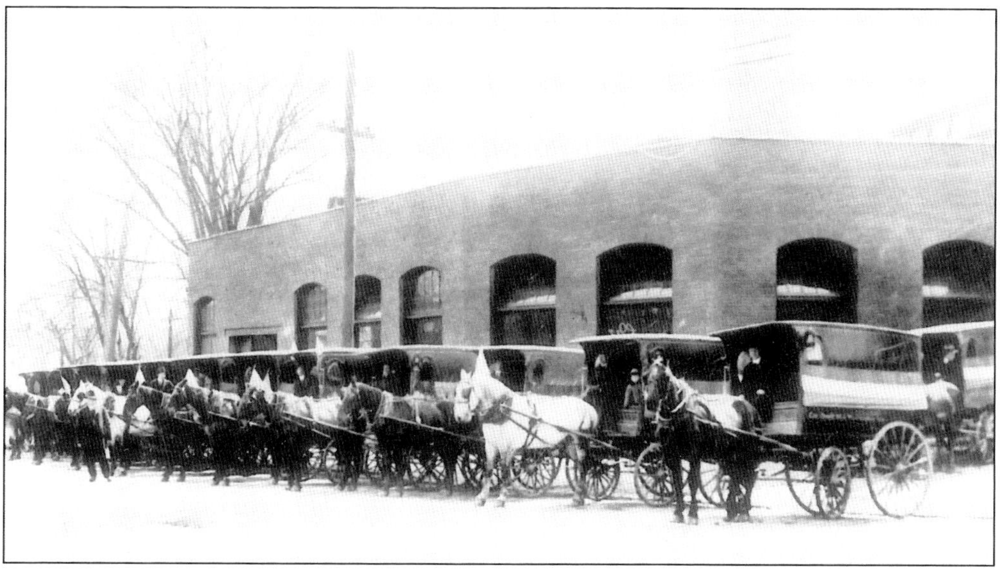

THE FREIHOFER BAKERY WITH WAGONS TO GO. When I was a boy in the 1960s, the clopclop of the horses drawing the wagons woke me up in the morning. It was also fun to pet the horses. Freihofer's sponsored a television show on local Channel 6 called "The Freddy Freihofer Show." The program was also called "Bread Time Stories," and it ran from 1949 until 1966. While it had several hosts, Jim Fisk is the best remembered for "squiggles," a cartoon that kids (in the audience) would help draw. If you appeared on the show, you left with chocolate chip cookies.

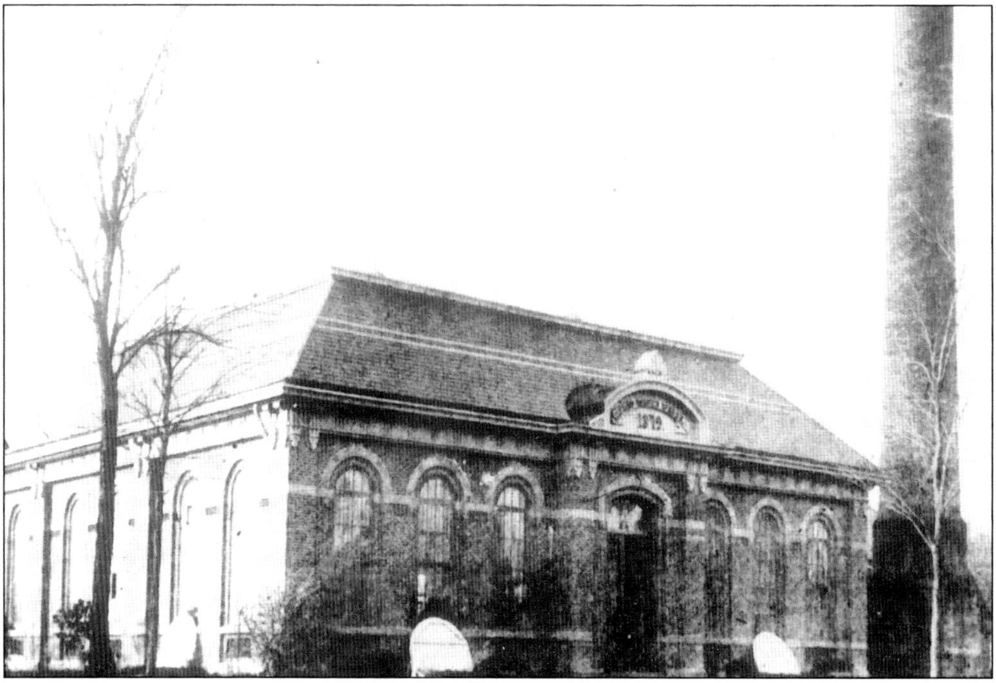

The Lansingburgh Water Works at the Northwest Corner of Second Avenue and 123rd Street, later Used as a Public Bath. A boat launch and park are now being created here.

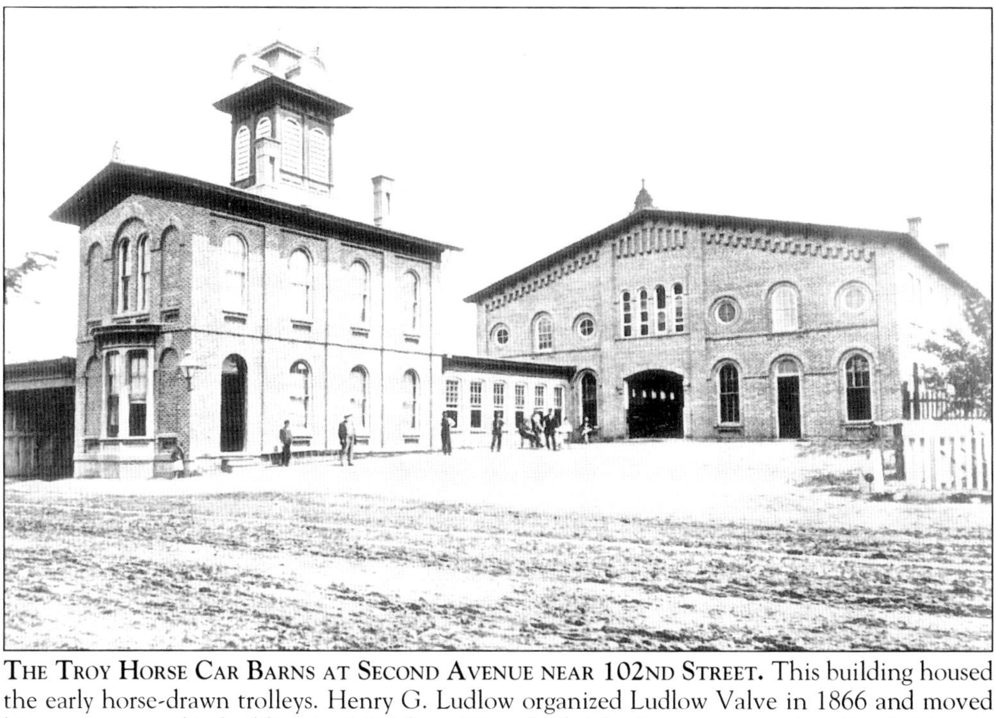

The Troy Horse Car Barns at Second Avenue near 102nd Street. This building housed the early horse-drawn trolleys. Henry G. Ludlow organized Ludlow Valve in 1866 and moved his company to this building in 1872 from Waterford. The business moved to South Troy in 1897 and became a worldwide supplier of all kinds of valves.

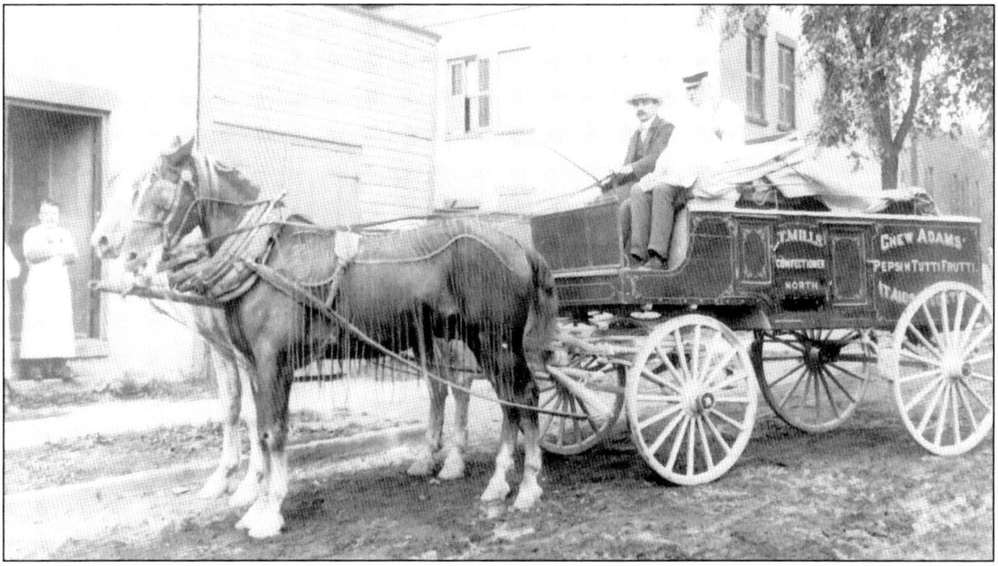

THOMAS MILLS, CANDY MANUFACTURER. This photograph shows the rear and south-side view of the main building, as well as the building behind 118th Street. The Mills Candy Wagon Store at the northeast corner of Second Avenue and 118th Street still stands. The advertisement on the side of the wagon says "Chew Adams' Pepsin Tutti Frutti. It Aids Digestion."

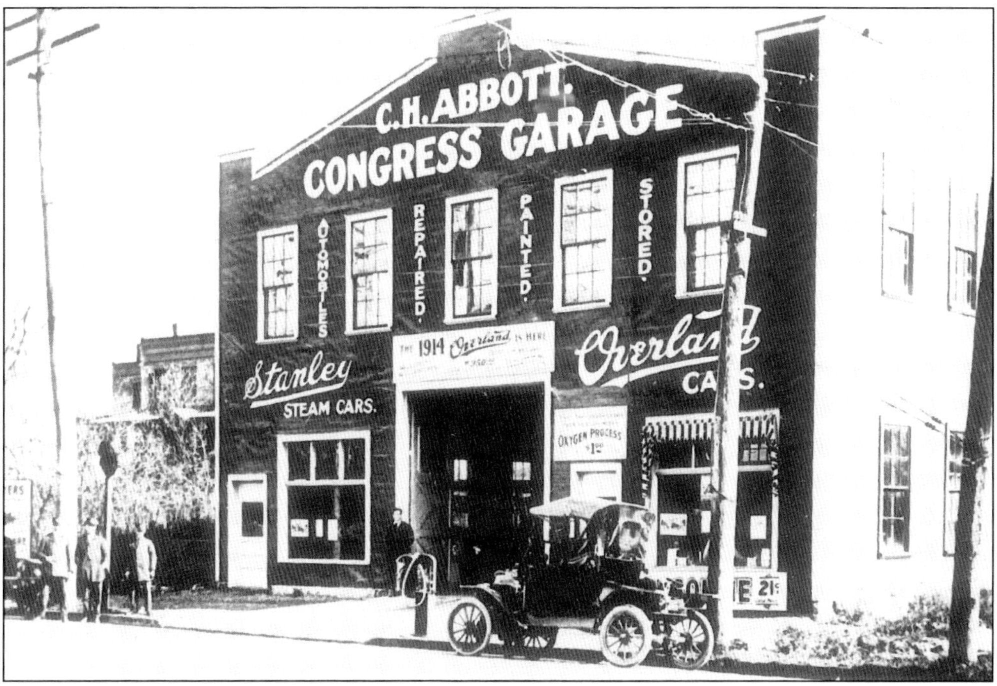

A 1915 PHOTOGRAPH OF C.H. ABBOTT AT THE CONGRESS GARAGE, LOCATED ON THE EAST SIDE OF SECOND AVENUE AT 126TH STREET. Notice the advertising for Stanley Steamers and Overland cars. One of the signs advertises the new 1914 Overland with 35 horsepower and a 114-inch wheelbase. It cost $950, although it was $125 extra for an electric starter and generator. It came completely equipped and featured electronic lighting.

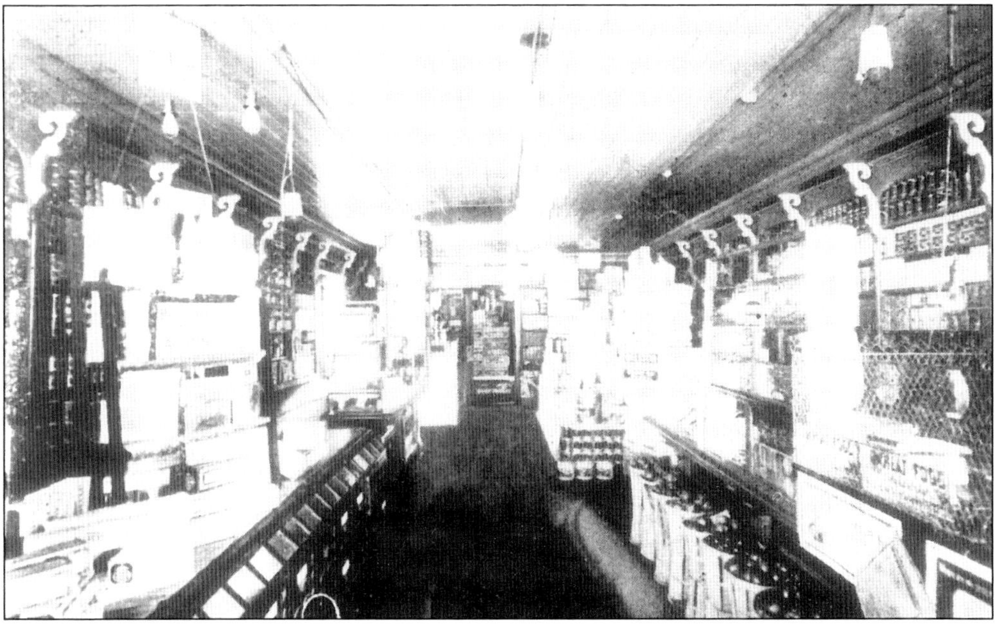

WILLIAM B. HALL'S GROCERY AND MEAT MARKET. Well stocked and neat, this store was located at the junction where Second and Third Avenues meet. At one time there was a gas station at this site.

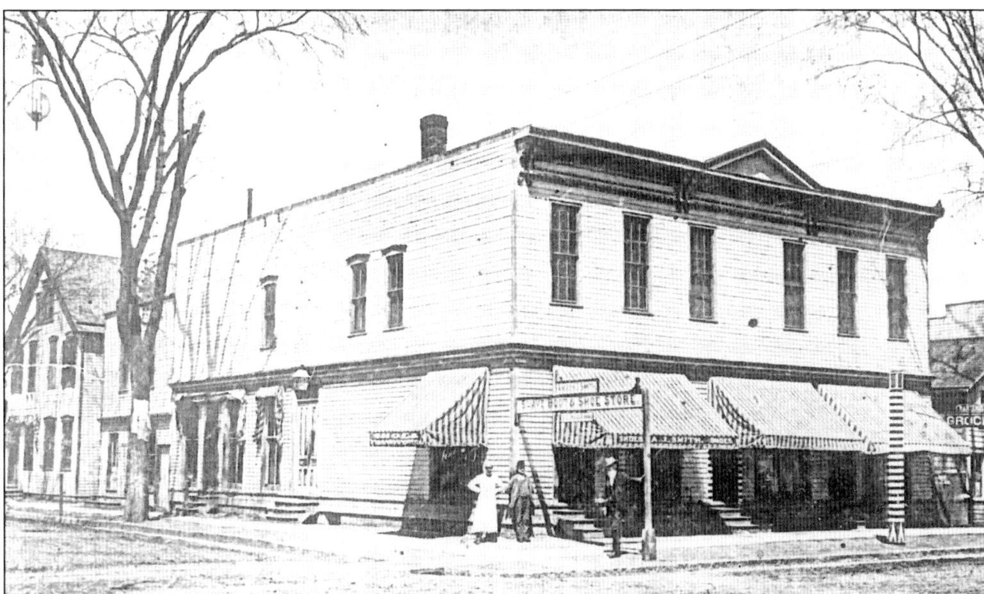

DANIA HALL, LOCATED AT THE NORTHWEST CORNER OF 471 FIFTH AVENUE AND 112TH STREET, IN 1902. The Godt Haab Council of the Danish Brotherhood owned this hall. Merchants in the building included Andrew J. Smith's Boots and Shoes and Martenus Howe Groceries. Unfortunately, the building was destroyed by fire on March 17, 1959.

Three

Transportation and Movement

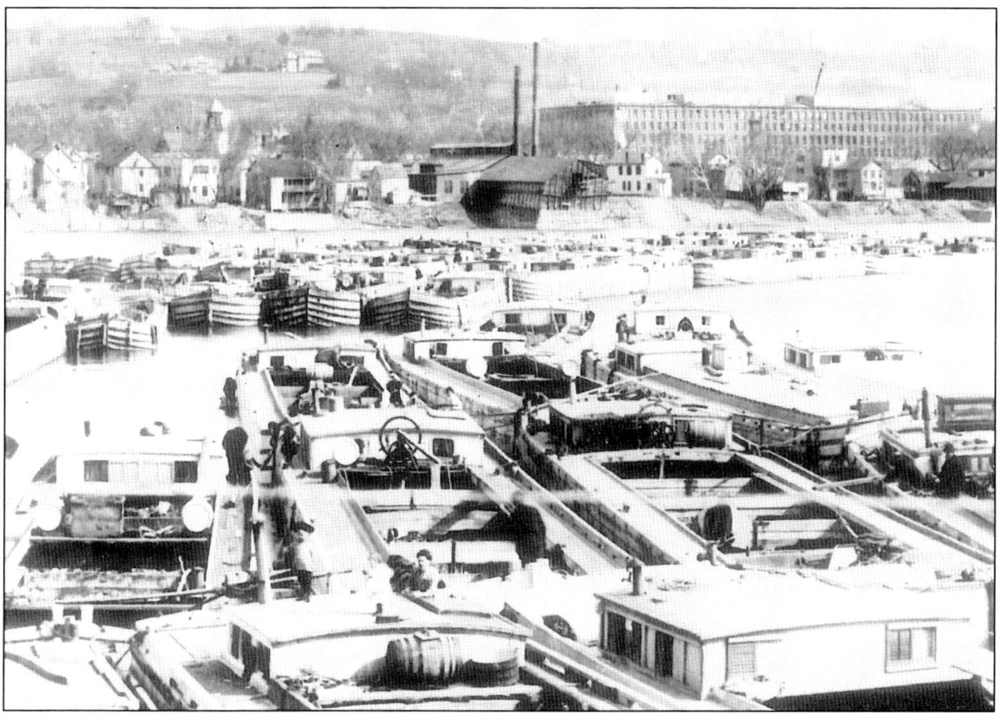

Canal Boats Waiting to Enter the Erie Canal at Waterford. The Lansingburgh shoreline, the United Shirt & Collar Company building, and the Lansingburgh Power Plant (the building with the smokestack) can be seen in the background. Both the Erie and Champlain Canals were located at Waterford.

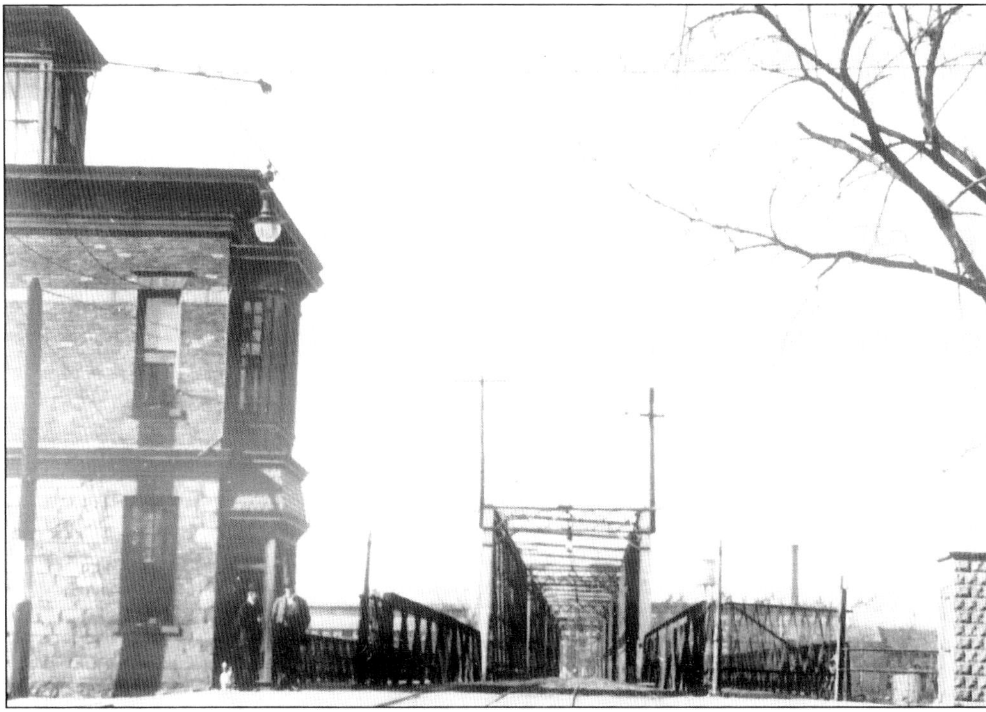

The Second Bridge to Connect Cohoes and Lansingburgh. This toll bridge was located at 112th Street. Cohoes and Lansingburgh were first connected by a bridge at 112th Street in 1880. Private companies built bridges and charged tolls in the early years. Four bridges have spanned the river at this location.

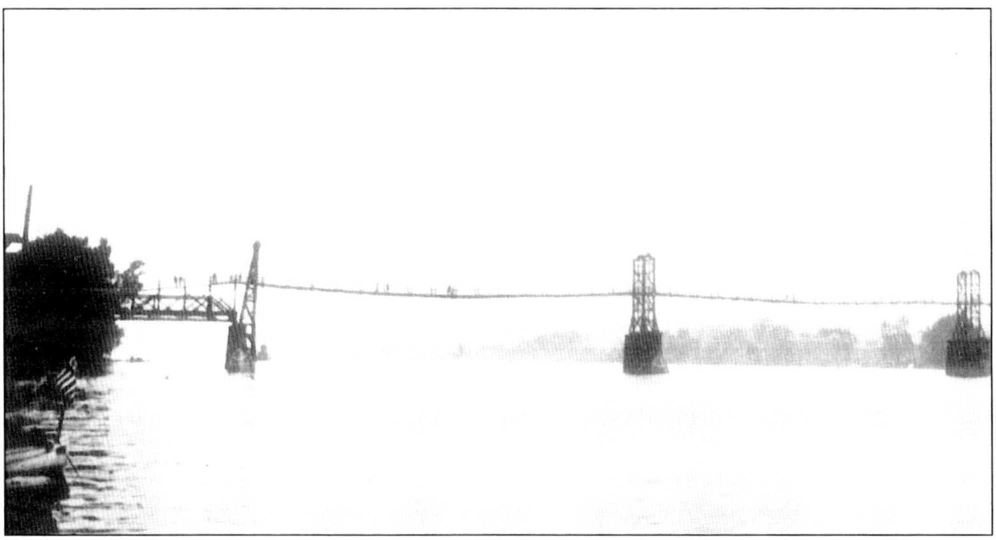

The Temporary Footbridge Built Following the Destruction by Fire of the Second Bridge. The wooden floor of the steel Cohoes Bridge caught fire on March 4, 1920, and according to accounts at the time, the fire was so intense that steel girders twisted and fell into the river. This temporary footbridge, which swayed in the wind, was built until a new ornamental concrete bridge was erected in 1923. The new one was free of tolls. A modern fourth bridge now crosses the river.

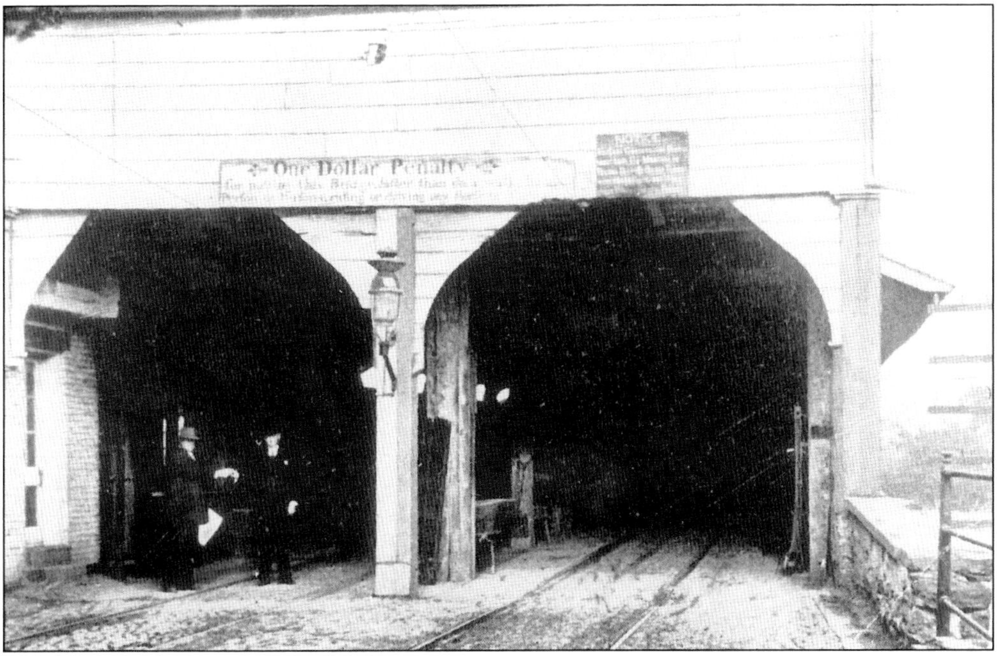

THE WATERFORD COVERED TOLL BRIDGE, BUILT IN 1804. When built, it was the only bridge between Lansingburgh and New York City, and when it burned on July 10, 1909, it was the oldest covered bridge in America. It was 800 feet long and 30 feet wide. The Waterford entrance looks east. The sign above says "One Dollar Penalty for passing this bridge faster than on a walk by any person or persons, or driving any horse or carriage."

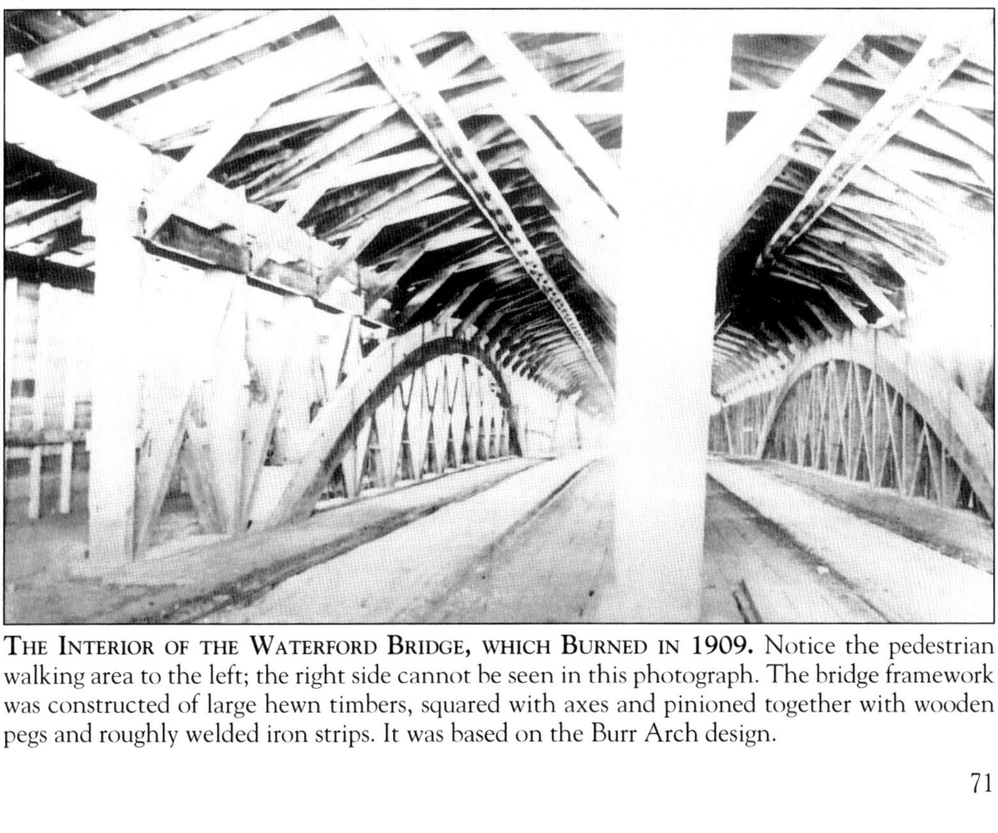

THE INTERIOR OF THE WATERFORD BRIDGE, WHICH BURNED IN 1909. Notice the pedestrian walking area to the left; the right side cannot be seen in this photograph. The bridge framework was constructed of large hewn timbers, squared with axes and pinioned together with wooden pegs and roughly welded iron strips. It was based on the Burr Arch design.

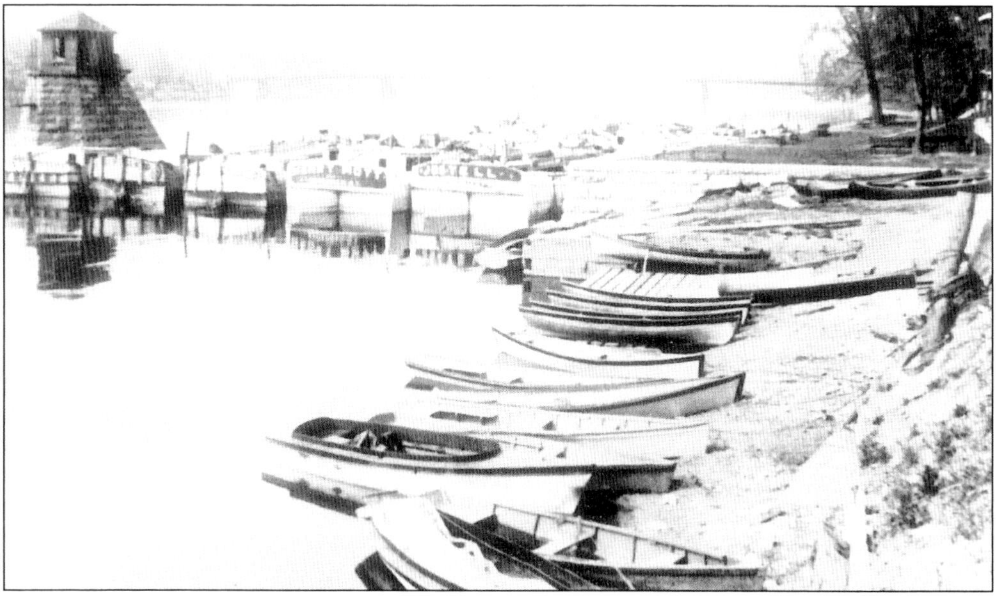

Pleasure Boats at the Lansingburgh Water Works Pumping Station at Second Avenue and 123rd Street. The Waterford Bridge is in the background. The area has now been restored as a boat launch and marina by the city of Troy.

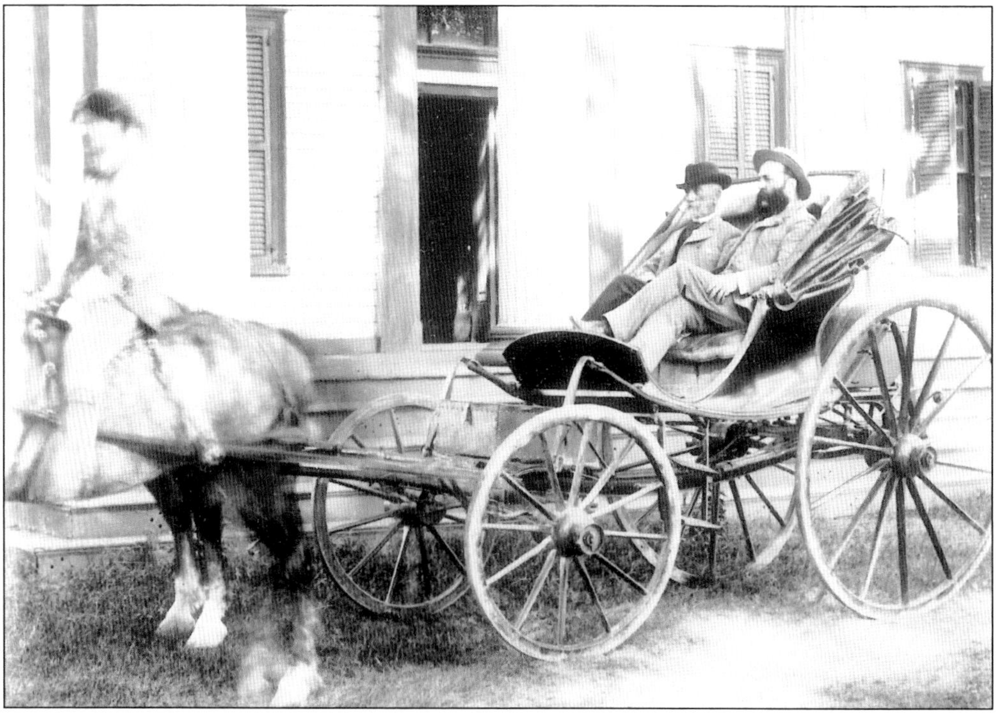

The Van Schoonhoven Family in front of Glenwood (the Eddy Residence). The Van Schoonhovens were a prominent family. James Van Schoonhoven and Lorenzo C. Fisk owned a wholesale dry goods and Yankee notions at 227 River Street (First Avenue) in the 1870s. Jacob Lansing Van Schoonhoven was president of the Central National Bank in Troy and was related to the Lansing family.

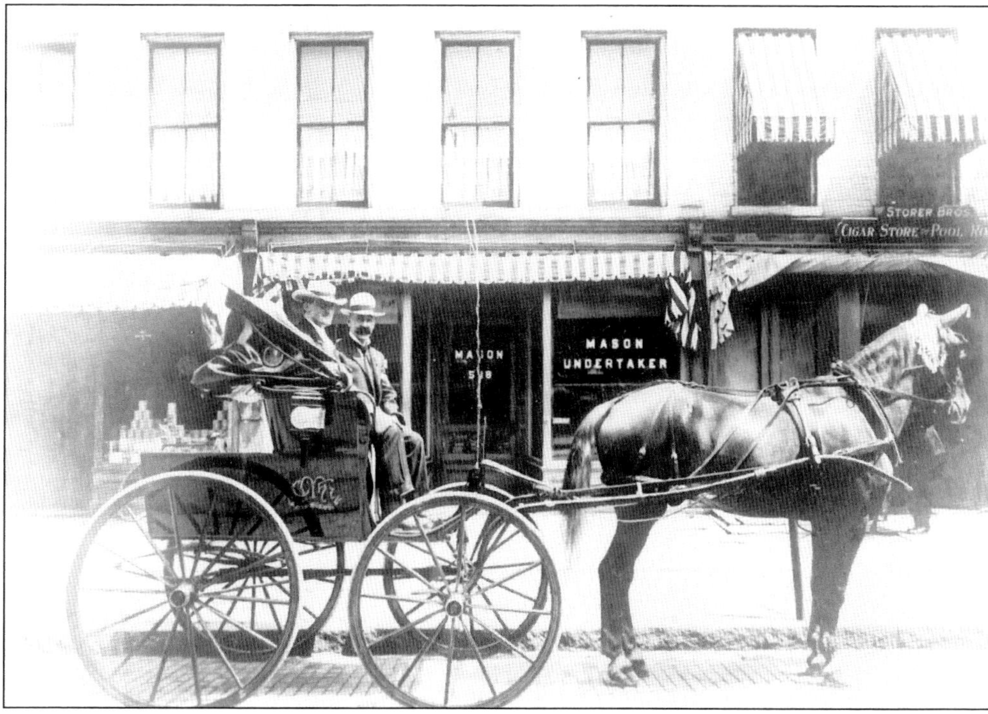

Peter A. Grogan (left) and John Carter (right), Clerks for Charles H. Mason Undertakers. The two are posing on the east side of 588 Second Avenue. Charles H. Mason Undertakers was adjacent and south of the Phoenix Hotel. The building no longer exists.

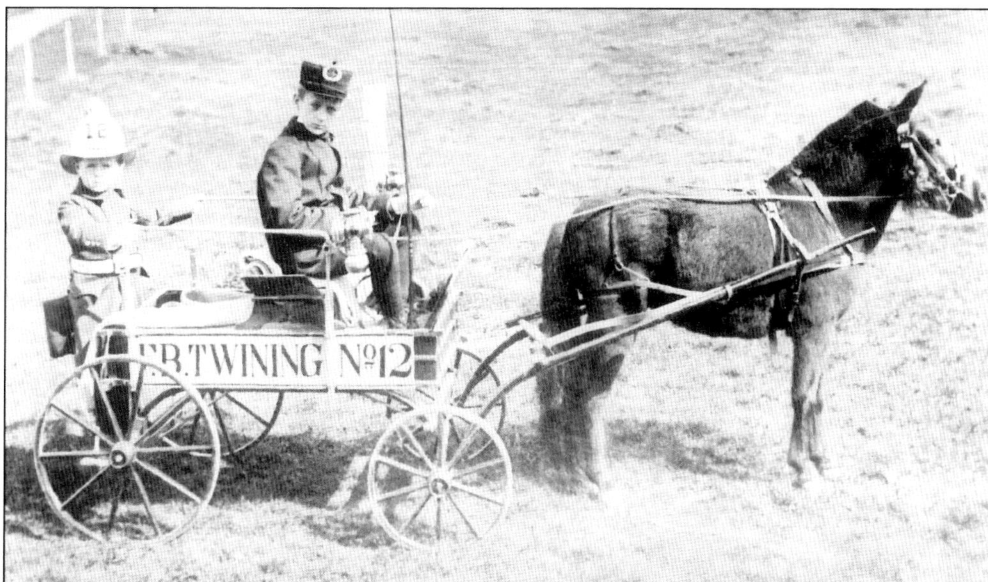

Even the Little Guys Had to Get Around. These kids were practicing to become firemen, no doubt, in this post-1900 photograph. The F.B. Twinning Fire Station was on the southwest corner at 122nd Street and Second Avenue. The station was built by the city of Troy after the village was annexed in 1900. Frank B. Twinning was a principle in George B. Ide's shirt, collar, and cuff company in Troy. Twinning lived at 865 Second Avenue in Lansingburgh.

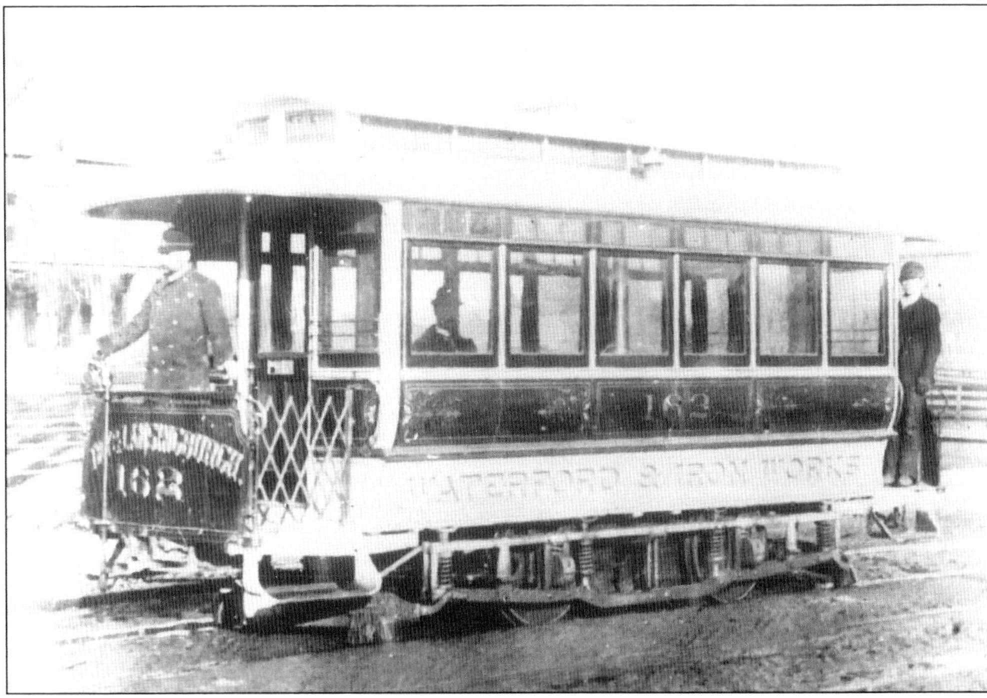

TROY AND LANSINGBURGH COMPANY TROLLEY #162 ON THE WATERFORD TO IRON WORKS LINE. The Lansingburgh Horse Railroad was a single track laid through River, Adams, and Second Streets to the Wyantskill, 6.5 miles away. The first car, called the Red Line, began in August 30, 1861, extending to Waterford in 1862.

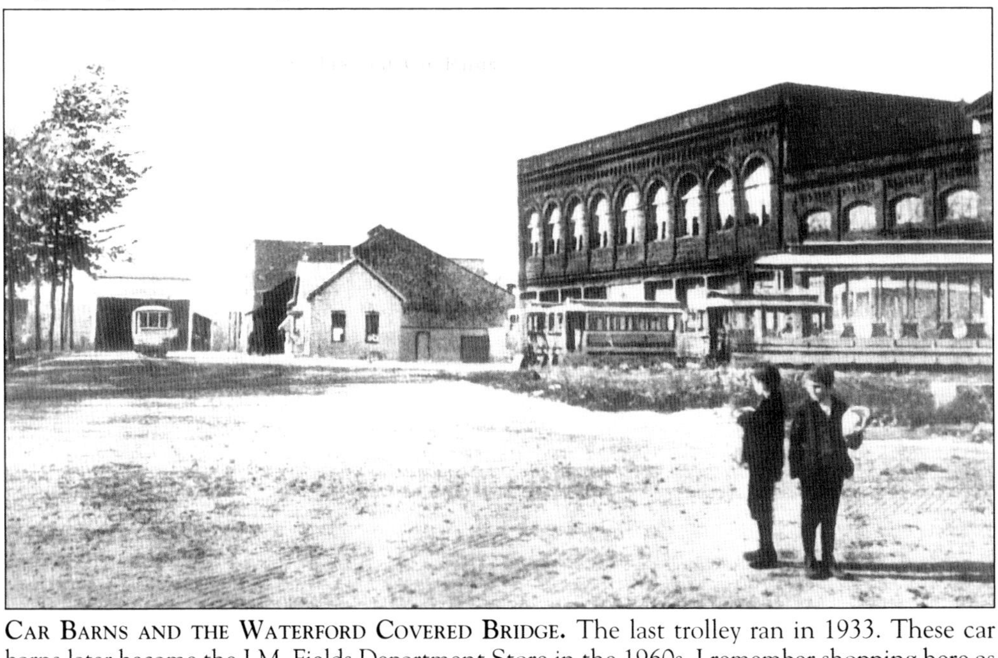

CAR BARNS AND THE WATERFORD COVERED BRIDGE. The last trolley ran in 1933. These car barns later became the J.M. Fields Department Store in the 1960s. I remember shopping here as a kid; parts of the floors dipped down as you walked across them and could make you dizzy. This site is now is a new Hannaford's supermarket.

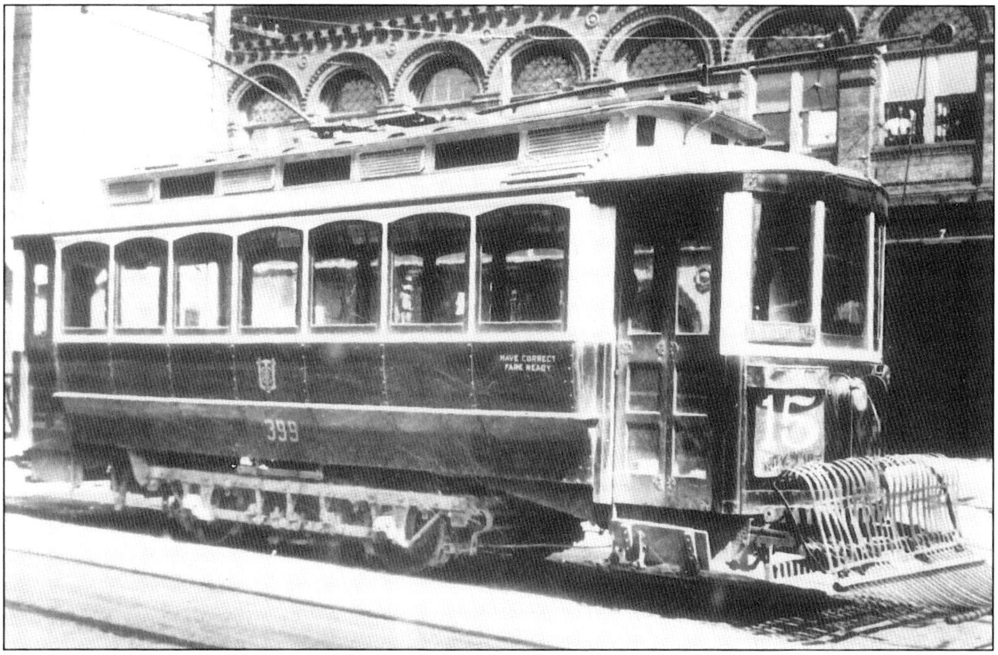

Trolley #399 of the United Traction Company. Route 15 was the Troy-Watervliet-12th Avenue route. In 1900, the streetcars of Troy, Albany, and the surrounding area combined under the United Traction Company. In 1906, the Delaware & Hudson Company purchased the UTC. In 1924, the electric trolley seen here began operating.

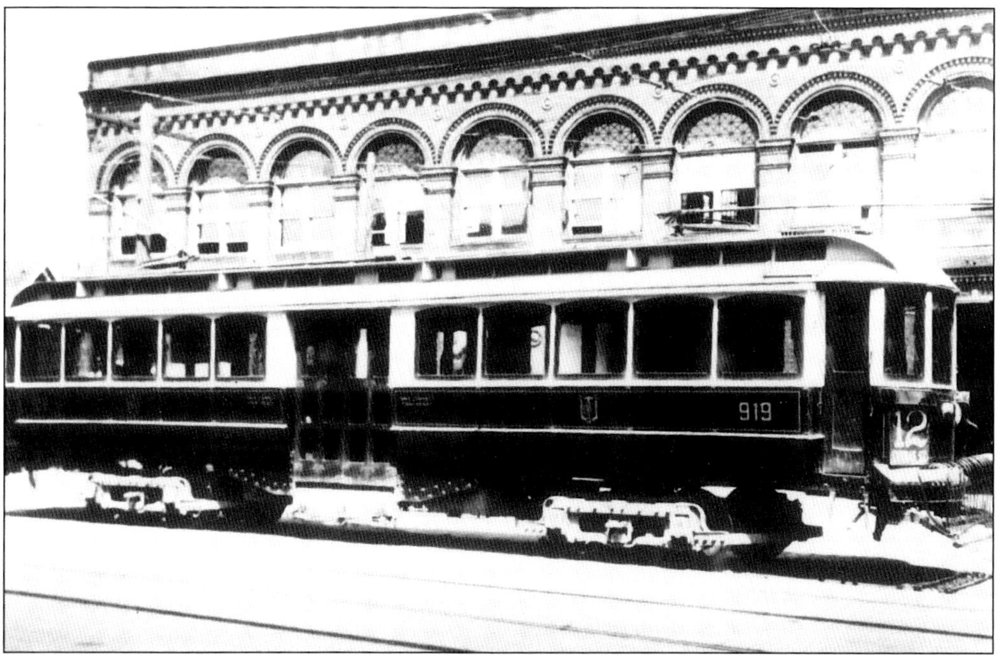

Trolley #919 in front of the Car Barns. Route 12 was the Waterford-Thomas Street route. Notice that the trolley shown here looks more like a railroad car. Even then you needed exact change.

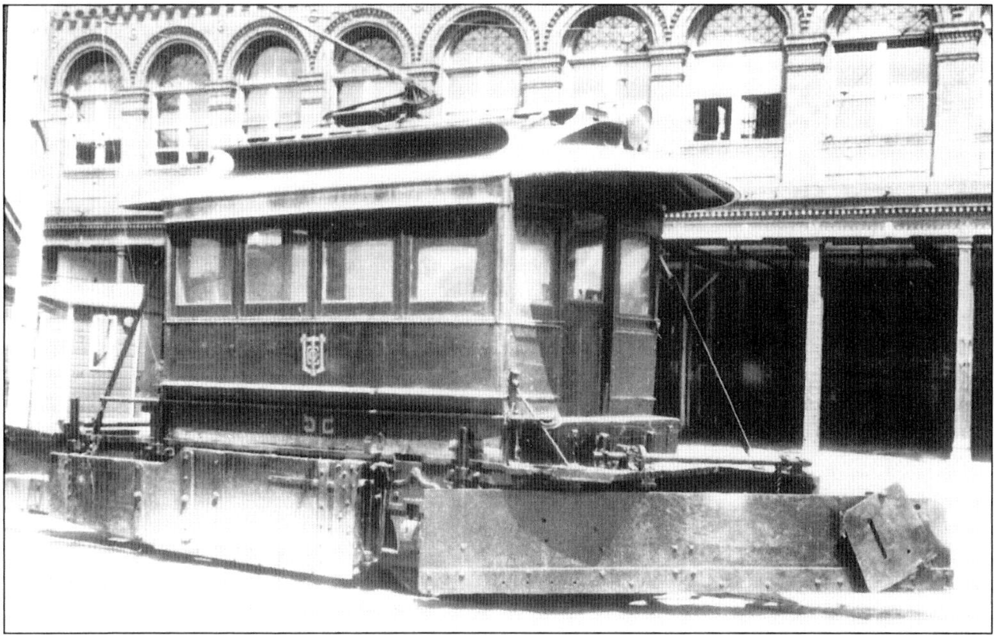

A TROLLEY SNOW PLOW. During winter months, it was necessary to keep the trolley car tracks clean of snow and debris. This trolley plow, like our modern snow plows would, be the first out of the barn on a snowy night or day.

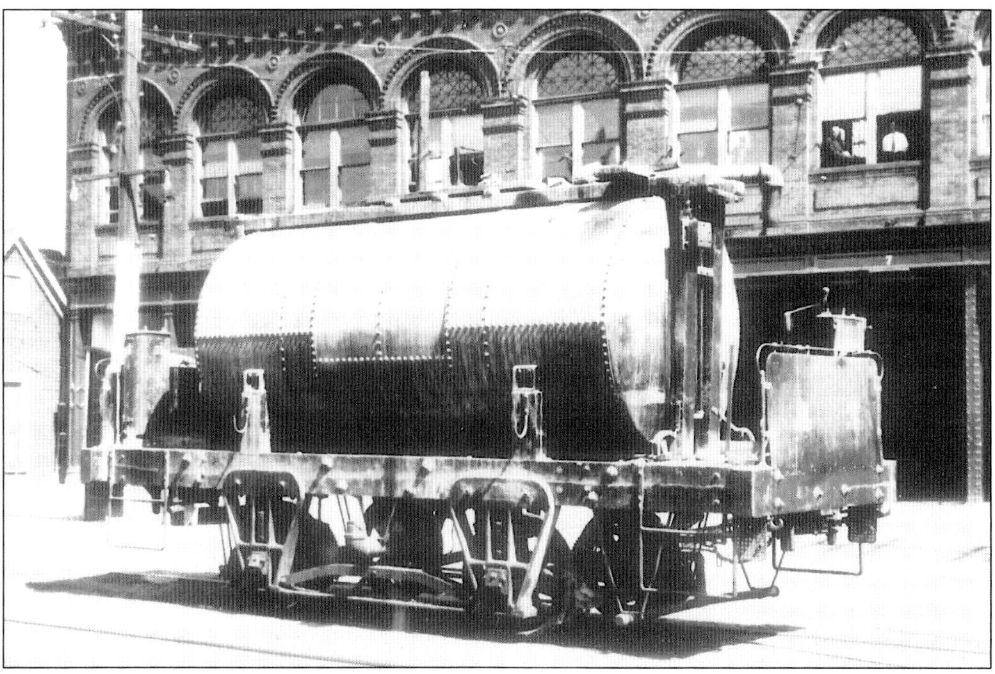

A TROLLEY WATER TANK. The tank was probably used to keep the dirt around the tracks down or perhaps even to keep the trolleys clean.

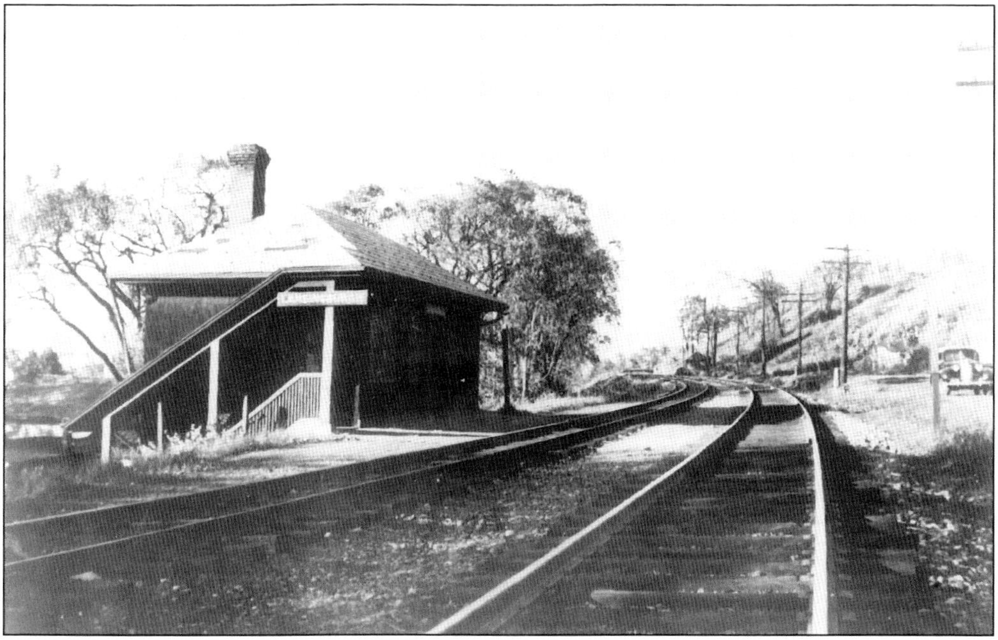

THE SECOND LANSINGBURGH TRAIN STATION, JUST WEST OF THE TRACKS, NEAR THE HEAD OF 115TH STREET. When no longer used as a station, it became the office of a coal company and was moved to the opposite side of the tracks. It was demolished in 1974. The first station was on the west side of tracks between 116th and 117th Streets.

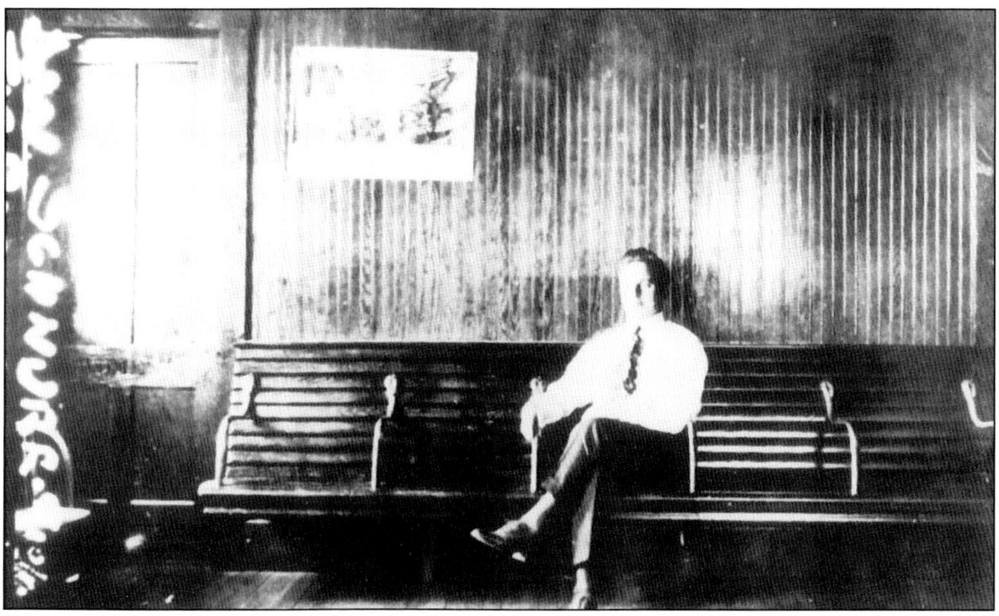

THE INTERIOR OF THE TRAIN STATION OF THE BOSTON & MAINE RAILROAD. J.W. Schnurr, president of the B&M, poses for a photograph. Originally these tracks were part of the Troy & Boston Railroad, and later the Fitchburg Railroad. The Boston & Maine Railroad Company absorbed the Fitchburg Railroad in 1905.

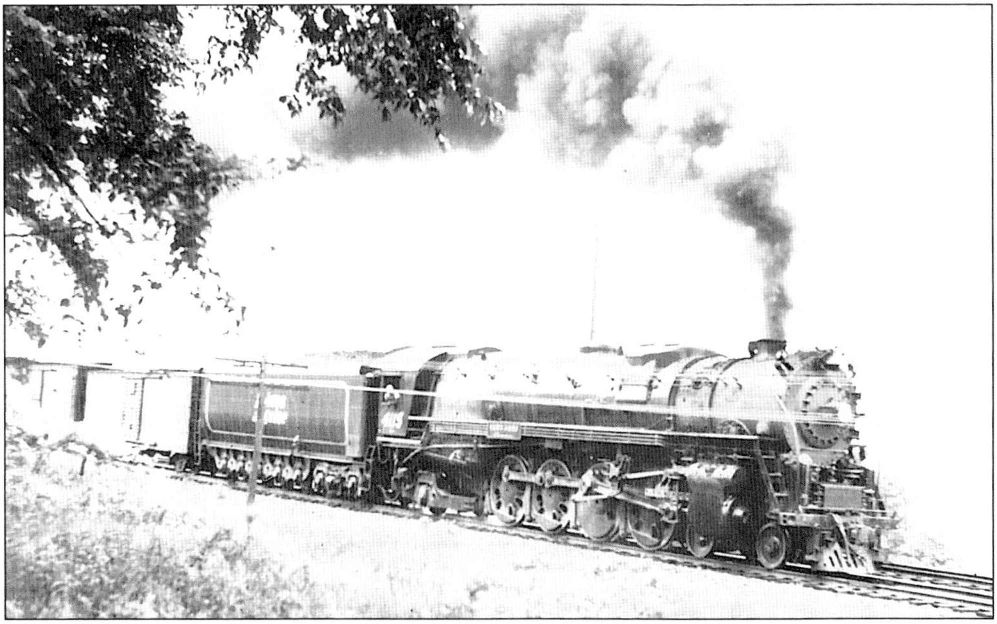

A Boston and Maine Train near St. John's Cemetery, c. 1940s. Engine 4115, the "Casey Jones," was a 4-8-2 Mountain type, built in 1941 at the Baldwin Locomotive Works in Philadelphia, Pennsylvania. It weighed 415,200 pounds and was retired from service on September 19, 1956. It had a centipede tender. Starting in late 1937, a contest was held for schoolchildren to name certain engines in the Pacific and Mountain types. The names were applied in white (silver in the Speed Lettering scheme) to a plate mounted below the running board, with the name of the child who won the contest and the school he/she attended below in smaller letters.

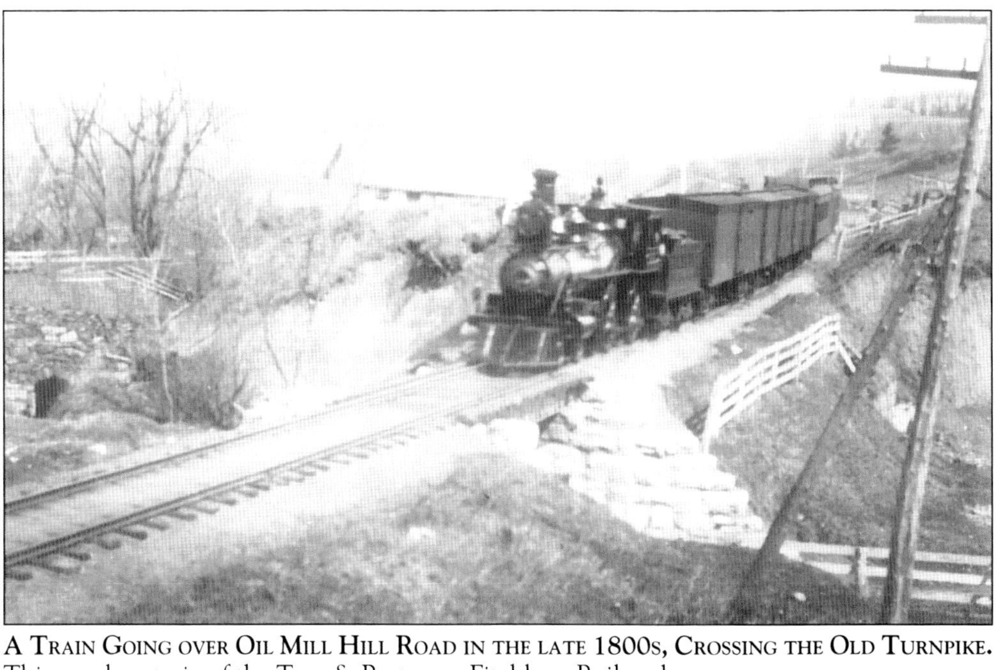

A Train Going over Oil Mill Hill Road in the late 1800s, Crossing the Old Turnpike. This may be a train of the Troy & Boston or Fitchburg Railroad.

Boston & Maine Engine 3663 or 3669 around 116th Street in the 1930s. Engine numbers 3660 to 3679 were built in 1913 at the Alco plant in Schenectady (American Locomotive) and were of the 4-6-2 Pacific type. They weighed 247,700 pounds and were retired from service on September 1, 1956.

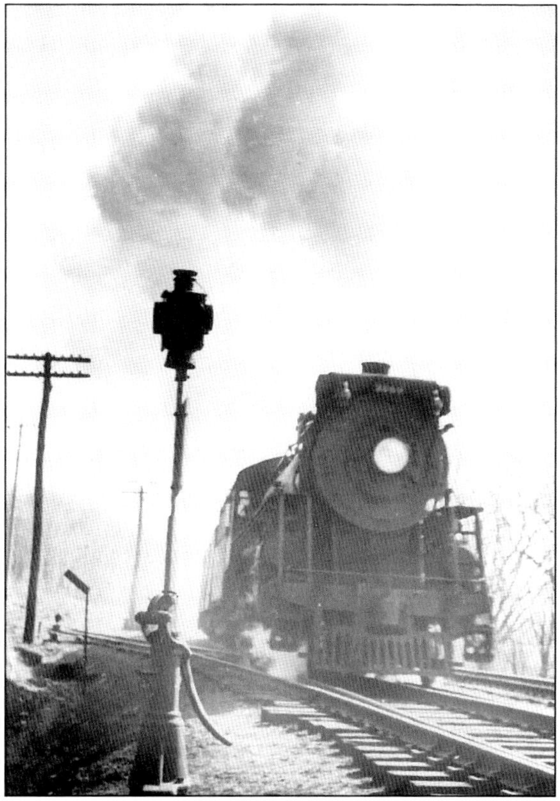

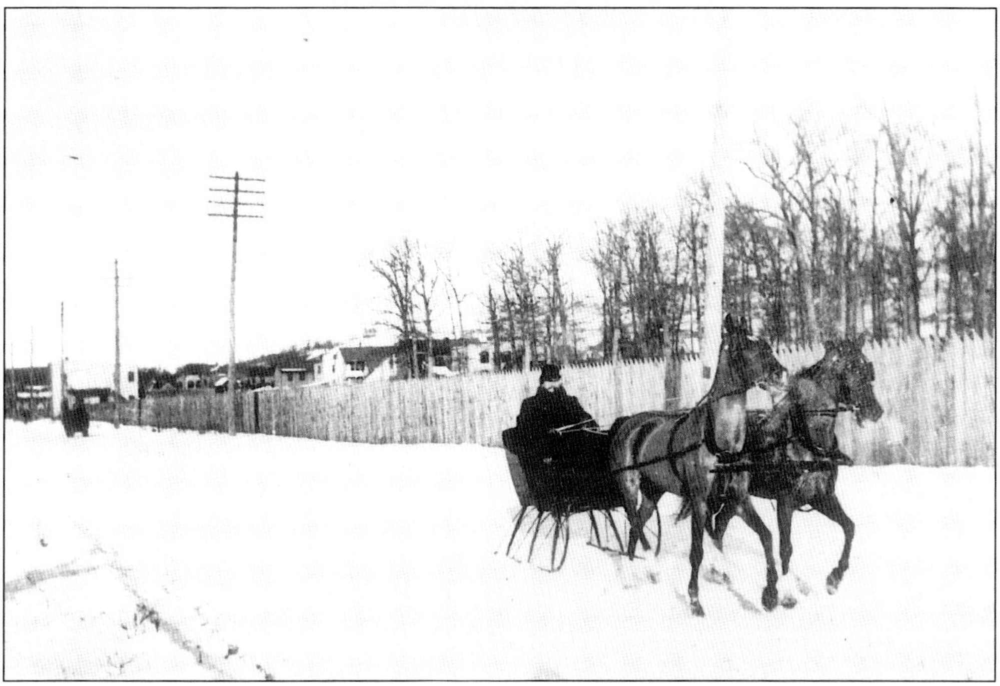

Horses and a Cutter on Fifth Avenue, perhaps around 108th Street. Sled races were common on Fifth Avenue.

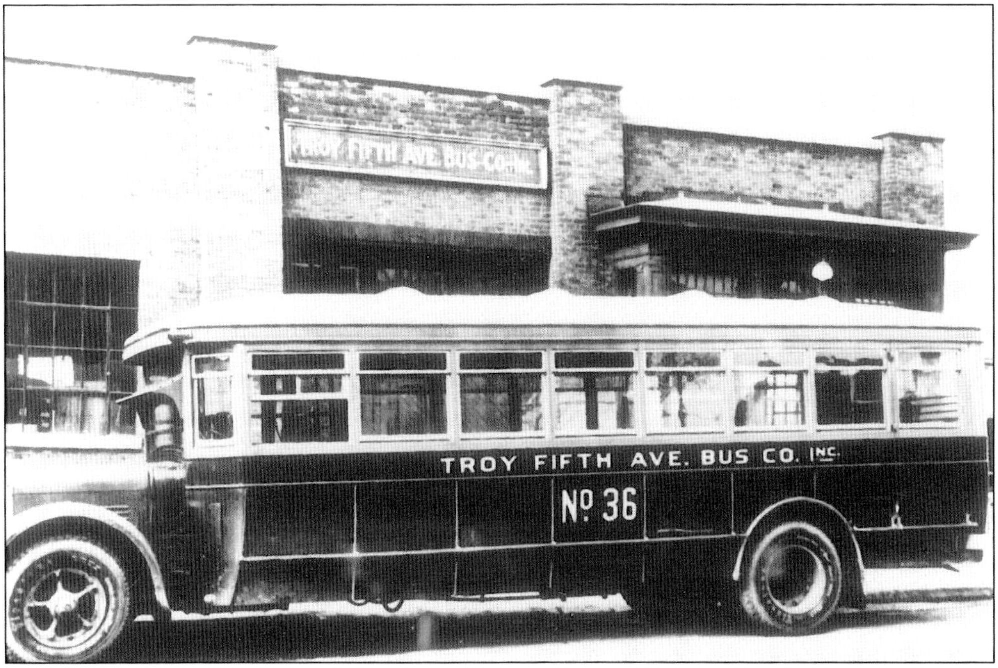

The Troy Auto Car Company (later the Troy Fifth Avenue Bus Company), which Served Troy and Lansingburgh. The company began operating on May 16, 1915, and ran northward on Fifth and Sixth Avenues to 125th Street. Fares were 5¢. It was still running in the 1960s. My buddy Paul and I would ride it for the complete circuit. Its original location was at 119th Street and Fifth Avenue.

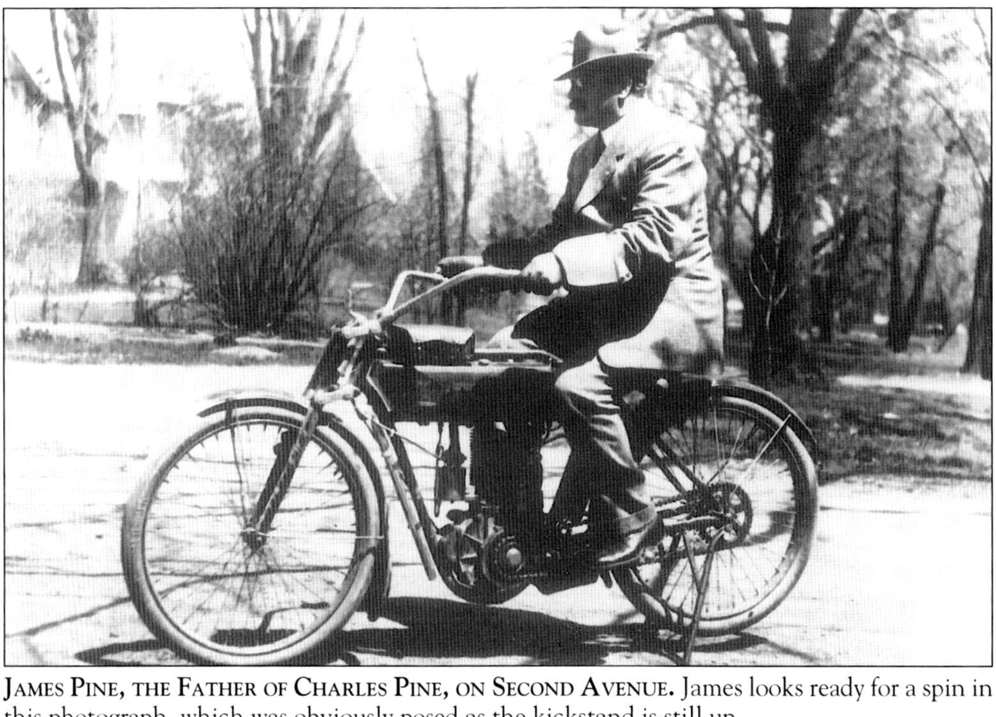

James Pine, the Father of Charles Pine, on Second Avenue. James looks ready for a spin in this photograph, which was obviously posed as the kickstand is still up.

Four

VITAL INSTITUTIONS

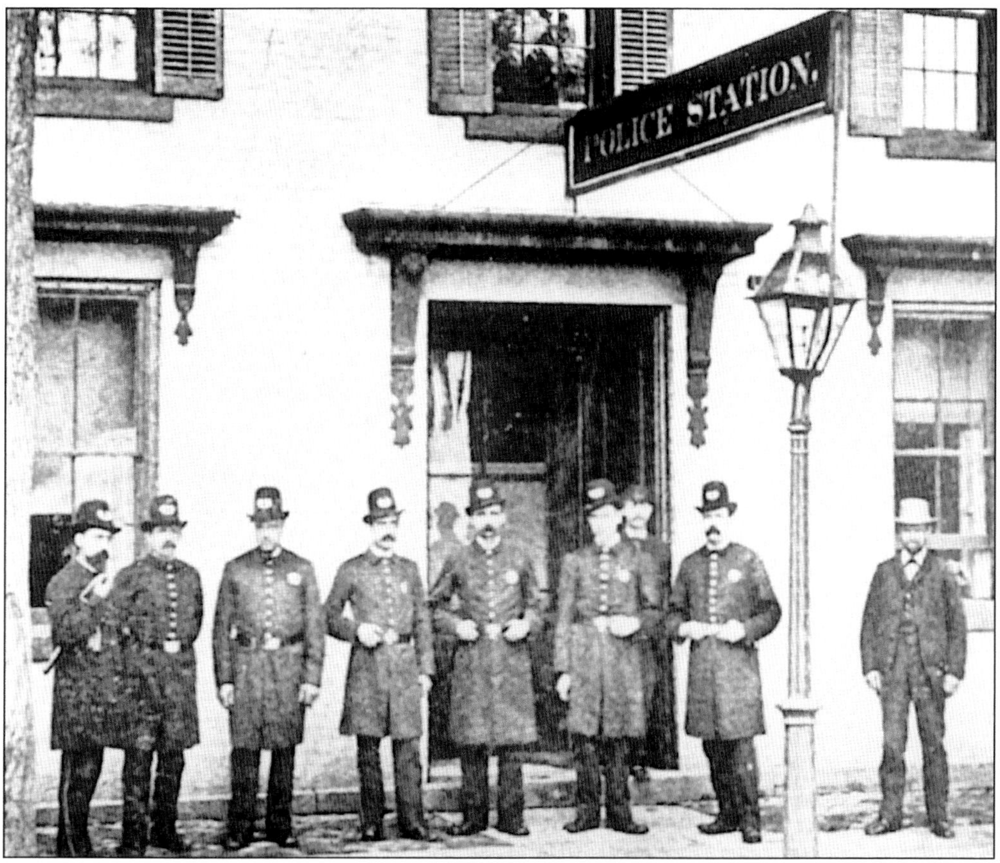

LANSINGBURGH POLICE, C. 1880. Lansingburgh had its own police force from 1871 until the village was annexed to Troy in 1900. It was then turned into the city's Fourth Precinct.

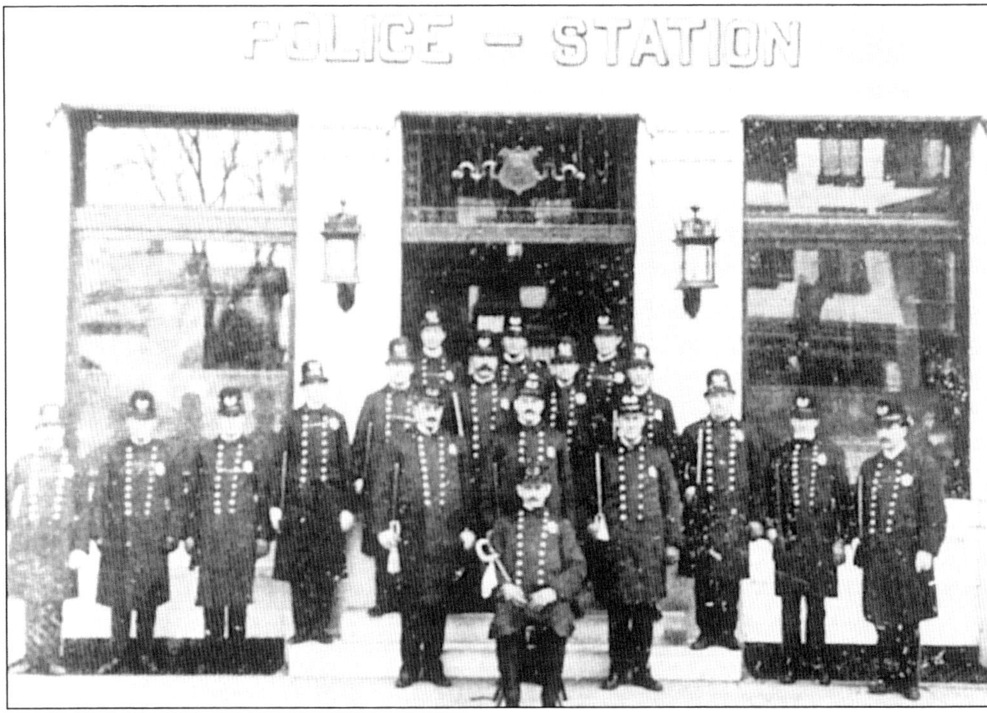

Lansingburgh Police, Fourth Precinct, post-1900. This building still stands with the police sign on the east side of Second Avenue, north of 116th Street. The Fellow sitting with sword is Morris Kirkpatrick, captain of the precinct. See page 34.

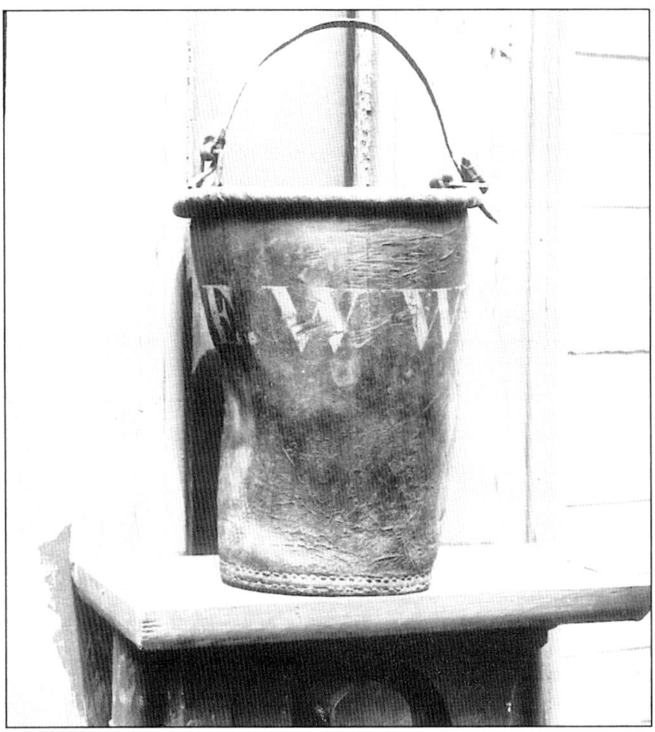

An early Leather Fire Bucket, Found in the Attic at 614 First Avenue, July 1973. The bucket belonged to Ebenezer William Walbridge (1779–1856), who settled in Lansingburgh in 1800. Everyone had a fire bucket to fight fires in those days.

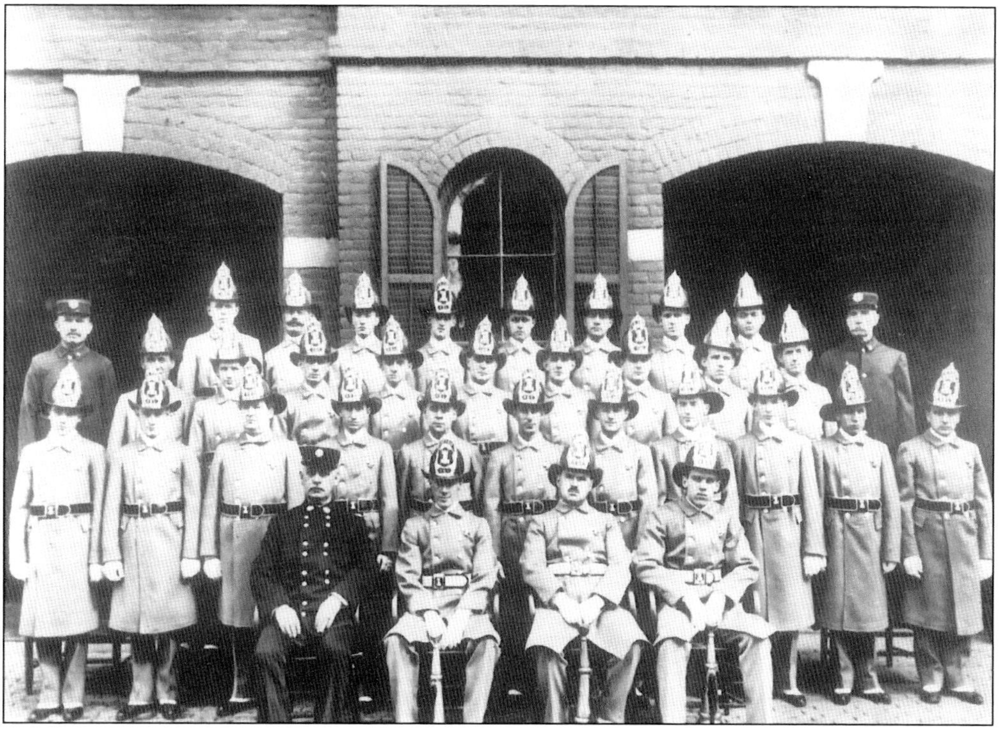

THE LANSINGBURGH FIRE DEPARTMENT. The Mason Hose and Fake Hook and Ladder Companies are shown here in front of the Central Fire Station on First Avenue and 115th Street. The structure, which sported the fireman's hall on the second floor, was later transformed into an apartment house.

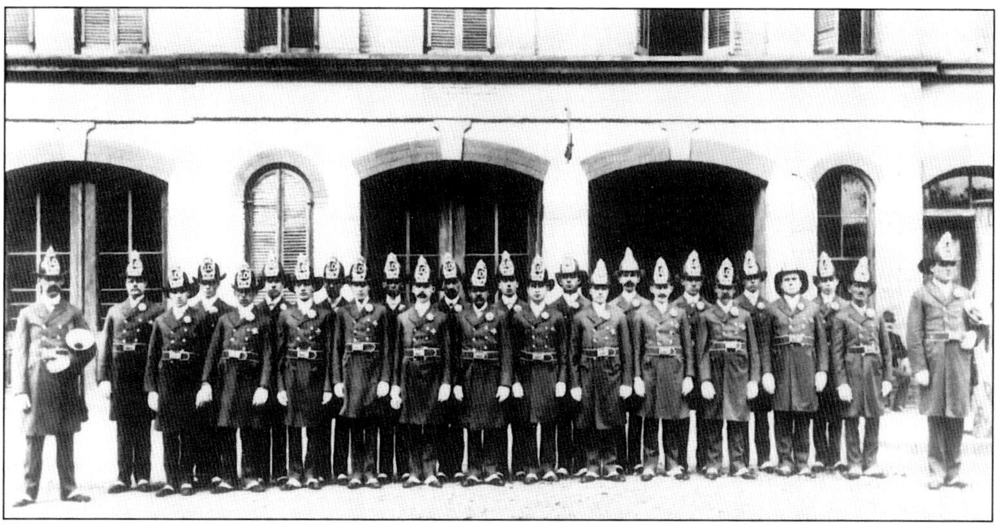

COMPANY NO. 10. Mason Hose firemen stand in front of the Central Fire Station. On Sunday, July 9, 1843, 30 to 40 buildings comprising the two blocks between State (Second Avenue), Congress (Third Avenue), Elizabeth (116th Street), and Grove (118th Street) Streets were destroyed by fire. Two weeks later, on July 23, 1912, more buildings burned on State Street (Second Avenue) between Richard (117th Avenue) and Elizabeth (116th Street) Streets. The street names changed in 1886.

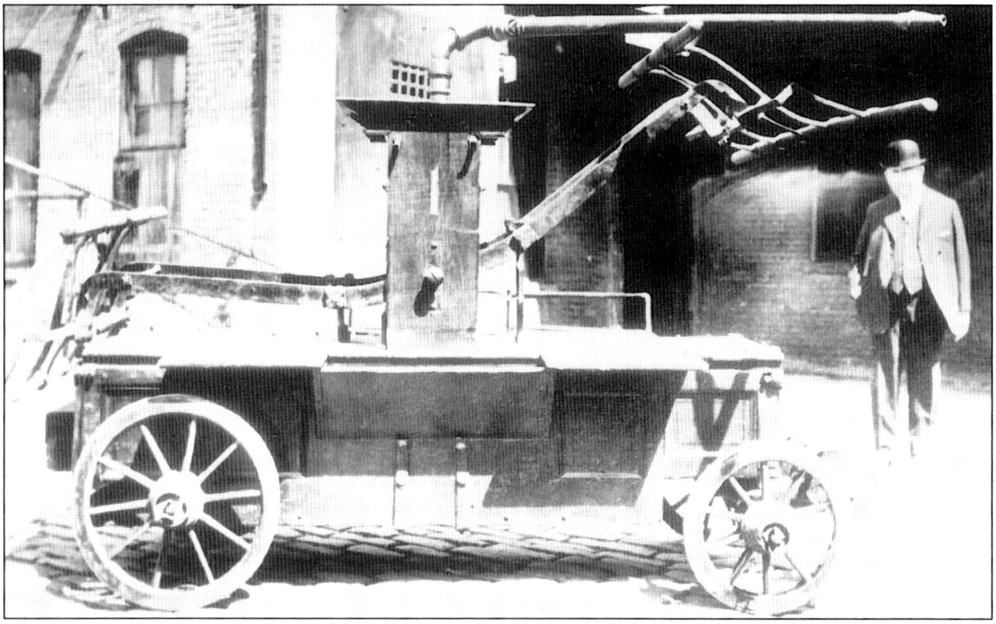

"Old Black Joke," Lansingburgh's First Fire Pump. Joseph Bolton of Bolton's Sons Brewery poses in this photograph next to the fire pump that he manned for years. Joke (one history book called it Joe) was purchased in 1791 from Richard Mason of Philadelphia. These were called "tubs" because they were hand-filled engines with buckets instead of hoses. The 2-cylinder, single acting pump threw a 140-foot stream through the brass-and-copper pipe. The John S. Fake Hook & Ladder Company gave Joke to the NYS Museum in 1937; it is still on display, some 208 years after its purchase.

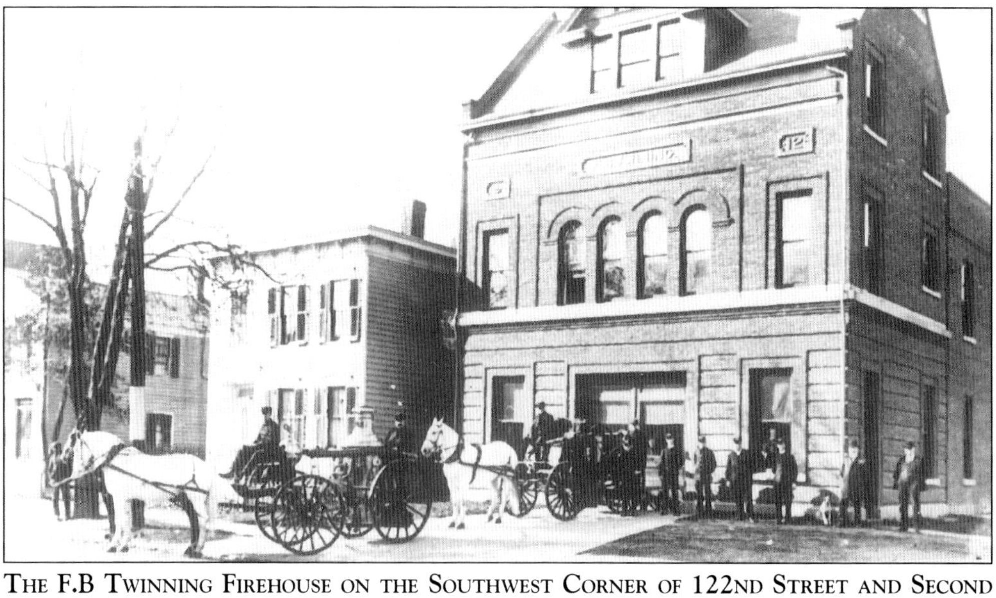

The F.B Twinning Firehouse on the Southwest Corner of 122nd Street and Second Avenue. This firehouse and the J.J. Childs Firehouse were built by the city of Troy after the village was annexed in 1900. From 1791 to 1874 the fire department was manned on a volunteer basis. Frank B. Twinning was a principle in George B. Ide's shirt, collar, and cuff company in Troy. Twinning lived at 865 Second Avenue in Lansingburgh.

THE J.J. CHILDS FIREHOUSE ON FIFTH AVENUE. Built after Lansingburgh became part of Troy in 1900, the J.J. Childs Firehouse is now the home of the Junior Museum. James J. Childs owned a coal company in his name at 600 Second Avenue. He was also the police commissioner in 1899, the last year Lansingburgh was a separate village. He lived at 166 Second Avenue.

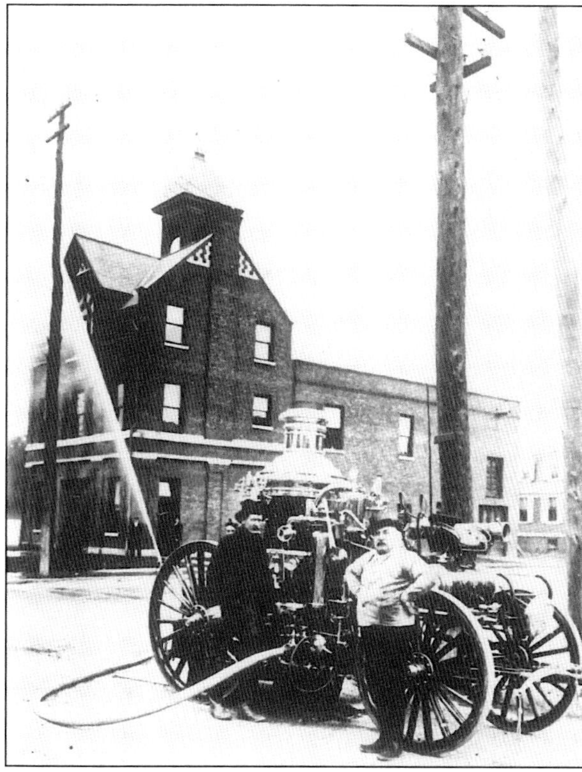

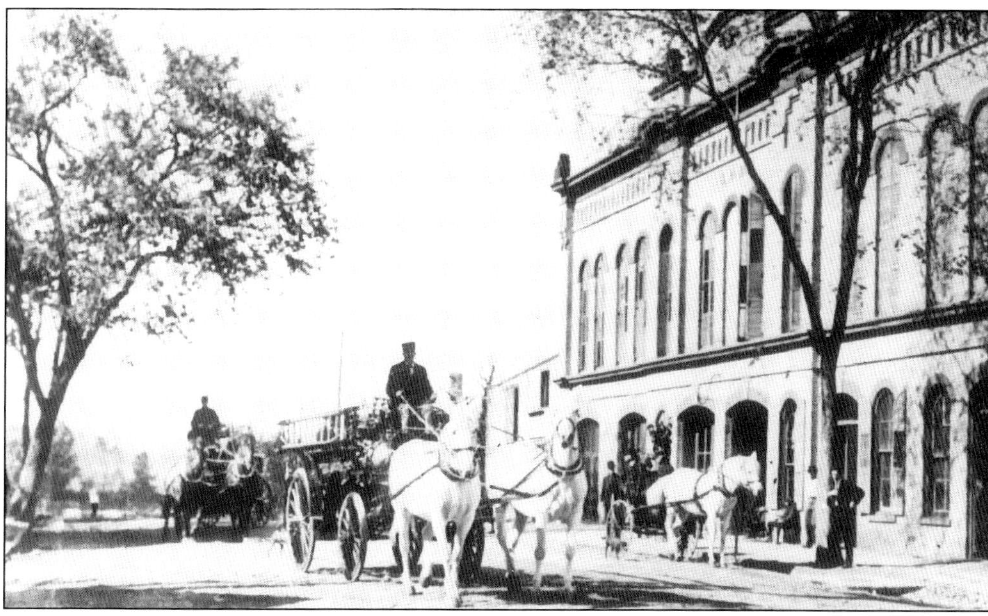

THE CENTRAL FIRE STATION, NORTH OF 115TH STREET, BETWEEN FIRST AND SECOND AVENUES. The Mason Hose and Fake Hook and Ladder Companies were stationed here. The volunteer fire departments were disbanded in 1874 to form a paid department, which became part of the greater Troy Fire Department when the Burgh was annexed in 1900. The building is now an apartment house.

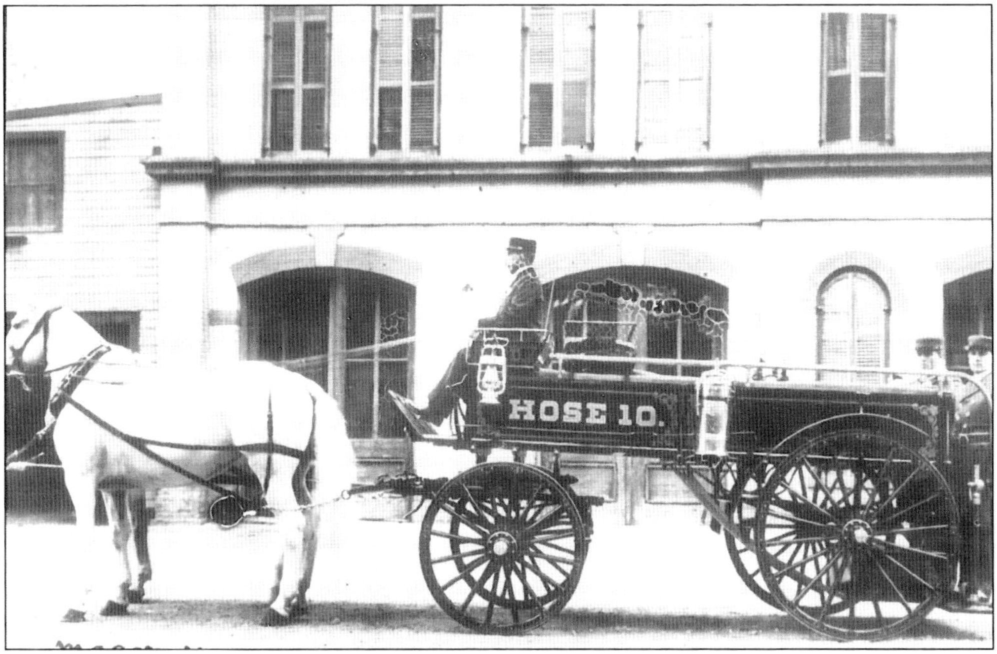

MASON HOSE NO. 10 AT THE CENTRAL FIRE STATION ON FIRST AVENUE AND 115TH STREET. Today you would never know this structure was a firehouse, as the front has been altered considerably. It is called "Ye Old Firehouse Apartments." The building to the left is gone.

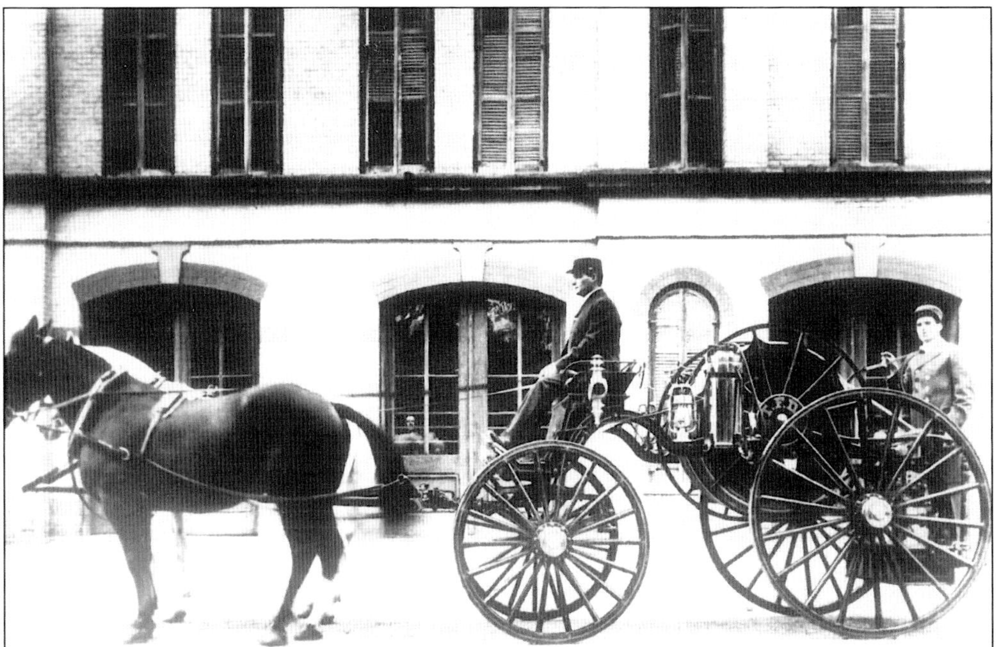

A HOSE CARRIAGE MARKED "TFD." This photograph was taken after 1900, when the fire department had become a part of the Troy Fire Department. The modern firehouse is located on Fifth Avenue.

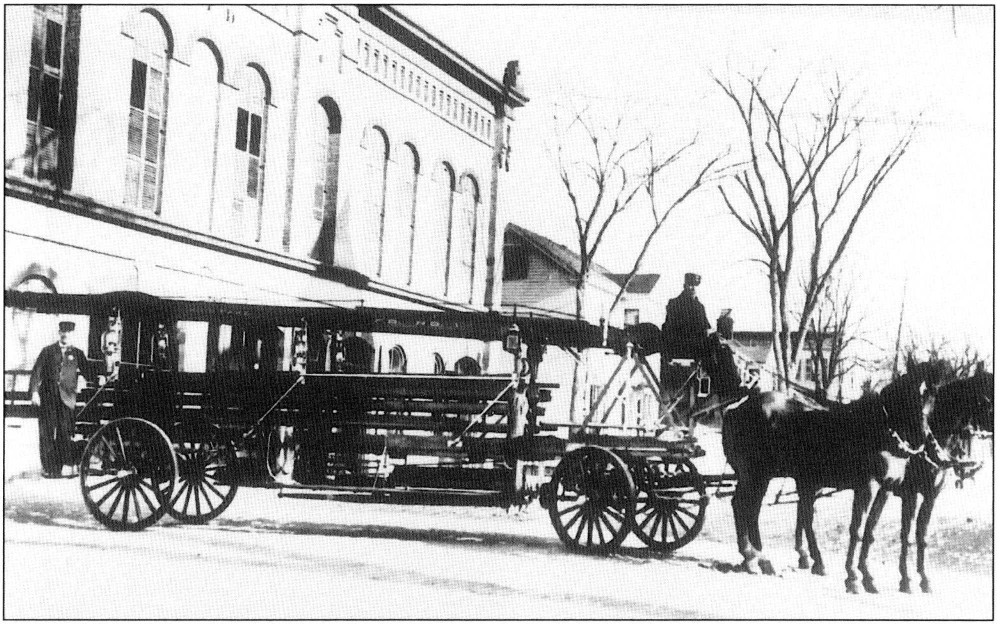

THE JOHN S. FAKE HOOK AND LADDER NO. 1, C. 1900. Notice on top of the building the initials "L.F.D.," which still show the Lansingburgh roots. This photograph was probably taken right after annexation.

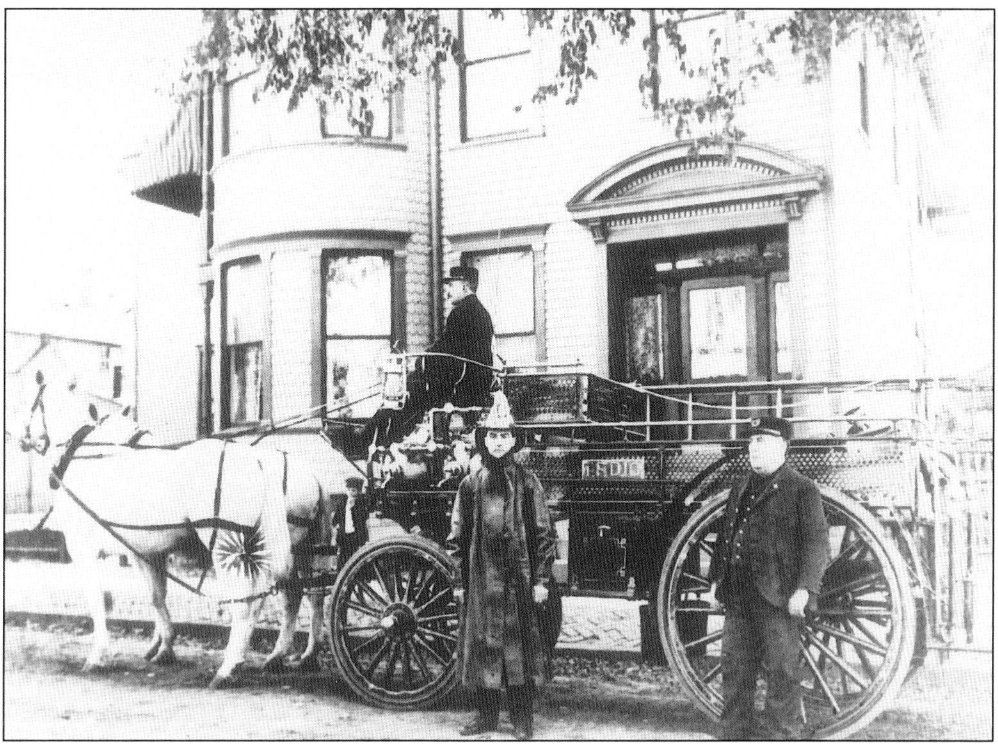

MASON HOSE IN FRONT OF THE JOSIAH WEST HOME AT NO. 4 115TH STREET. West was the owner of the West Paper Box Company of First Avenue. There is no indication as to why the hose wagon paused for a photograph here.

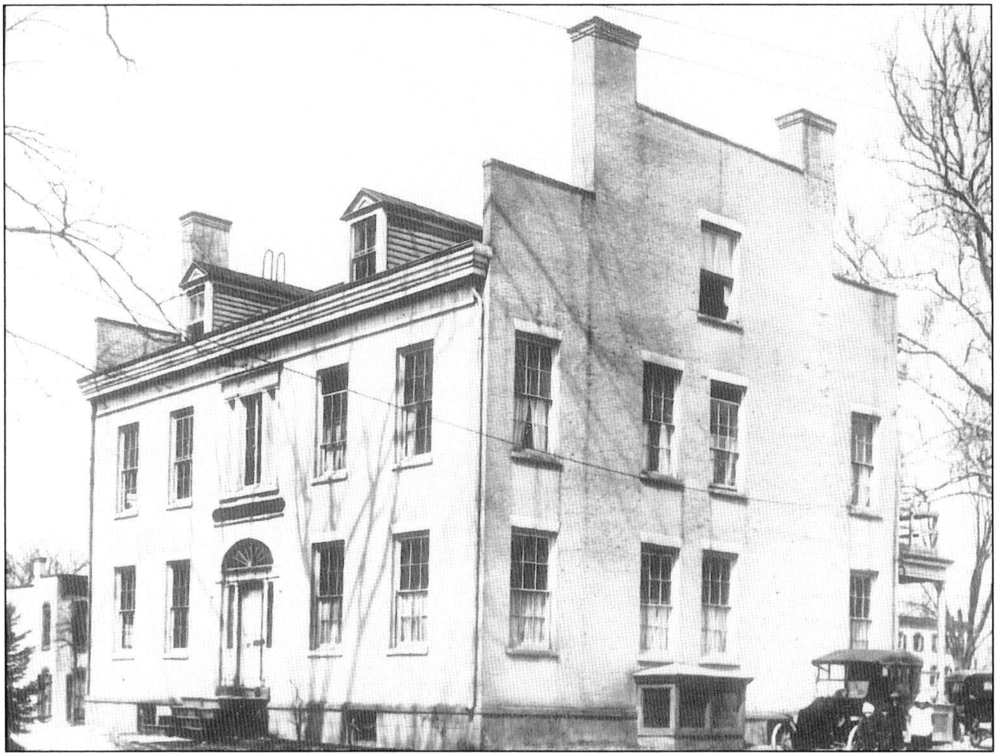

Leonard Hospital at 114th Street, between Sixth and Seventh Avenues. Dr. Frederick B. Leonard organized this Lansingburgh hospital in 1893. The structure was originally the home of his father, Timothy Leonard (d. 1814).

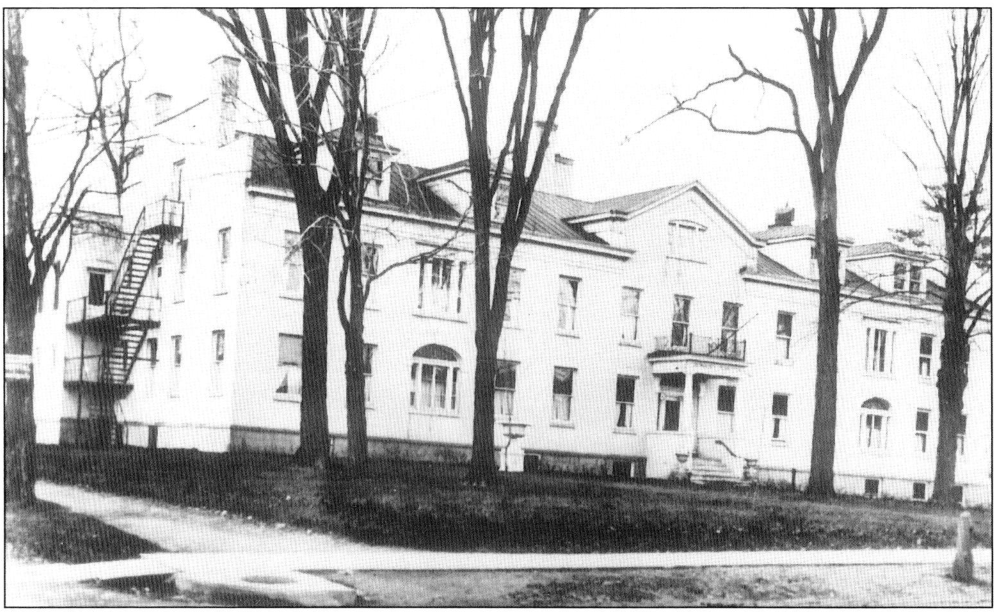

The Expanded Leonard Hospital. Leonard Hospital merged with St. Mary's Hospital to become Seton Health Services in 1995. This former hospital complex now serves as the Lansingburgh Apartments.

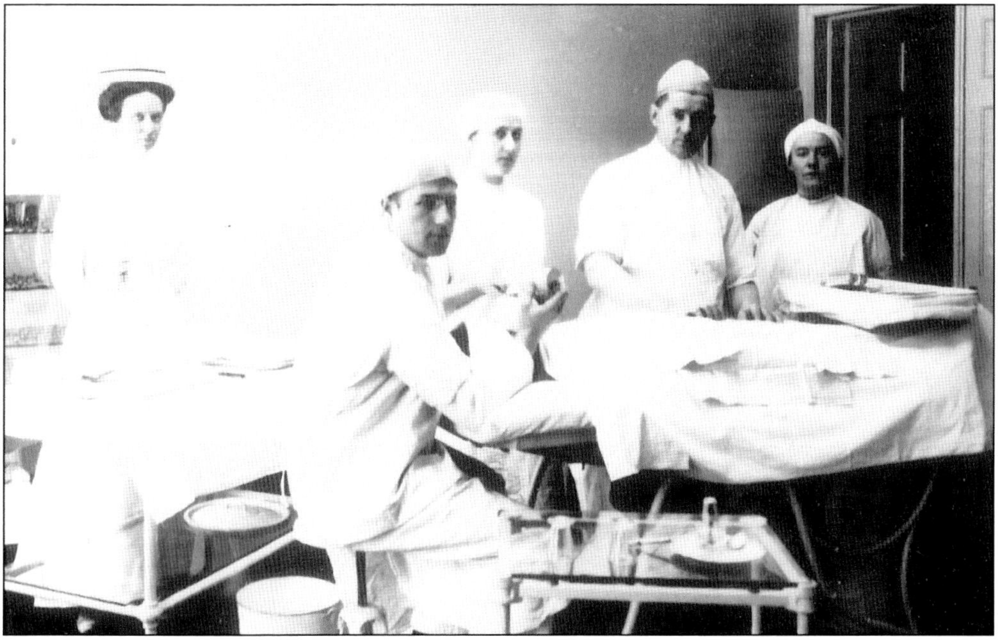

An Operating Room at Leonard Hospital. I wonder if the photographer had scrubs, or if the patient knew he or she was going to be photographed? The operating room looks rather sparse compared to its modern counterpart.

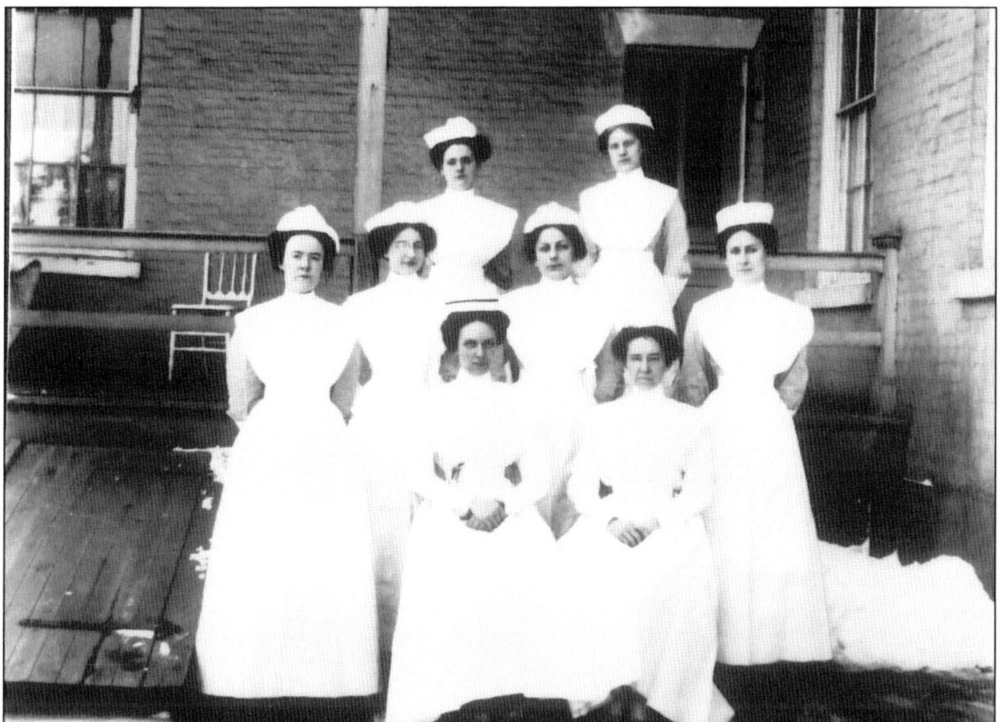

Nurses at Leonard Hospital. Certainly it must have been difficult keeping those uniforms pure white.

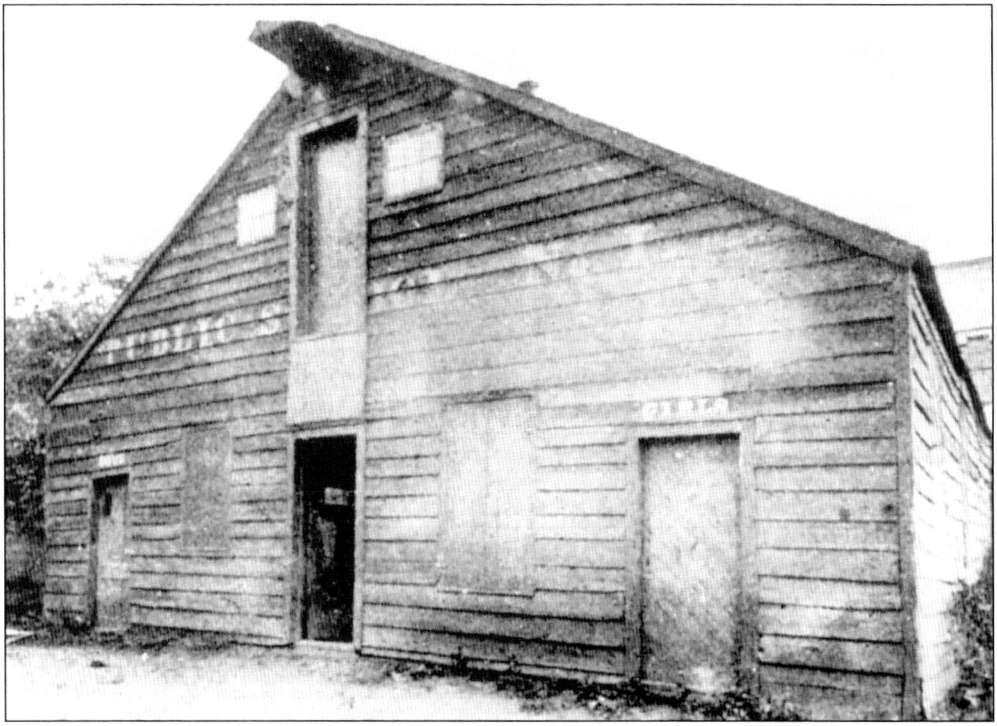

The First Free School, Built in 1820. Located on the west side of Fifth Avenue in the center of the block between 113th and 114th Streets, this school burned in 1897. Notice the separate entrances for boys and girls. When I went to grade school, we had separate entrances too, but still ended up in the same classrooms. So what was that about?

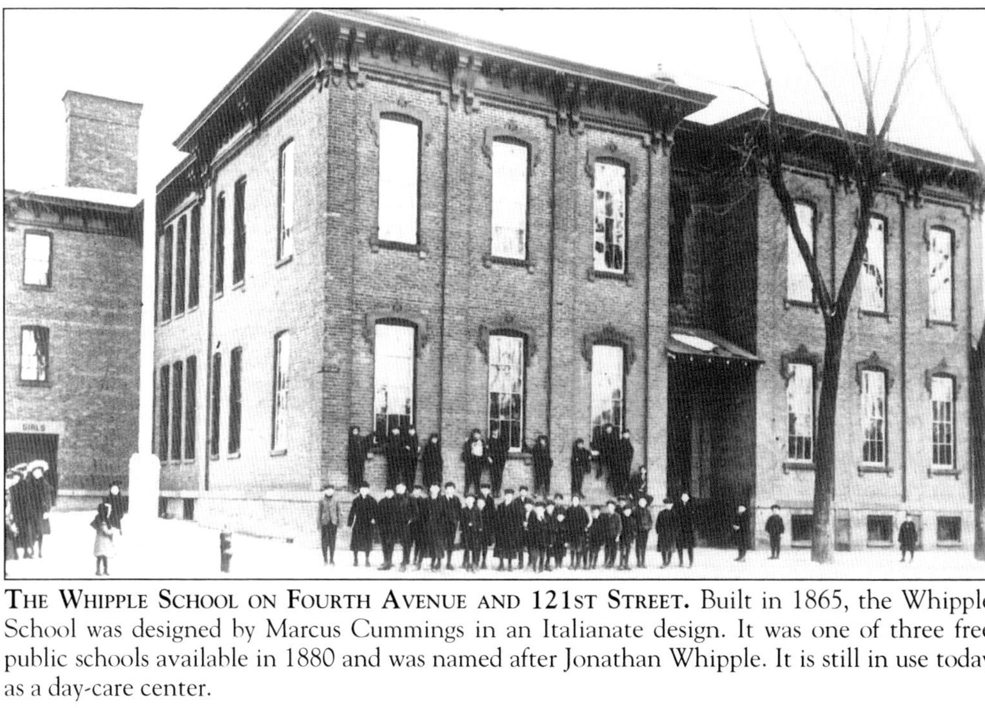

The Whipple School on Fourth Avenue and 121st Street. Built in 1865, the Whipple School was designed by Marcus Cummings in an Italianate design. It was one of three free public schools available in 1880 and was named after Jonathan Whipple. It is still in use today as a day-care center.

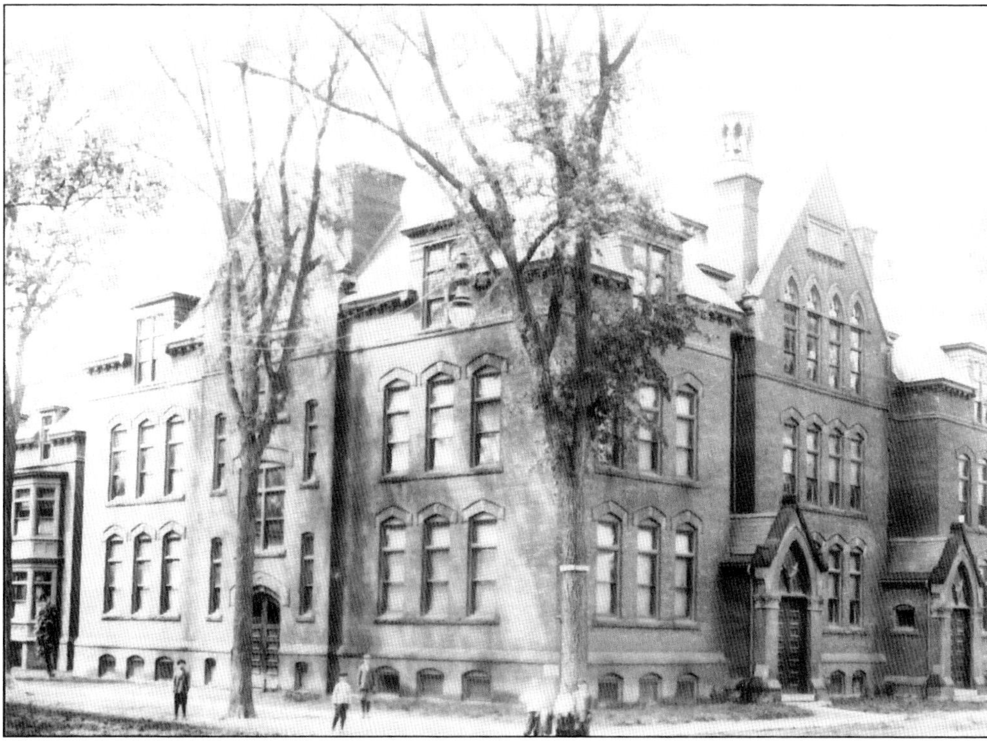

THE ST. AUGUSTINE ACADEMY. Located on the southwest corner of Fourth Avenue and 114th Street, the academy was designed by Frederick Cummings and built in 1899. St. Augustine's Church and parish first organized in 1842 as St. John's Church. The Gothic church was built in 1864.

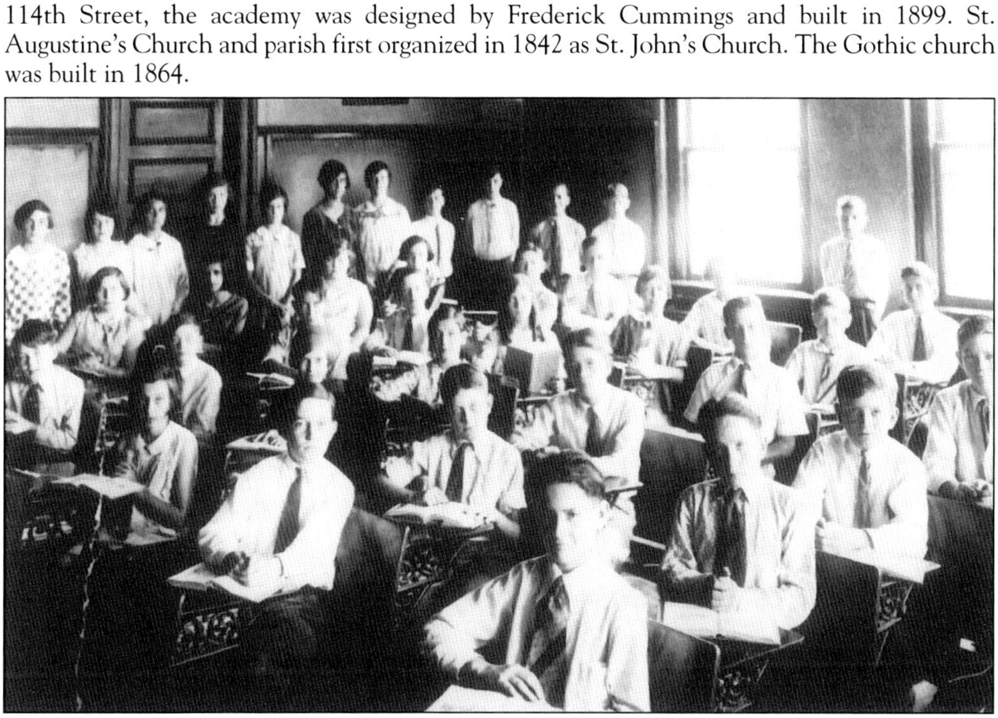

THE ST. AUGUSTINE ACADEMY, GRADE SIX, C. 1930. Sister Theresa Martin was the teacher. The school was opened in 1869.

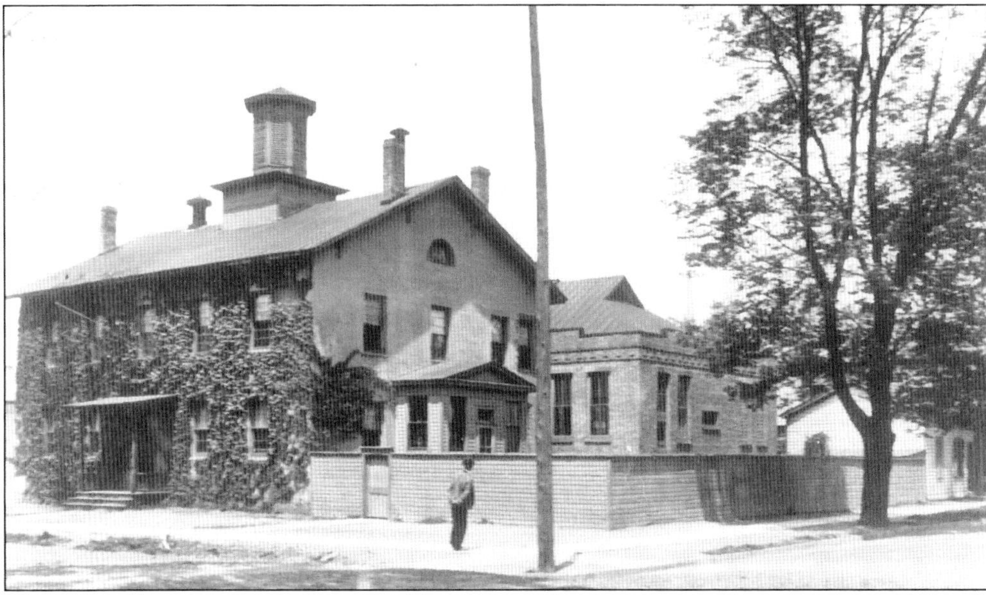

LANSINGBURGH ACADEMY, LOCATED ON THE CORNER OF 114TH STREET AND FOURTH AVENUE. Built in 1820 to replace an earlier academy building on the village green between 112th and 113th Streets, the academy served as the high school until a new one was built in 1912 (the building now serves as district offices). The academy, originally chartered in 1796, was the centerpiece of Lansingburgh education.

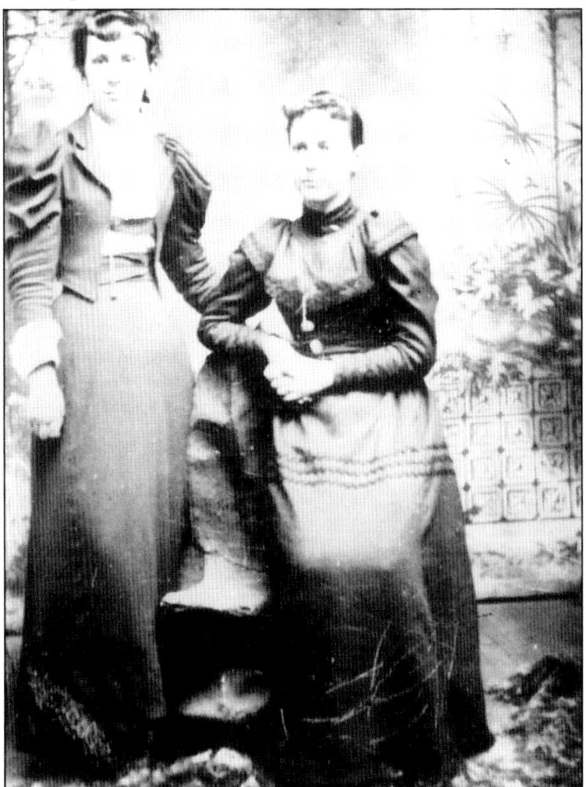

TWO STUDENTS AT THE ACADEMY. This photograph of Ellen Sherman (left) and Lottie Smith was taken in the fall of 1893 or the spring of 1894. Herman Melville and Chester Arthur were students at the academy. The St. Augustine Academy was located right across the street.

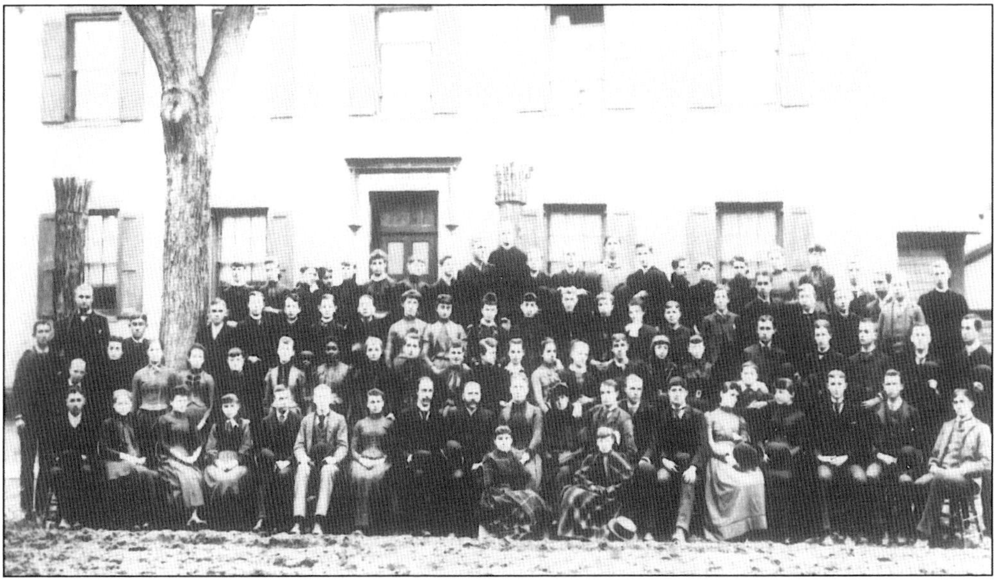

The Full Academy Class of Both Students and Teachers. This photograph was taken before the front portico was built. The sign over the door reads "Lansingburgh Academy, 1820." The academy lasted for 150 years.

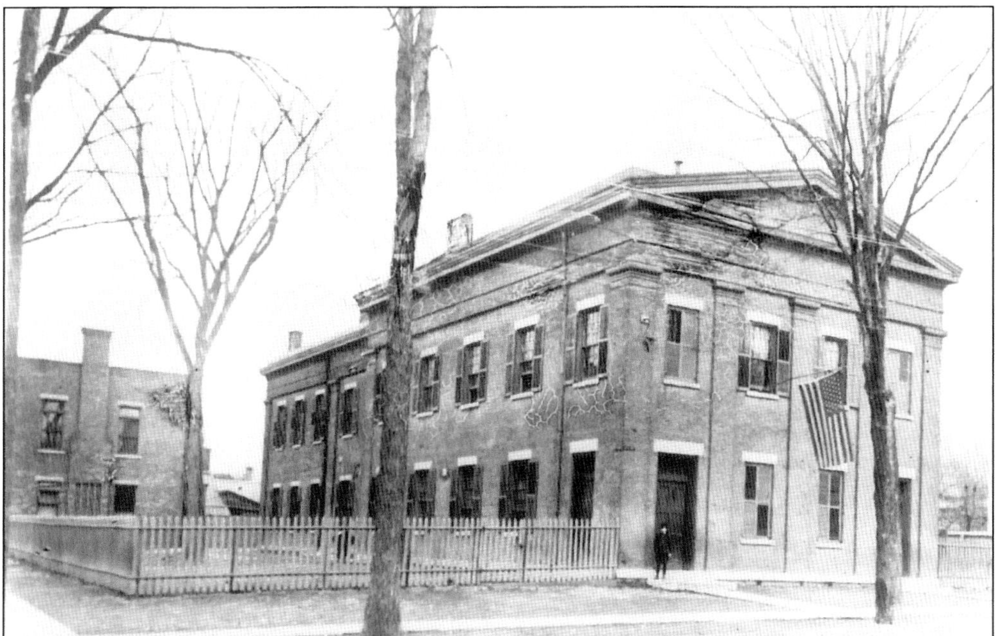

The Comstock School (the Market Street School), Located on the Northeast Corner of 115th Street And Fifth Avenue. The Lansingburgh Board of Education building is on the left. The school was torn down when the present high school was built on this site in 1910; that school opened in 1912. The school board building was moved to west side of Fifth Avenue, north of 120th Street, and used as a dwelling; a third floor was added later. In 1854, this school had six teachers and one principal. Originally built in 1845, the addition in the rear was added in 1874. The Powers family donated $1,000 for construction costs.

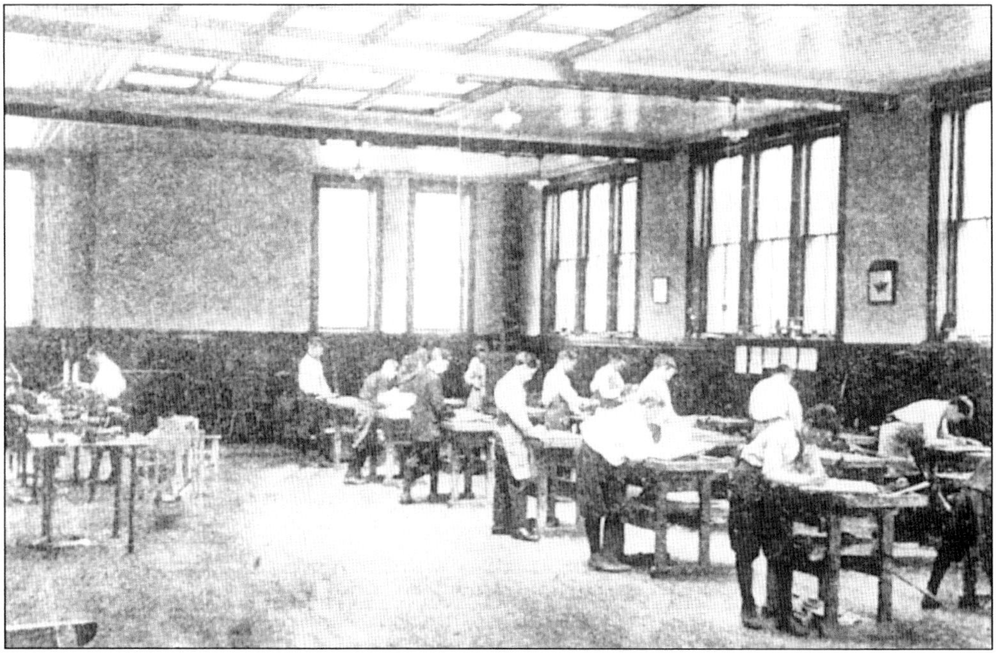

THE BENCH ROOM OF THE LANSINGBURGH VOCATION SCHOOL. This school, a part of the Lansingburgh Academy, was in the brick addition added to the school in 1911. It served as a high school until a new one was built in 1912.

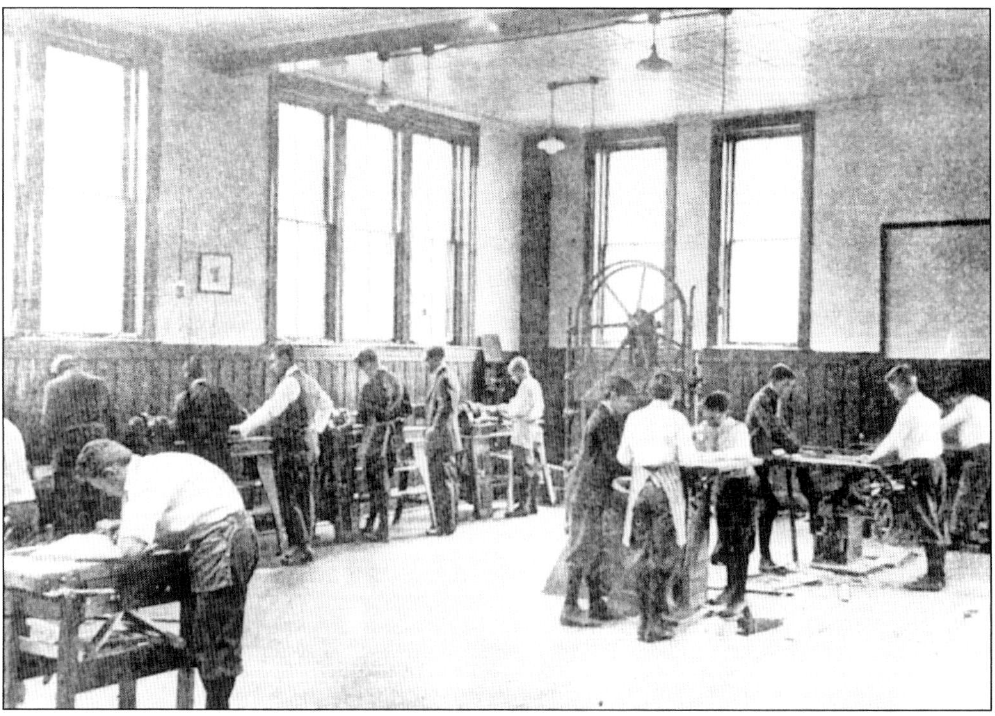

THE MACHINE ROOM OF THE LANSINGBURGH VOCATIONAL SCHOOL. The academy complex still serves residents of the area. The library is located there.

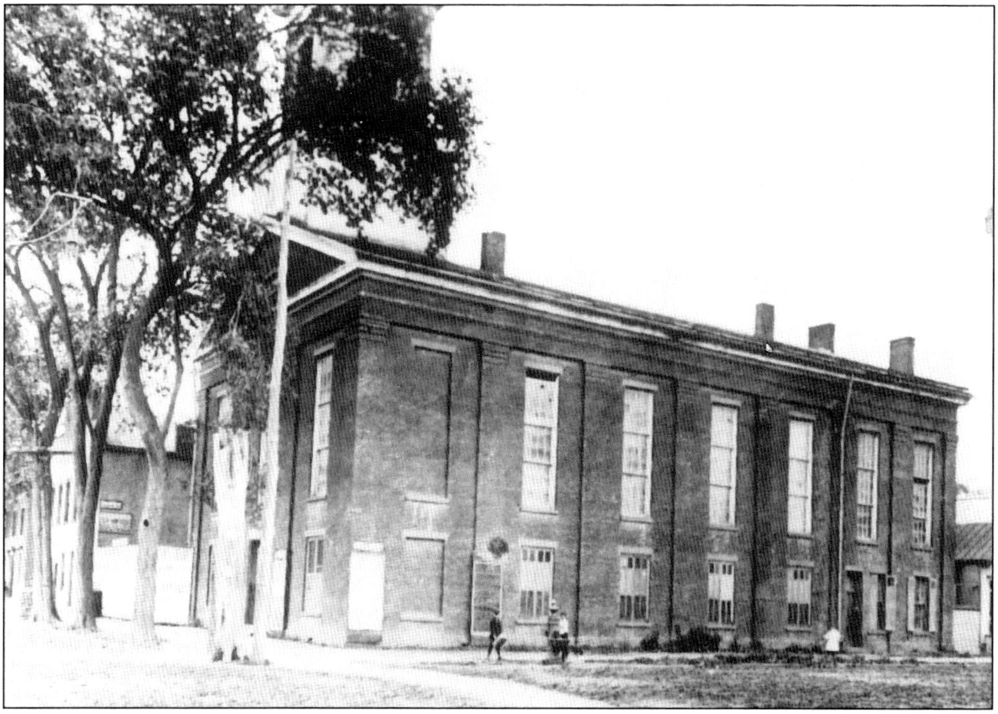

The Powers Opera House, Northwest Corner of 117th Street and Third Avenue, Facing 117th Street. Rev. William Arthur, the father of President Chester A. Arthur, preached in this building, which was originally a Baptist church. The structure burned on March 25, 1917. The top was removed and it now serves as a warehouse.

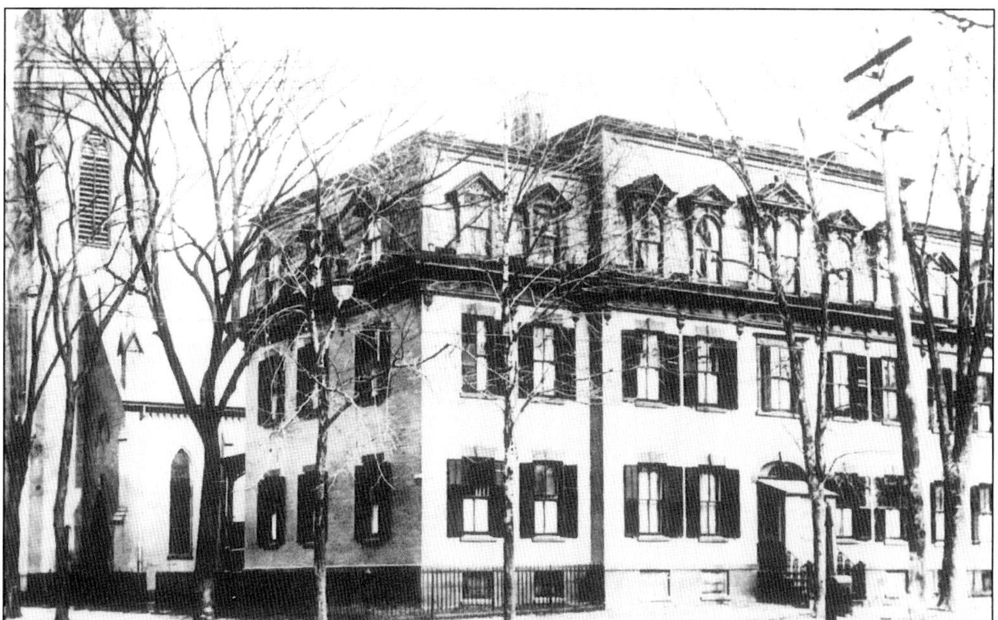

Saint Augustine's Rectory and Church. Erected c. 1864–65, the rectory originally had a pitched roof, but that roof was eventually removed to add the third story visible here.

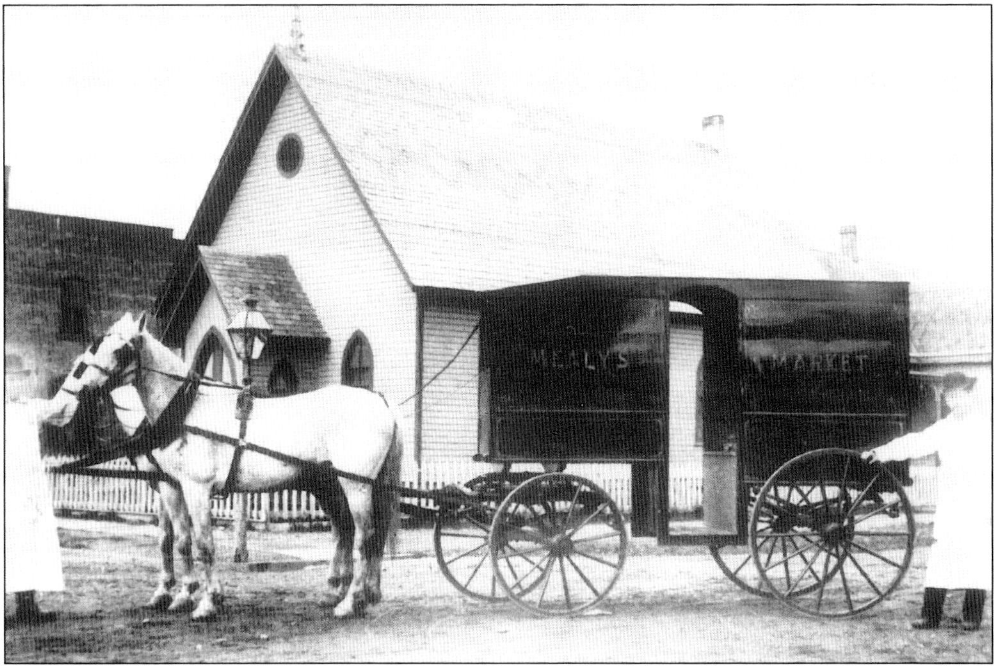

THE PRESBYTERIAN CHAPEL AT FOURTH AVENUE AND 105TH STREET. This Presbyterian chapel was built in connection with the First Presbyterian Church for the convenience of people in this end of the village. G. Frank Mealy's Meat Wagon (104 Second Avenue) is in front. Frank Mealy died in 1906.

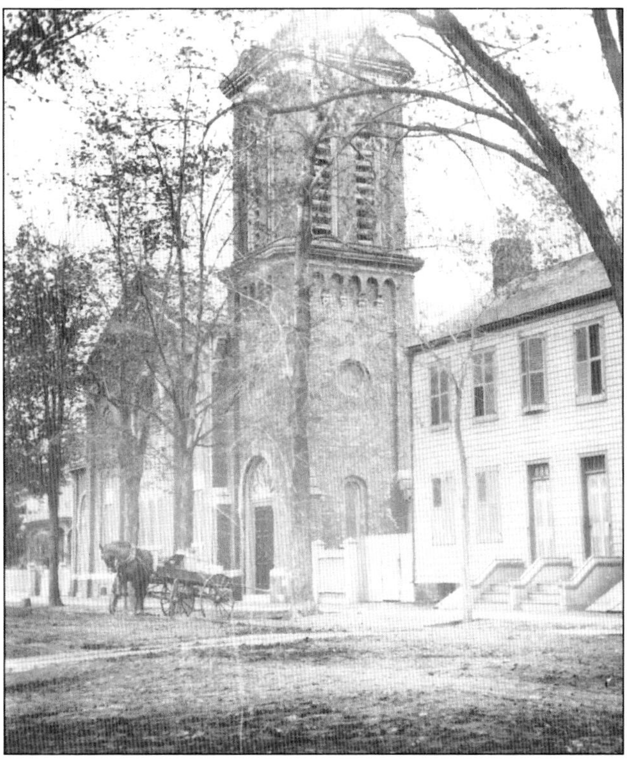

THE FIRST PRESBYTERIAN CHURCH, THIRD AVENUE AND 115TH STREET, SECOND BUILDING. Built in 1844, the church opened in April 22, 1845. The First Presbyterian Church of Lansingburgh was organized on August 9, 1792, at the same time as the one in Troy. The original church was built in 1793 with brick imported from Holland.

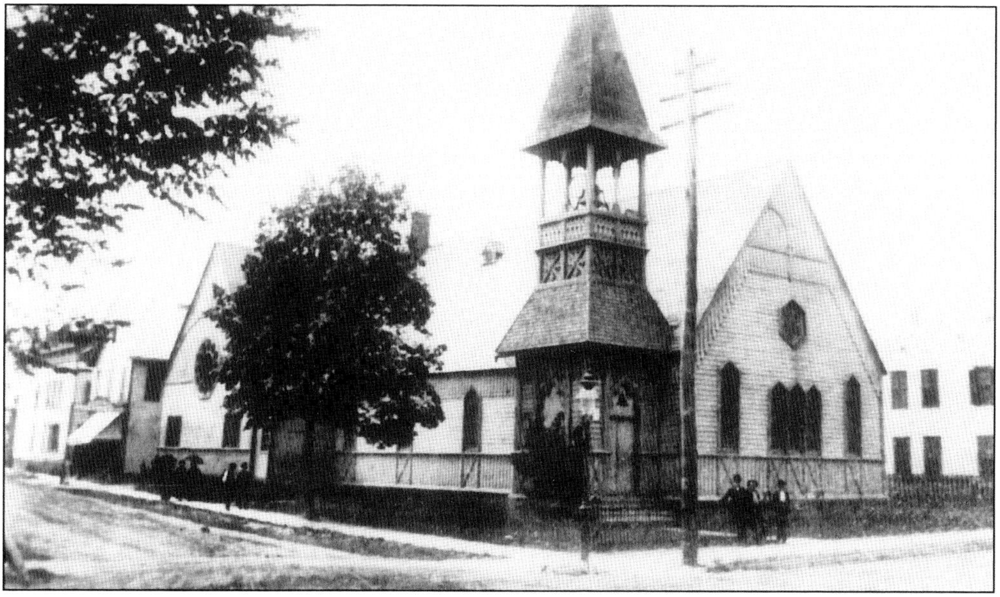

THE ORIGINAL BUILDING OF THE WESTMINSTER PRESBYTERIAN CHURCH ON FIFTH AVENUE AND 101ST STREET. The Westminster Presbyterian Church was organized on November 2, 1871, in Troy as an outgrowth of a mission Sunday school started by the Second Street Presbyterian Church in 1868. They moved here in 1882.

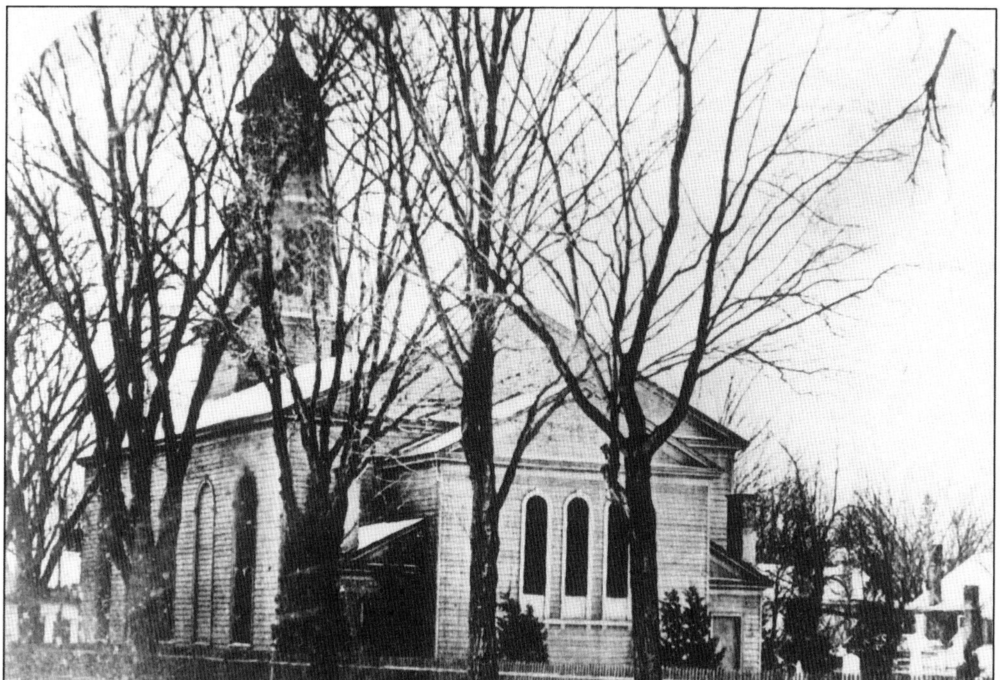

TRINITY CHURCH, NORTHWEST CORNER OF FOURTH AVENUE AND 115TH STREET. Trinity (Protestant Episcopal) was organized in 1804. The original building, designed by Philip Hooker, was built in 1806 and destroyed by fire in 1868. The present building, built in 1869, was designed by Henry Dudley and is on the National Register of Historic Places.

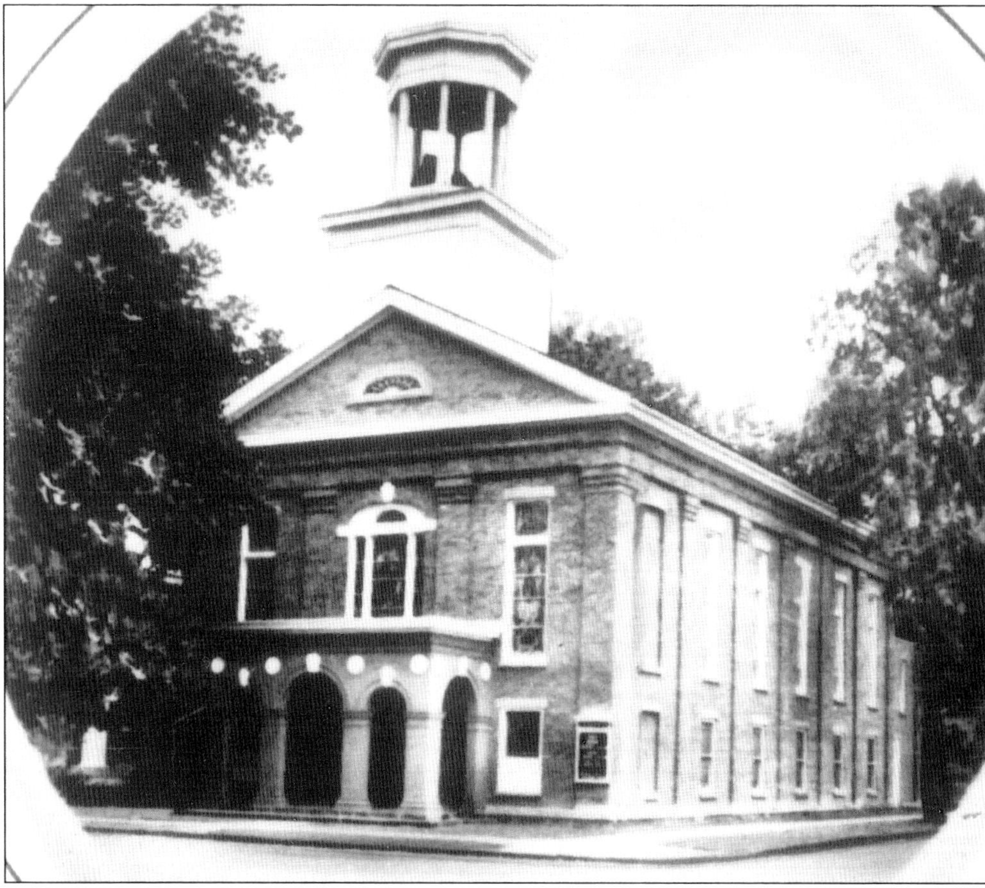

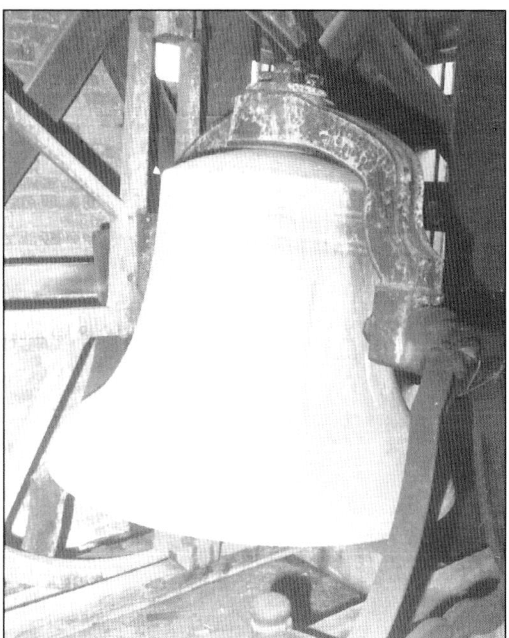

The United Methodist Church. This third building of the Methodist Society was built in 1848 on the northeast corner of 116th Street and Third Avenue. The formal organization of the Methodist Society took place in 1827, though there were Methodists preaching in the area as early as the 1790s.

The Meneely Bell of the First Presbyterian Church. This bell was made in West Troy and given to the church by John G. McMurray in 1870. The Meneely Bell Foundry was world famous for the quality of its bells, especially church bells. The foundry started in Troy.

Five

People and Events

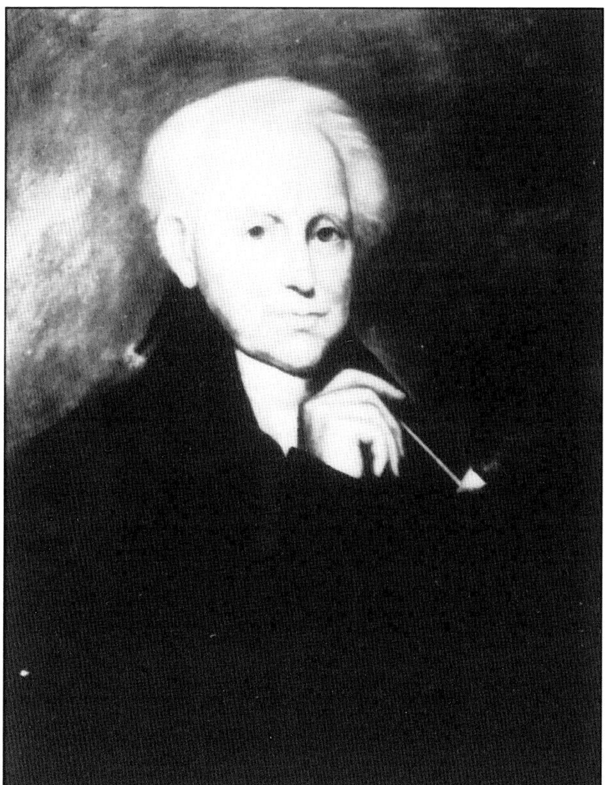

Cornelius Lansing (1752–1842). No image of village founder Abraham Jacob Lansing has been found, but his son, Cornelius Lansing, is shown here. The Abbey, a Dutch-styled house on the west side of Second Avenue, was built by Cornelius in the 1700s. It was later purchased and remodeled by Lansingburgh businessman J.K.P. Pine.

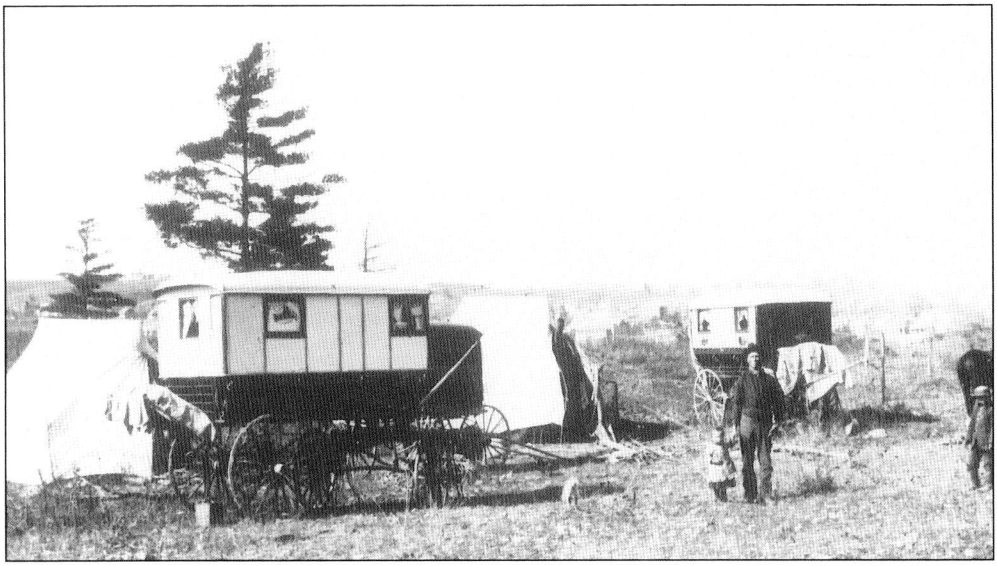

A GYPSY FAMILY TEMPORARILY LIVING SOMEWHERE IN THE DIAMOND ROCK AREA. The Diamond Rock area was great for rock climbing, picnicking, and even fireworks. It also was a favorite camping spot for gypsies.

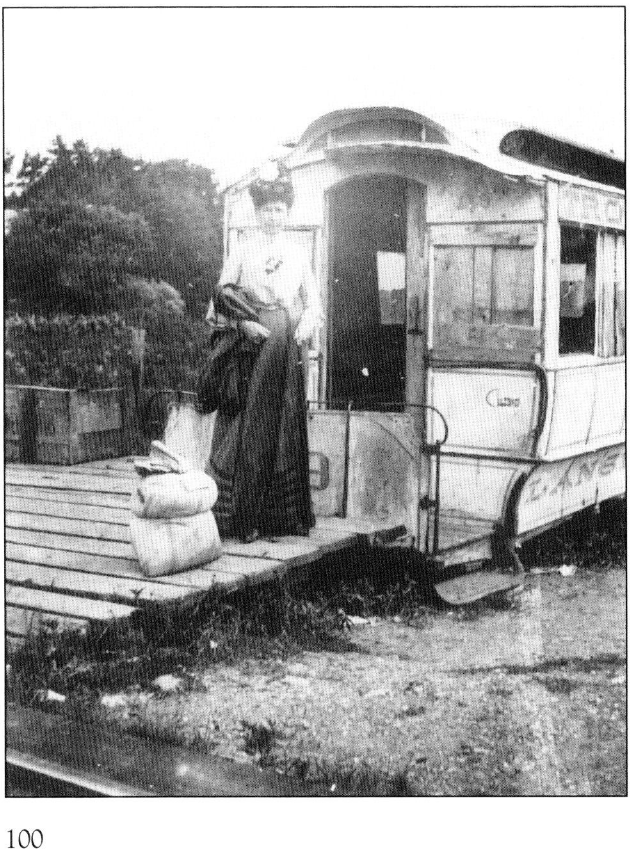

A TROY AND LANSINGBURGH RAILWAY CAR. This abandoned car was perhaps near the Lansingburgh Train Station or the Iron Works Station in South Troy, as tracks can be seen in front. The woman has her packed bag and is evidently waiting patiently for the train.

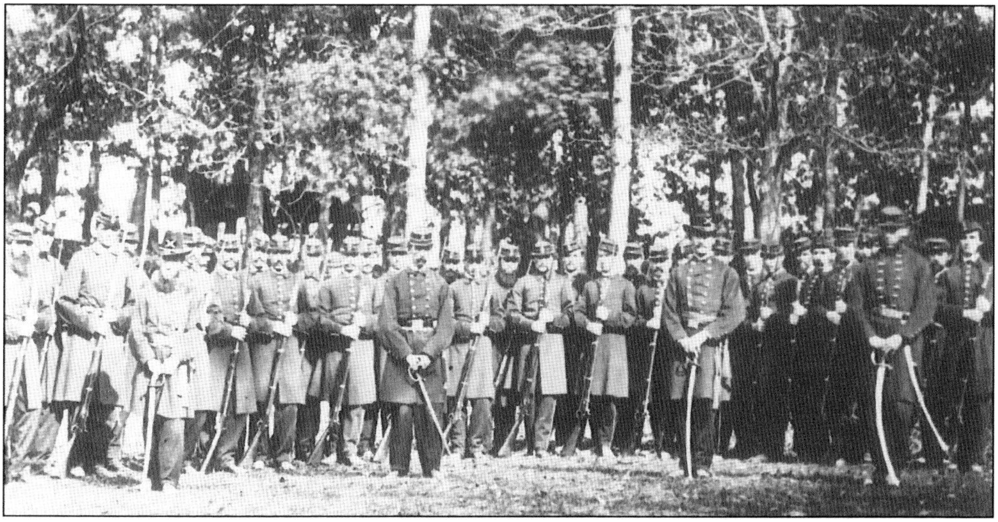

A CIVIL WAR COMPANY AT YOUNG'S GROVE, SOUTH OF RENSSELAER PARK, BEFORE GOING TO BATTLE. There are 35 soldiers here. The first company to organize in Lansingburgh was Company A, a part of the 13th Regiment of New York State Volunteers, commanded by Colonel Frisby. Seven men were killed from Company A during the first Battle of Bull Run.

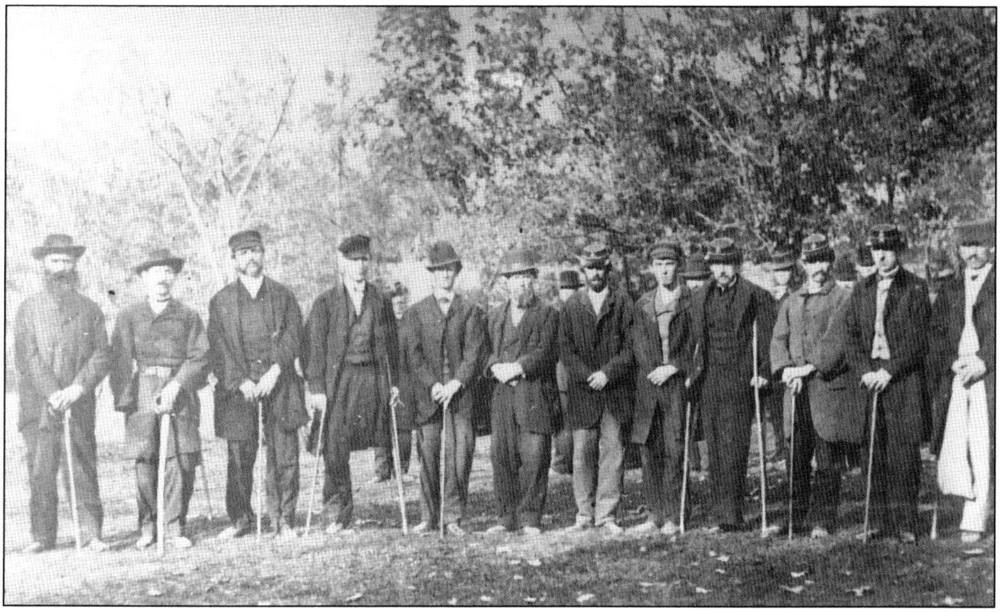

A CIVIL WAR COMPANY REUNION AT YOUNG'S GROVE AFTER THE WAR. Only 13 men are shown here, and five of them have lost a leg or hand. Company K of the 169th Regiment was the second group of Lansingburgh men organized during the Civil War. With Capt. Daniel Ferguson commanding, they saw a lot of fighting. Other regiments, including the 22nd, 125th, and 192nd Regiments and the Griswold Cavalry, had large numbers of Lansingburgh men in them during the War between the States.

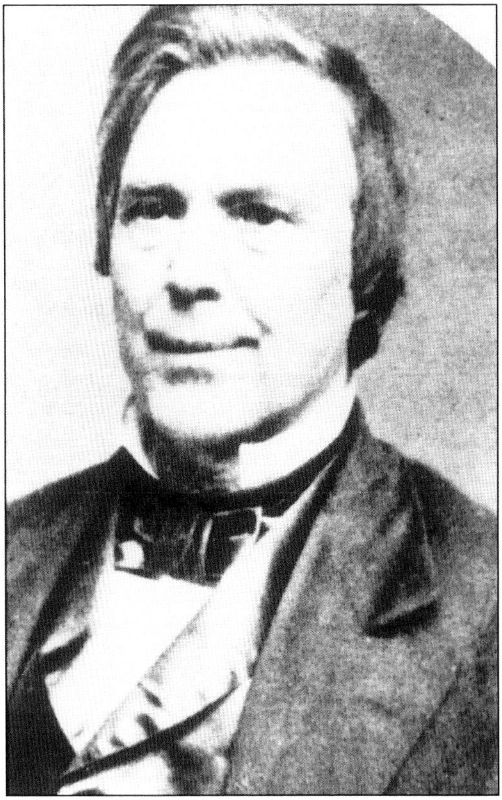

Reverend William Arthur, the Father of Chester A. Arthur, President of the United States. The Arthurs lived at 626 First Avenue. Reverend Arthur preached at the Baptist church at the northwest corner of 117th Street and Third Avenue (later the Powers Opera House). The building burned on March 25, 1917. The top of the church has been removed and it is now used as a warehouse.

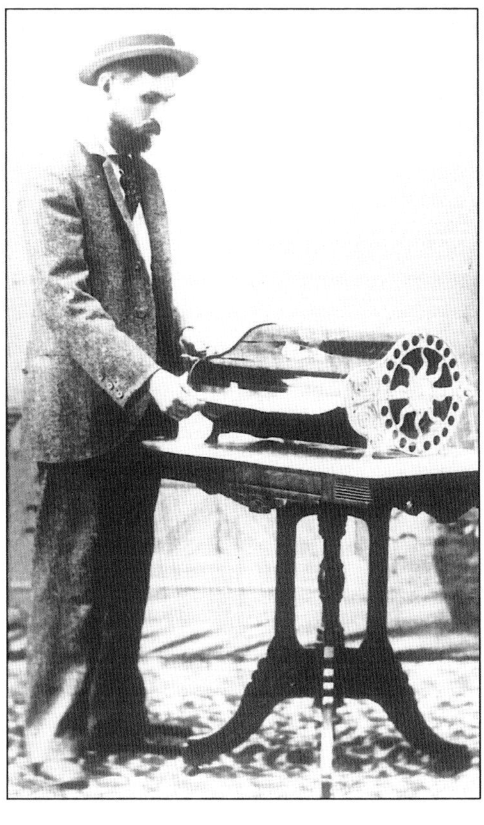

Mr. Parks, Inventor of a Paper Machine. This may be Clarence W. or Stephen Parks of Parks & Parks at 523 Fifth Avenue.

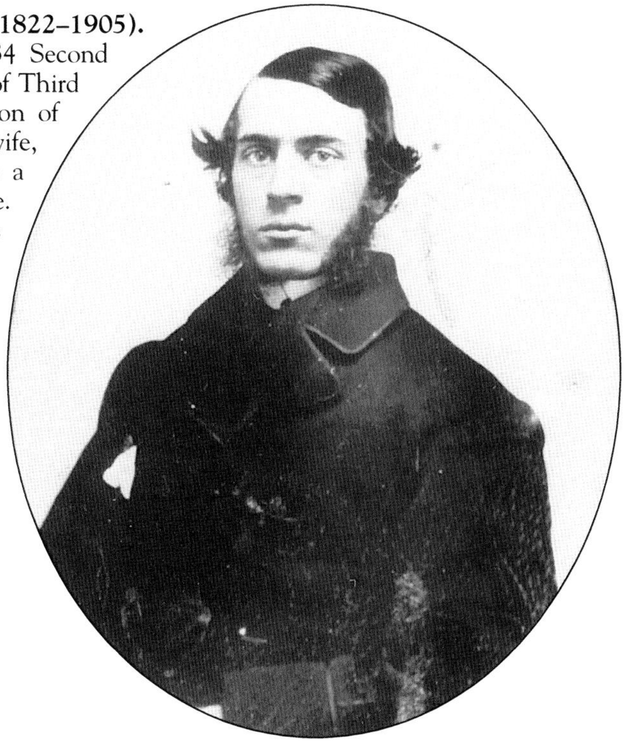

ANTHONY AUGUSTUS PEEBLES (1822–1905). Peebles was born and died at 534 Second Avenue, on the southeast corner of Third Avenue and 114th Street. The son of Gerrit Peebles and his second wife, Maria VanSchaick, Anthony was a second cousin to Herman Melville. His wife, Mary Louise Peebles, was a well-known author.

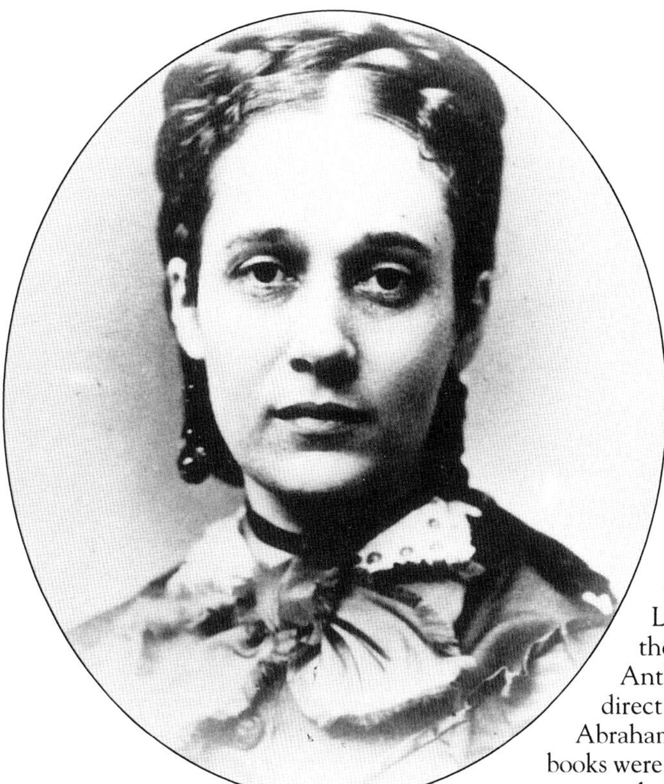

MARY LOUISE (PARMELEE) PEEBLES (1834–1915). The daughter of Elias Ripley and his second wife, Eleanor (Allen), Mary Louise wrote books under the name Lynde Palmer from 1860s to the 1890s. She was the wife of Anthony Augustus Peebles and a direct descendent of village founder Abraham Jacob Lansing. Some of her books were inspired by the death of her two young sons, her only children.

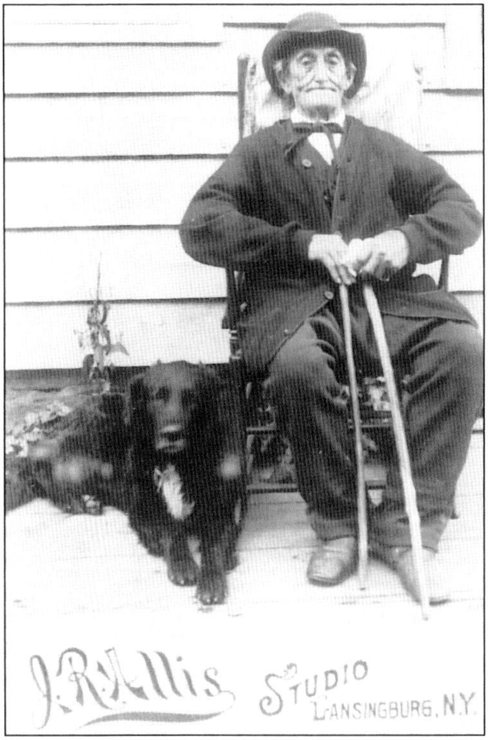

Captain Joseph King (1791–1897). This photograph was taken on his 106th birthday at his residence on First Avenue, south of 112th Street. King was born on Peebles Island.

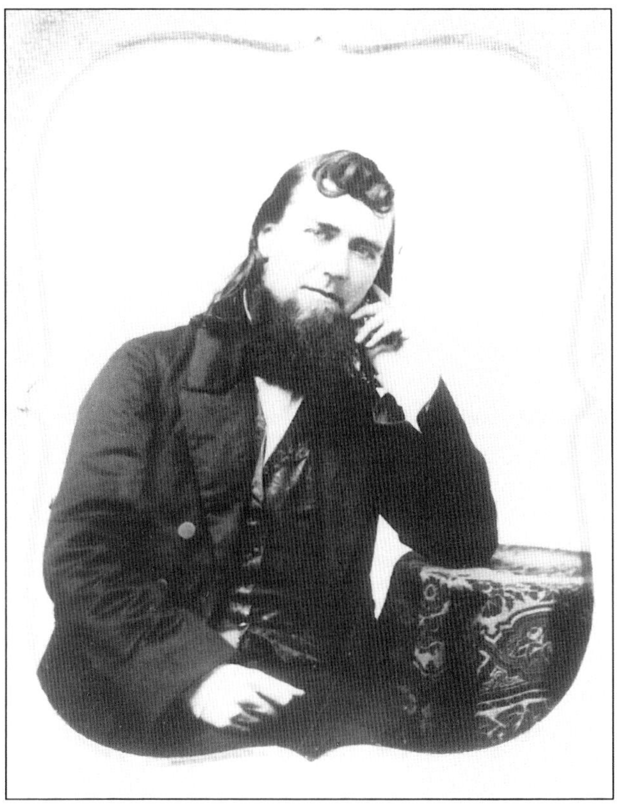

George R. Poulton, Composer. George composed the song "Aura Lee," which became the melody for Elvis Presley's "Love Me Tender." A colorful character, he was tarred and feathered for having an affair with a young student.

LUCIEN R. BURLEIGH. Lucien made Burleigh Lithographs, and located the offices of the Burleigh Lithographing Company in Troy on Fulton Street. He lived at 350 Second Avenue. His lithographs of Lansingburgh are outstanding.

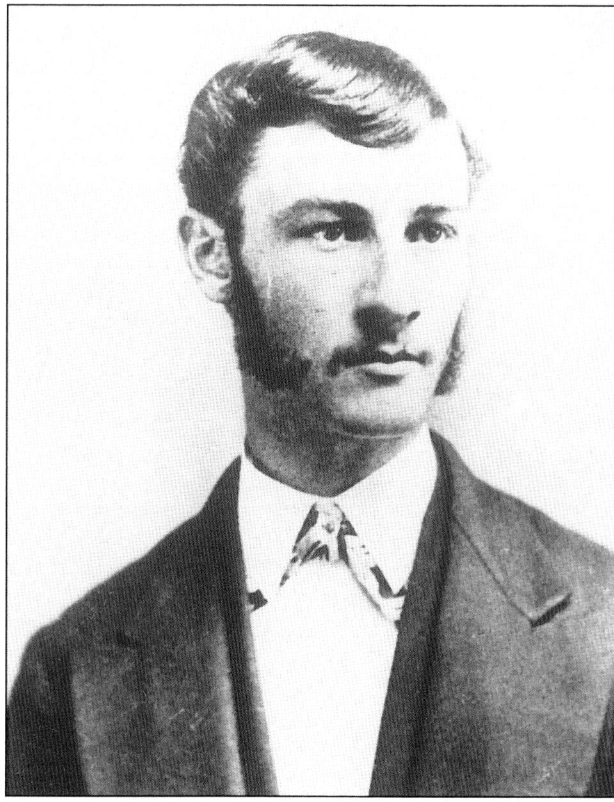

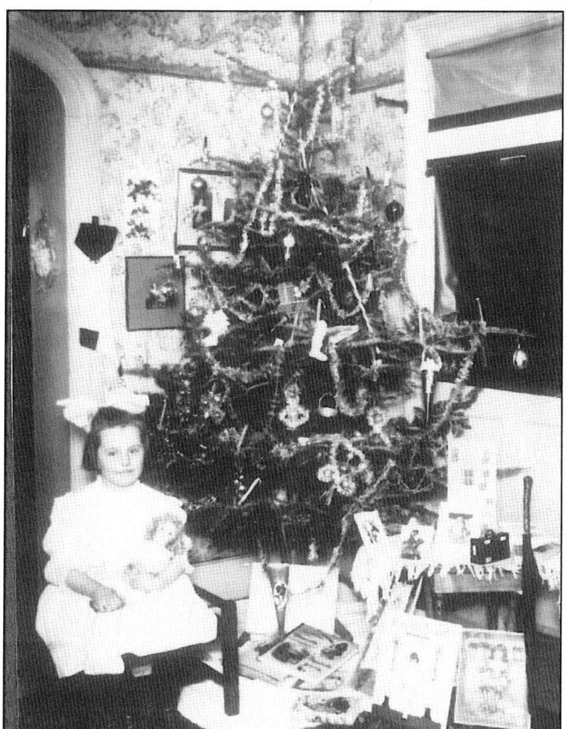

CHRISTMAS AT THE VAN SCHOONHOVEN RESIDENCE. The house, built in 1846, is still at 114th Street and Third Avenue. Jacob Lansing Van Schoonhoven was president of the Central National Bank in Troy and was related to the Lansing family.

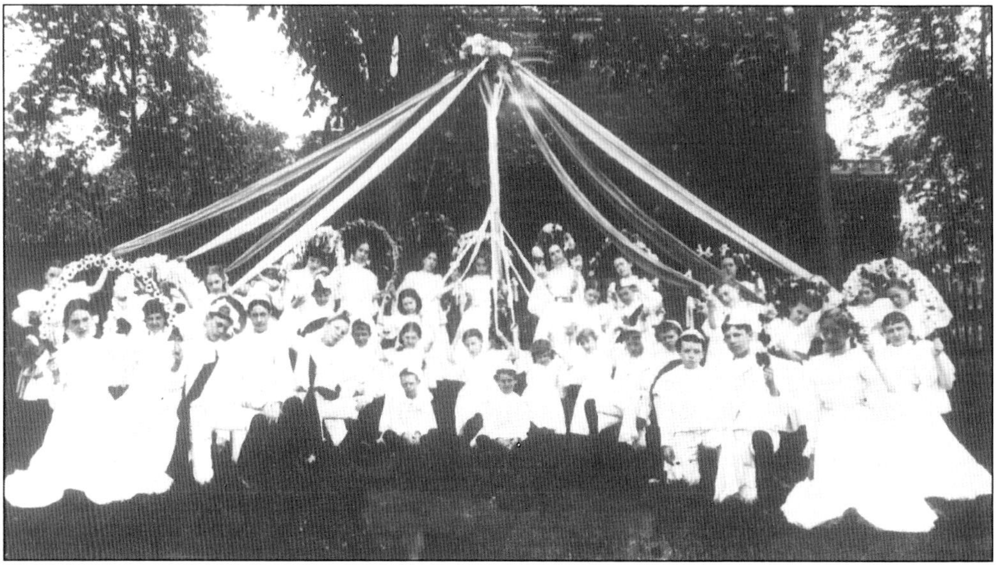

A Maypole Dance at the David Judson Mansion at 442 Second Avenue. David A. Judson owned a coal company at 125 River Road (First Avenue). He had a coal site in Troy as well.

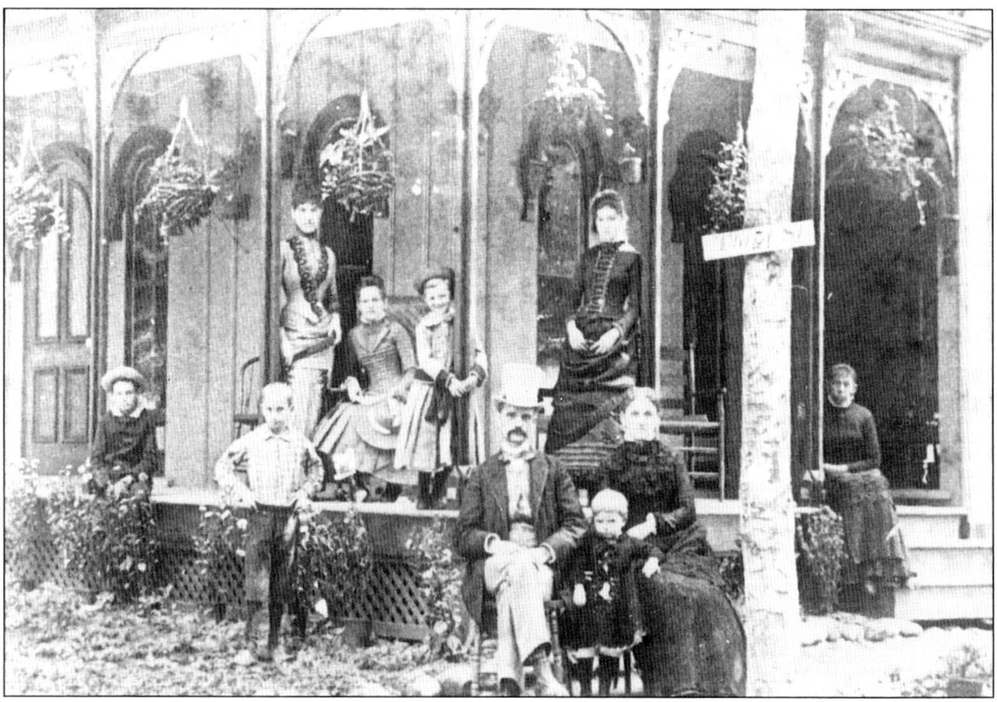

"Oaklands," the Gould Estate. The (George and Sarah) Gould Mansion was located just north of 103rd Street and set back on Seventh Avenue. Sarah died here in 1899. The mansion is still standing.

Six

Recreation and Leisure

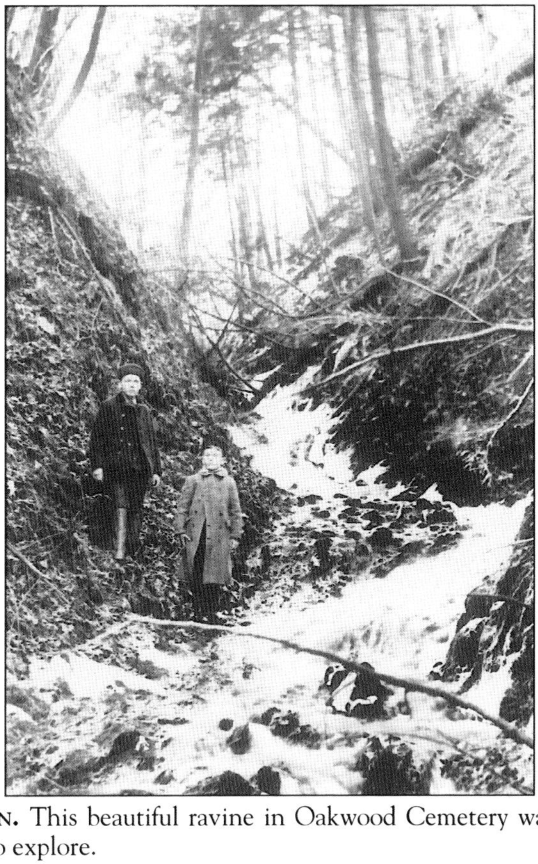

The Devil's Kitchen. This beautiful ravine in Oakwood Cemetery was a popular place for young and old alike to explore.

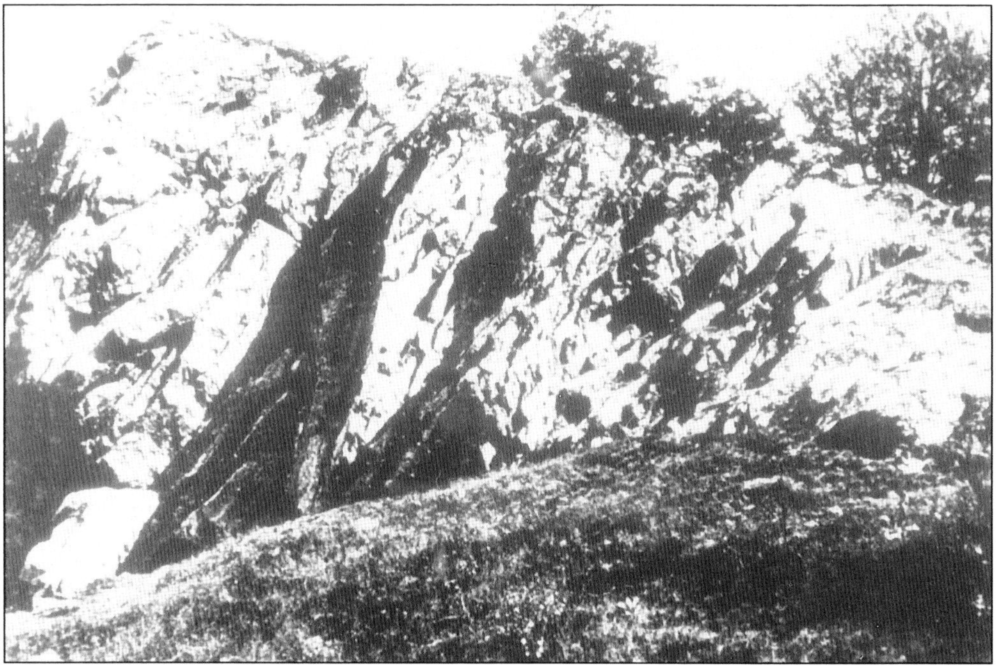

THE LEGEND OF DIAMOND ROCK. This hill has streaks (veins) of quartz crystals throughout that give the appearance of diamonds. A Native-American legend, "The Old Indian's Story of Moneta," written by Nathaniel Sylvester in 1877 says the quartz represents tears that froze to diamonds from an Indian maiden named Moneta who lost her sons.

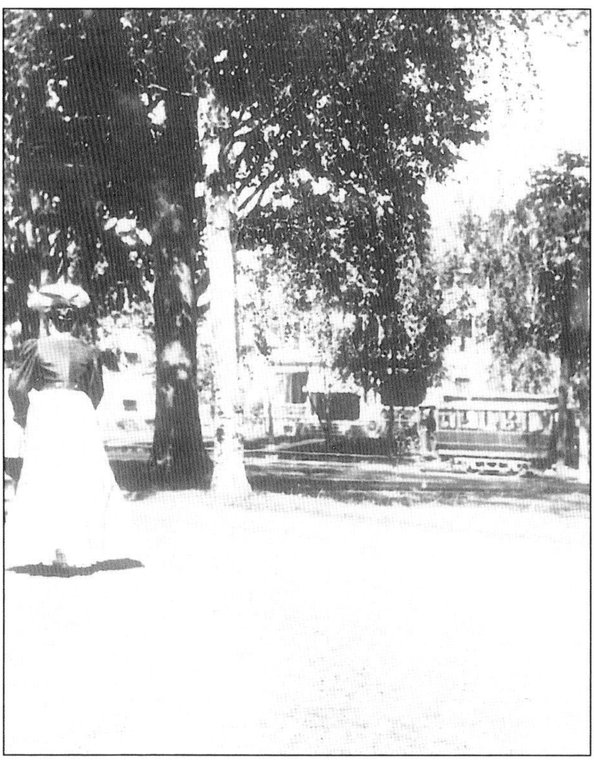

STROLLING IN THE PARK ON UPPER SECOND AVENUE. A trolley heads down the road as a woman pushes a baby carriage.

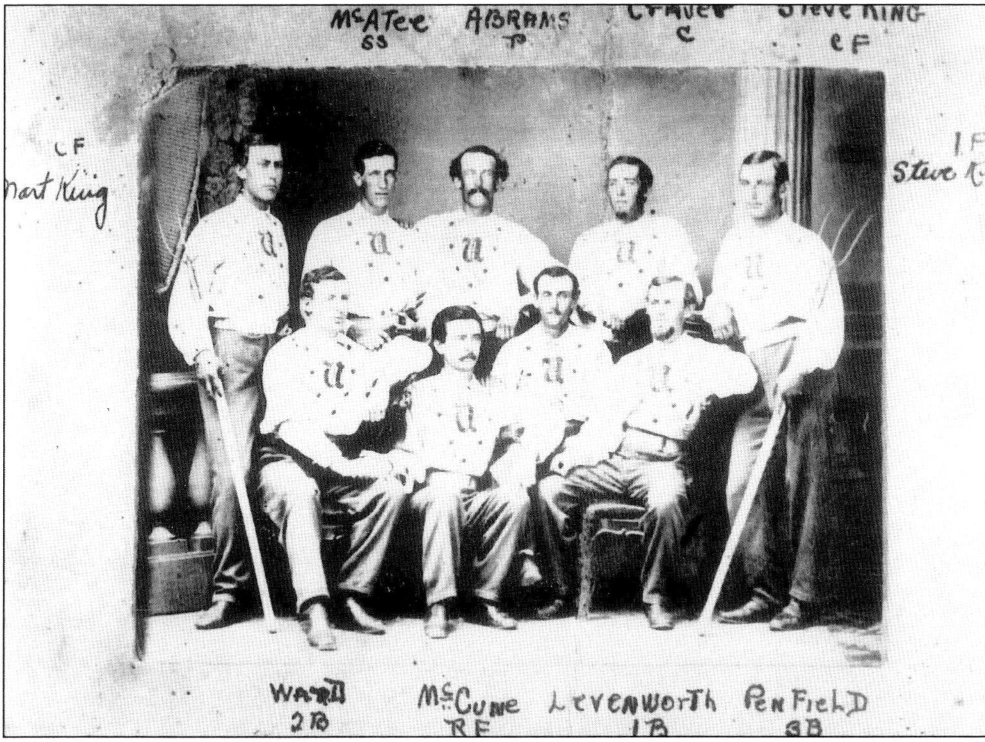

THE UNION (HAYMAKERS) NINE. The Haymakers baseball team was one of the first teams admitted into the new National League in 1876. Six players, Buck Ewing, Tim Keefe, Roger Connor, Mickey Welch, Del Gillespie, and Fred Pfeffer, went to New York and formed the nucleus of the New York Giants. To this day, Troy is an honorary member of the National League.

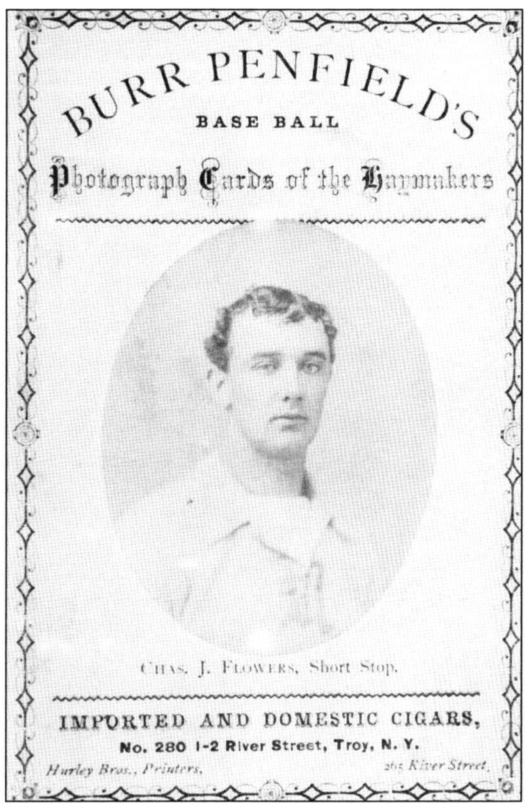

A UNION (HAYMAKERS) BASEBALL CARD OF SHORT STOP CHARLES. J. FLOWERS. Four members eventually made it to the Baseball Hall of Fame: outfielder Roger Connor (1976), catcher-infielder William "Buck" Ewing (1939), pitcher Timothy Keefe (1964), and pitcher Michael "Smiling Mickey" Welch (1973). First baseman Dan Brouthers (1945) only played one season with Troy before signing with Buffalo.

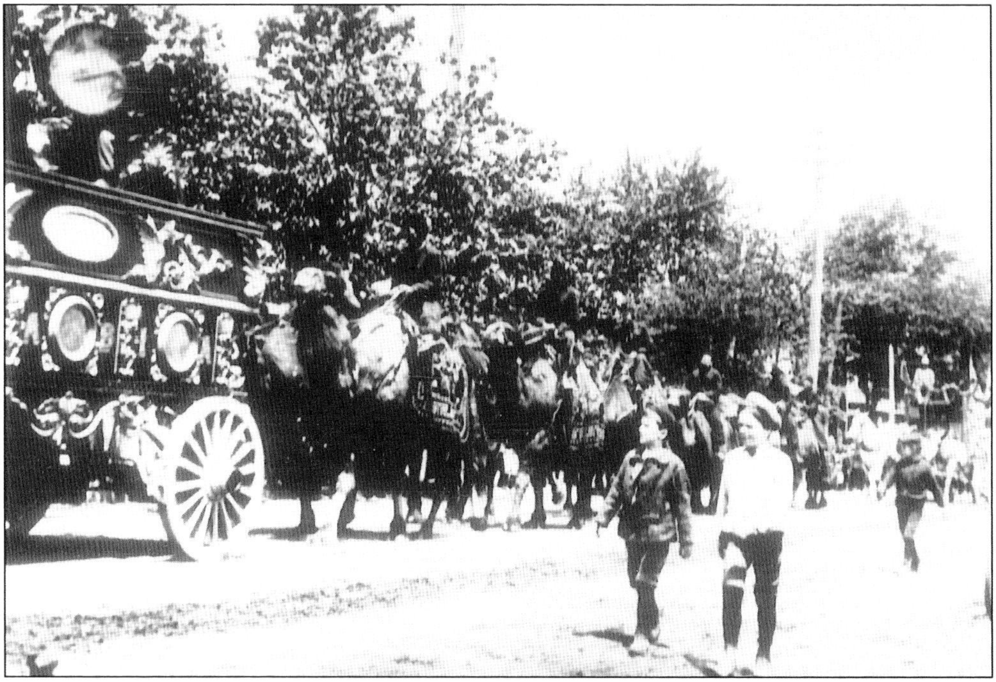

THE RINGLING BROTHERS CIRCUS. Everyone loves a circus. The Ringling Brothers Circus is shown here in 1903 parading down Fifth Avenue, perhaps on their way to Young's Grove, also located on Fifth Avenue. When I was a kid, O.C. Buck and the James Straits shows used to come to the area. They used the flat lands in Menands where the Village One Apartments now sit. I tried to run away with the Straits show (too much influence from Disney's Toby Tyler!).

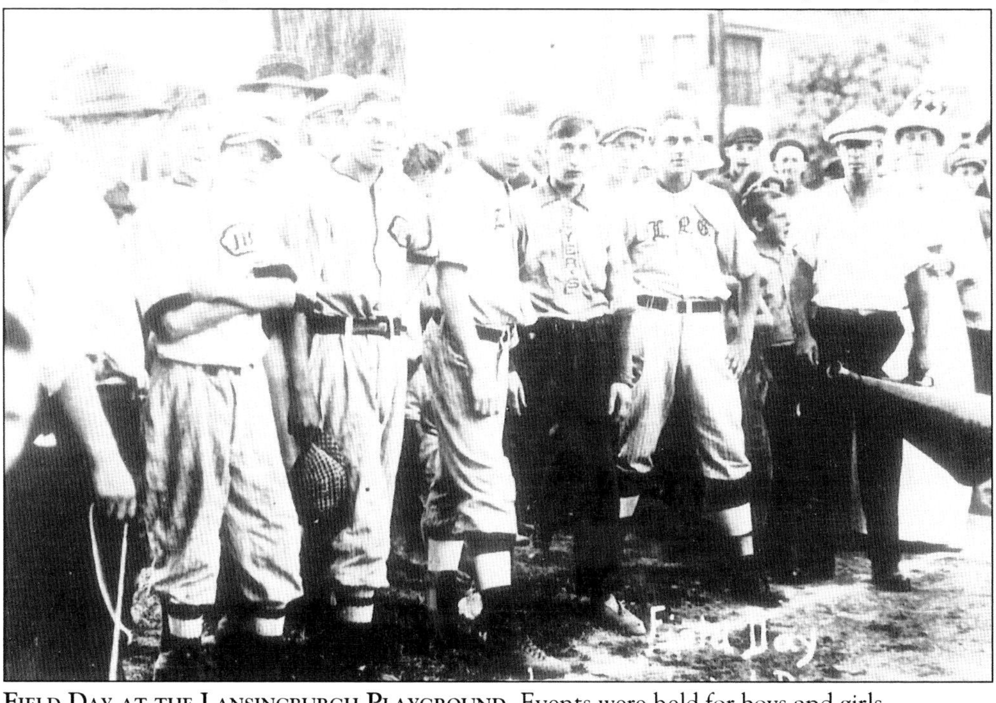

FIELD DAY AT THE LANSINGBURGH PLAYGROUND. Events were held for boys and girls.

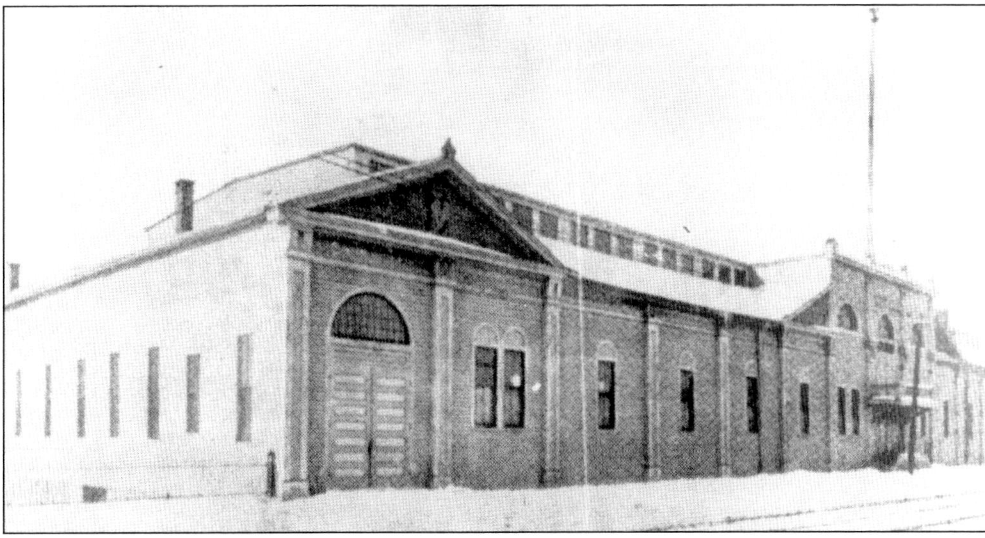

Bolton Hall. Located on the riverbank, on the west side of Second Avenue, not far from 106th Street, Bolton Hall was a roller rink in 1907. Bolton Hall was built by the Bolton family, and was used for political rallies, fraternal order drills, industrial expos, bike races, and spring events. William Jennings Bryan spoke here while campaigning in 1900.

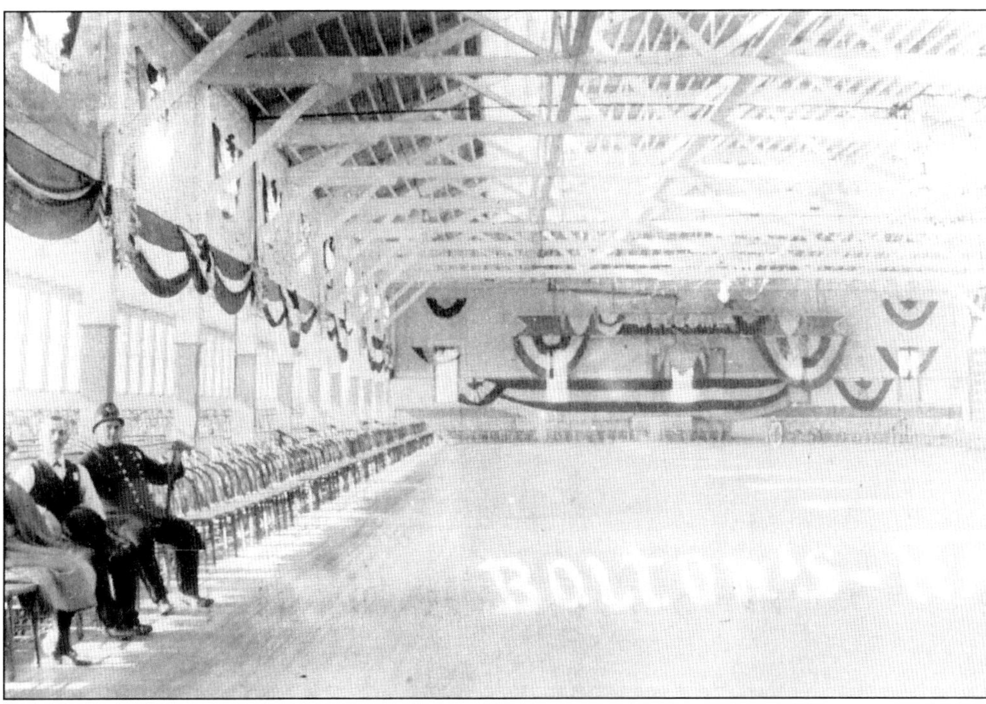

The Interior of Bolton Hall. This picture was taken on September 29, 1897, for the J.S. Fake Concert (the Hook & Ladder Company). Notice the policeman's uniform. The hall burned on February 17, 1924.

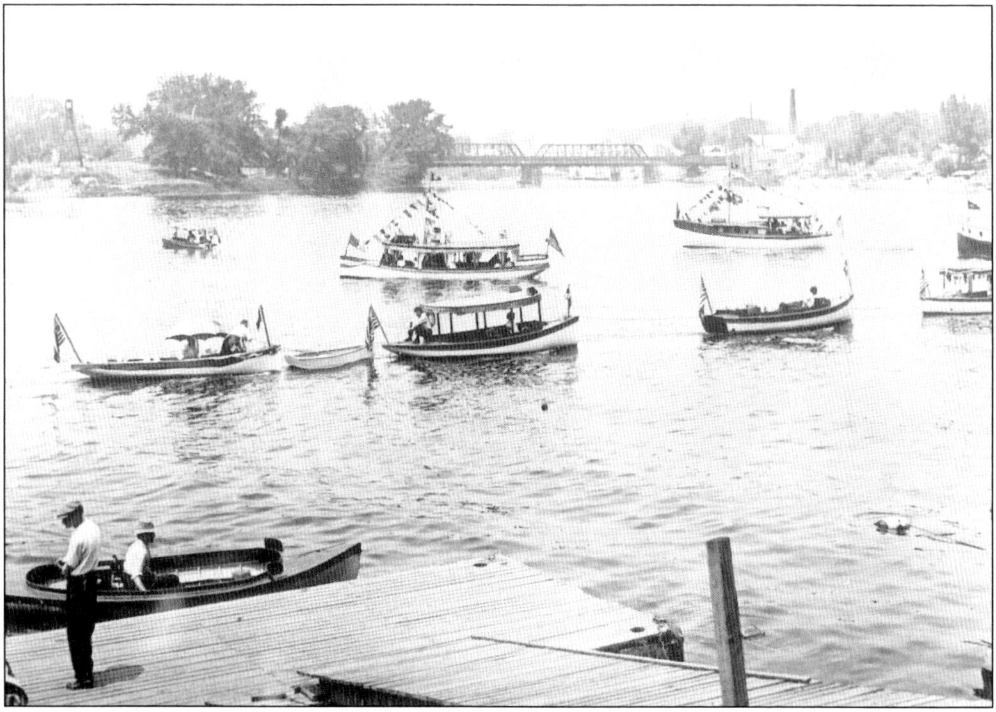

Street Docks at 123rd Street during the First Quarter of the 20th Century. Most of the boats shown here were built in Lansingburgh. Peebles Island and Waterford are in the background. The marina and boat launch have been restored.

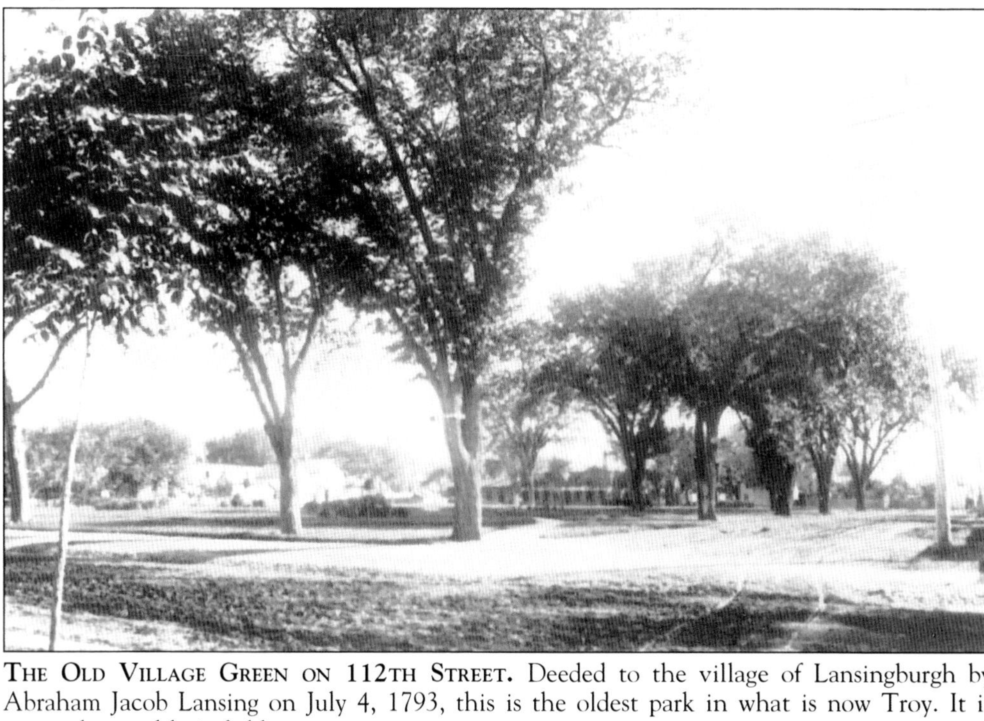

The Old Village Green on 112th Street. Deeded to the village of Lansingburgh by Abraham Jacob Lansing on July 4, 1793, this is the oldest park in what is now Troy. It is currently an athletic field.

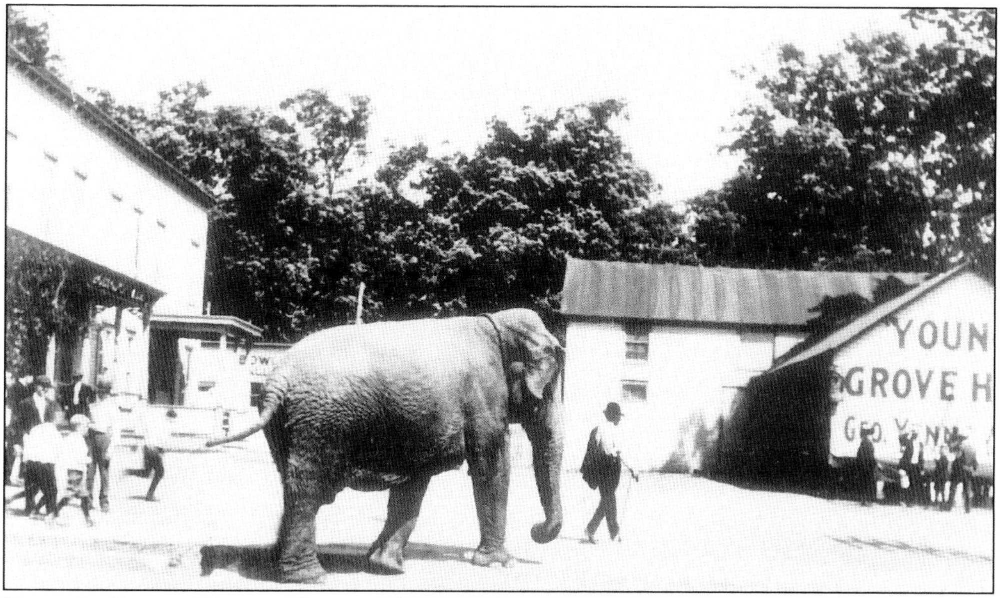

YOUNG'S GROVE HOTEL. This popular spot for picnickers (sometimes drawing from 2,000 to 5,000 people a day!) was located just south of Rensselaer Park at 243 Fifth Avenue. The year-round attraction, which featured a famous dance hall, circus grounds, and a bowling alley, was later known as Phelan's Hotel. The elephant probably belonged to the Ringling Brothers Circus.

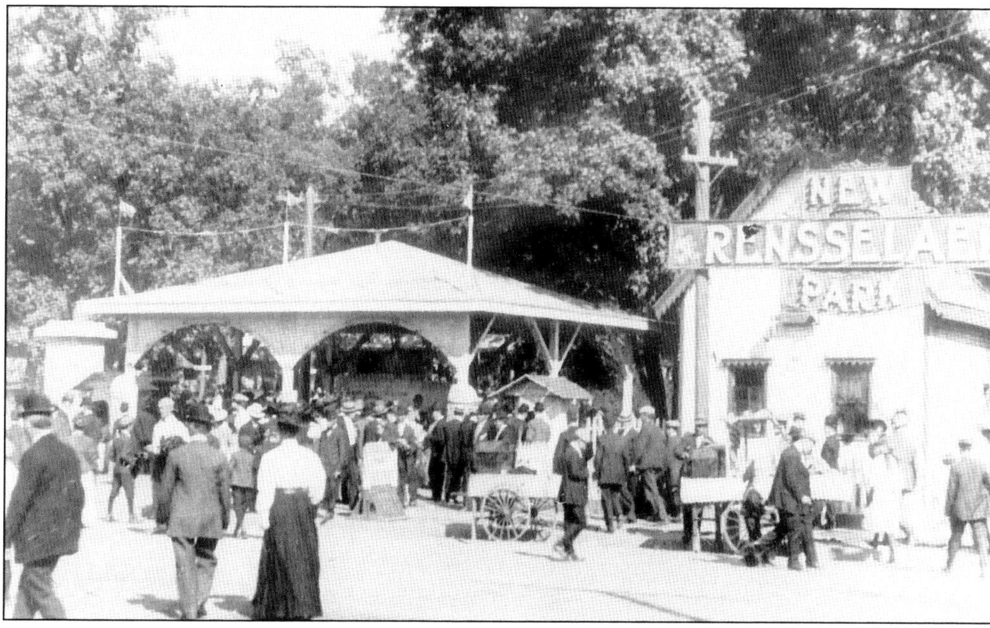

THE ENTRANCE TO THE NEW RENSSELAER PARK. Located east of Fifth Avenue and 108th Street, between 108 and 110th Streets, the 42-acre park reopened in 1906. It had a racetrack and an amusement park. During the Civil War, the area served as Camp Williard, a training area for Union soldiers. It also housed the Rensselaer County Fair until 1920. The following several pictures show various activities at the park. It closed in 1917, and the land was sold in 1919. It is now occupied by homes; no trace of the park exists.

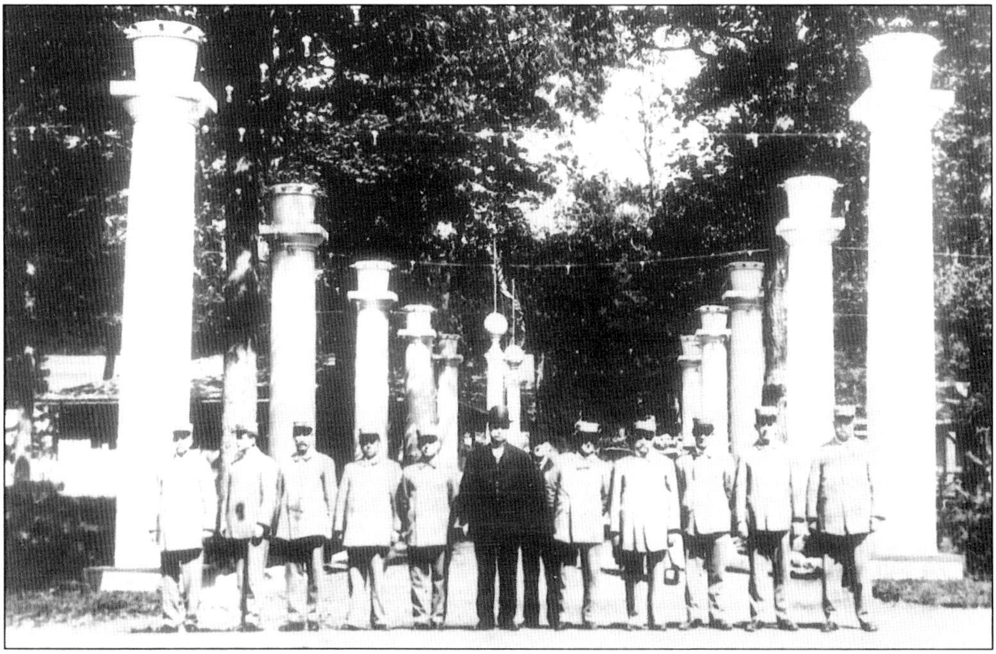

PARK POLICE. The park had their own security to keep control of crowds. Notice the directions for horse teams on the bottom left and right columns. Those columns were originally used in the Troy "Old Home Week" of 1908, before they found their way to the park.

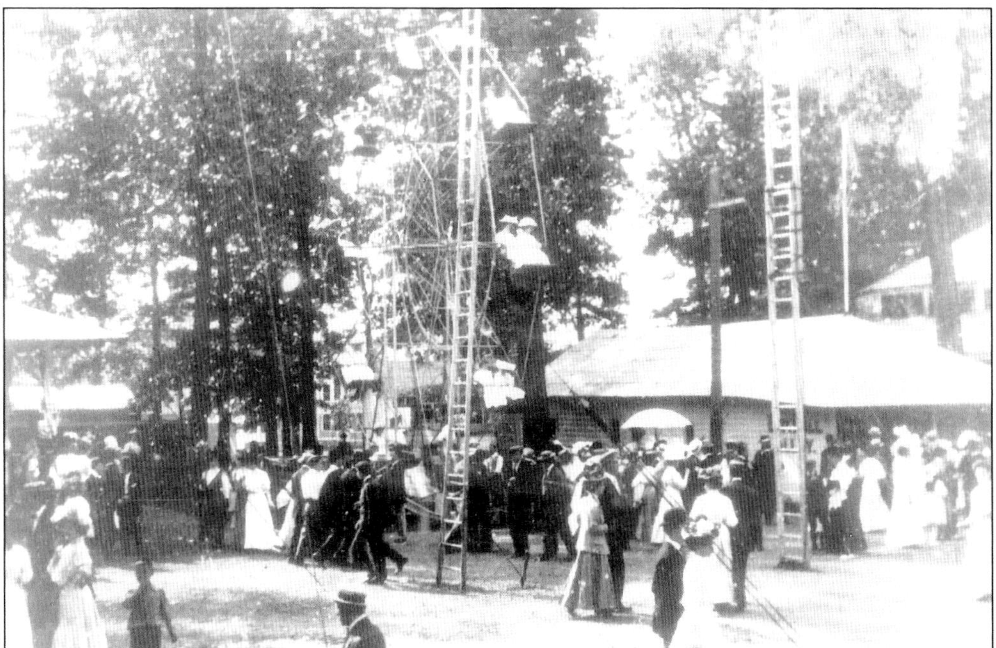

THE FERRIS WHEEL. An RPI graduate, George Ferris, invented the Ferris wheel. The first Ferris wheel debuted at the 1893 World's Colombian Exposition in Paris. It had 36 buckets (seats). This one had about 10. Notice the bowling alley to the right, the carousel next to that, and the high wire act in front.

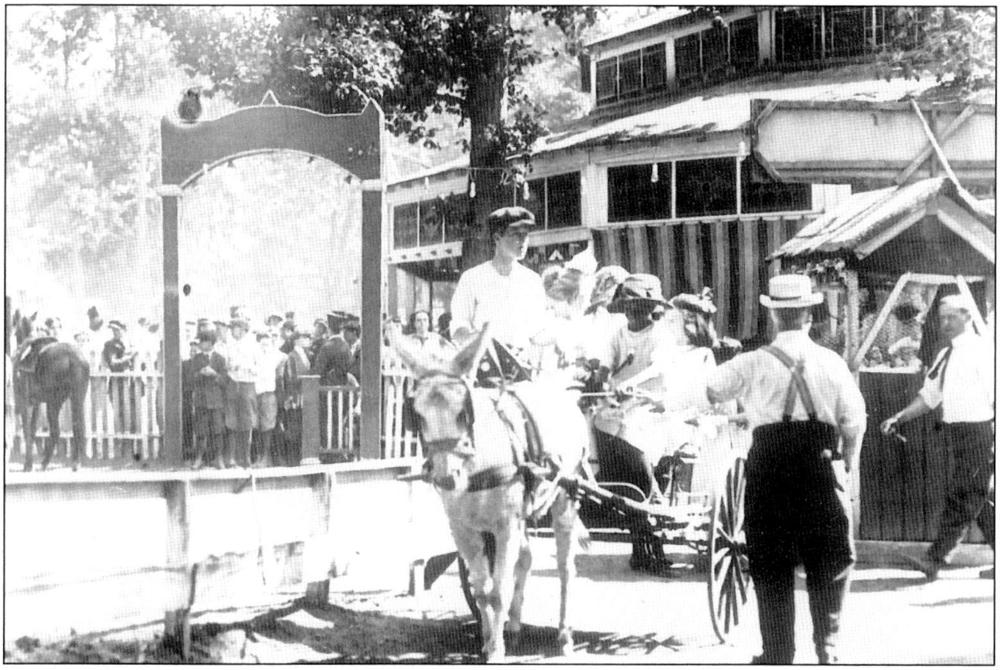

A Pony Ride. Behind the pony ride is the carousel and a line of people waiting to get on. A tag line for the park was "The Real Pleasure Ground for the Pleasure Bound."

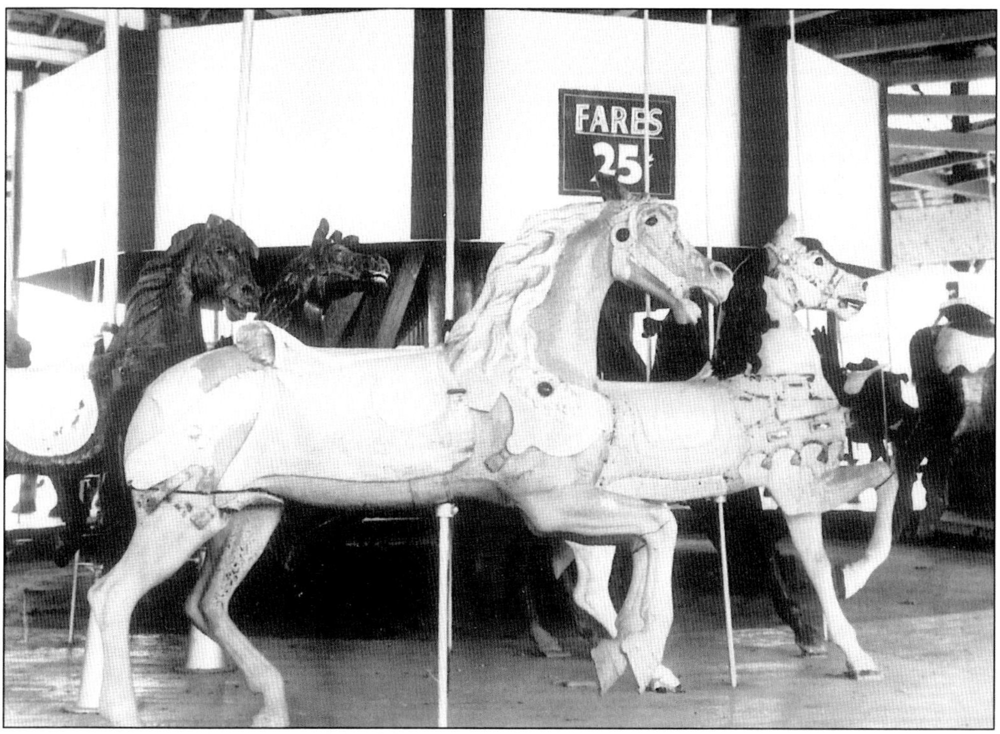

The Menagerie. This carousel had horses, bears, giraffes, camels, lions, elephants, and goats to ride. After the park closed, the carousel was moved to Crystal Lake and then to Halfmoon Beach. Eventually, it and the individual animals were sold.

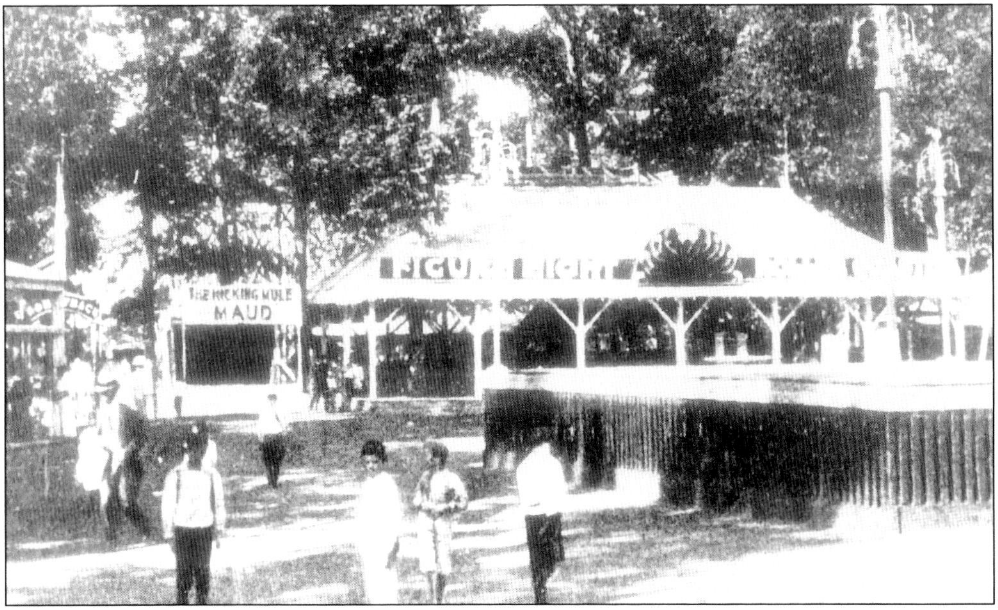

The Entrance to the Wooden Figure Eight Roller Coaster Ride. All of the rides were neatly tucked away within the grove of woods. A drive down the area now reveals nothing of the activity that was so vital to Lansingburgh residents 80 years ago.

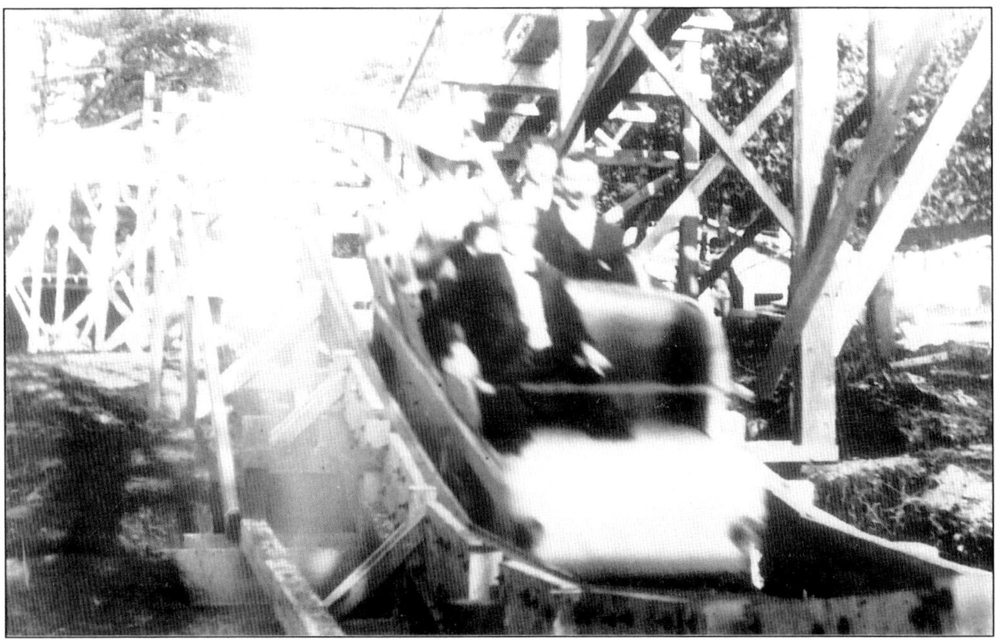

No Fast Shutters on Cameras Then! Notice the woman with her hat still on! All but the rails were made of wood. One local resident tells me her house sits on the former site of this roller coaster.

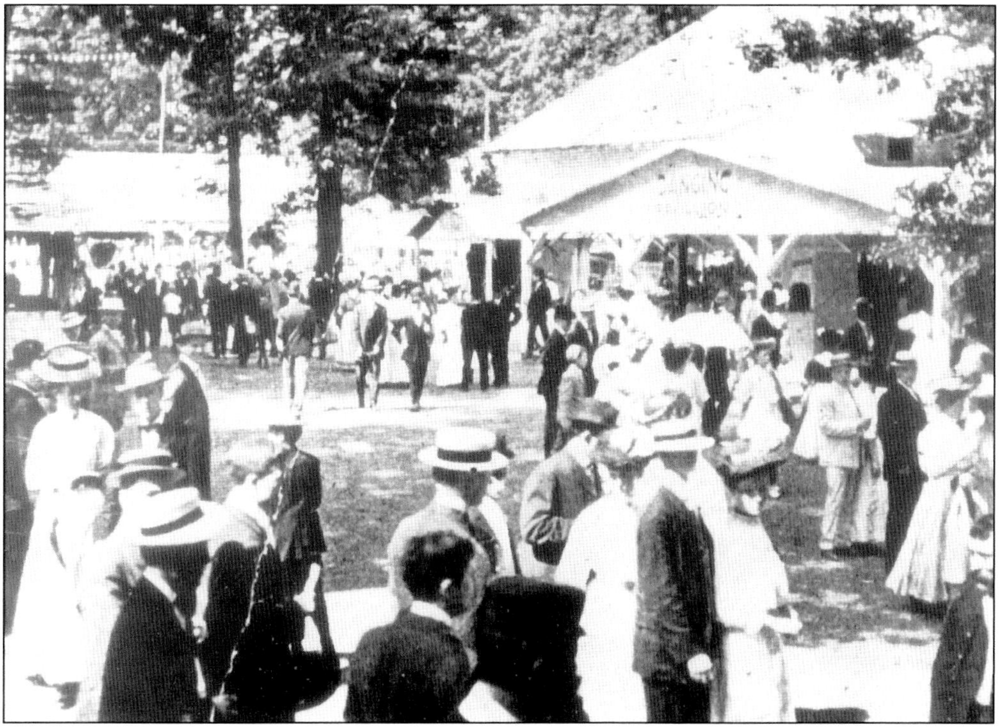

THE DANCING PAVILION. The park was also the home of the Rensselaer County Fair and the buildings of the Rensselaer County Agricultural Society, which were used for military drills during the Civil War.

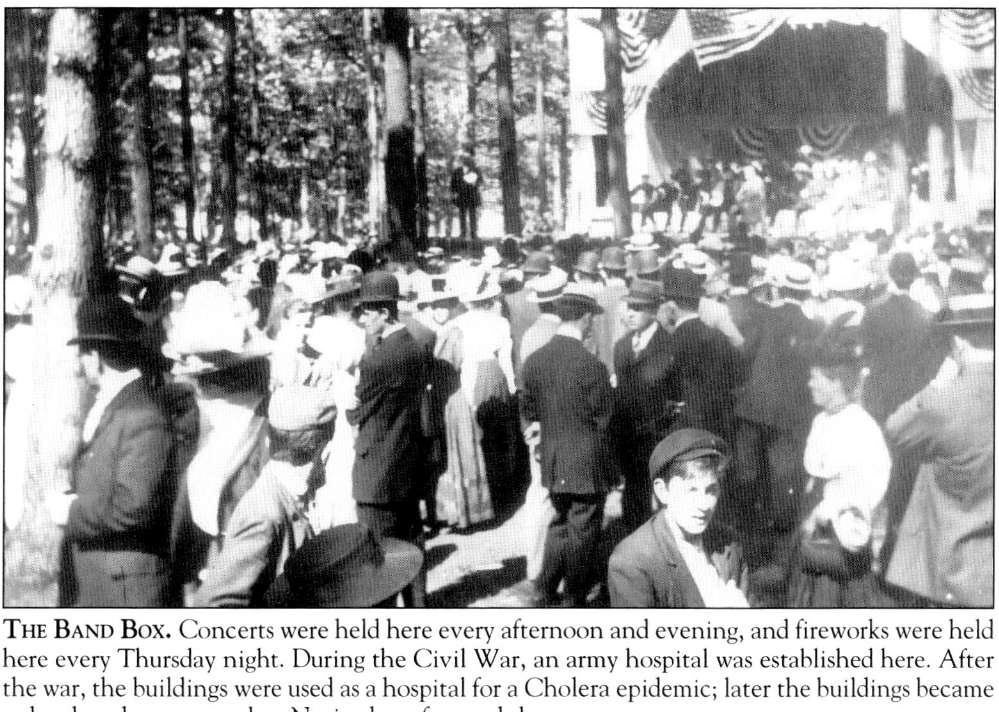

THE BAND BOX. Concerts were held here every afternoon and evening, and fireworks were held here every Thursday night. During the Civil War, an army hospital was established here. After the war, the buildings were used as a hospital for a Cholera epidemic; later the buildings became a slaughter house complex. Notice how forested the area was.

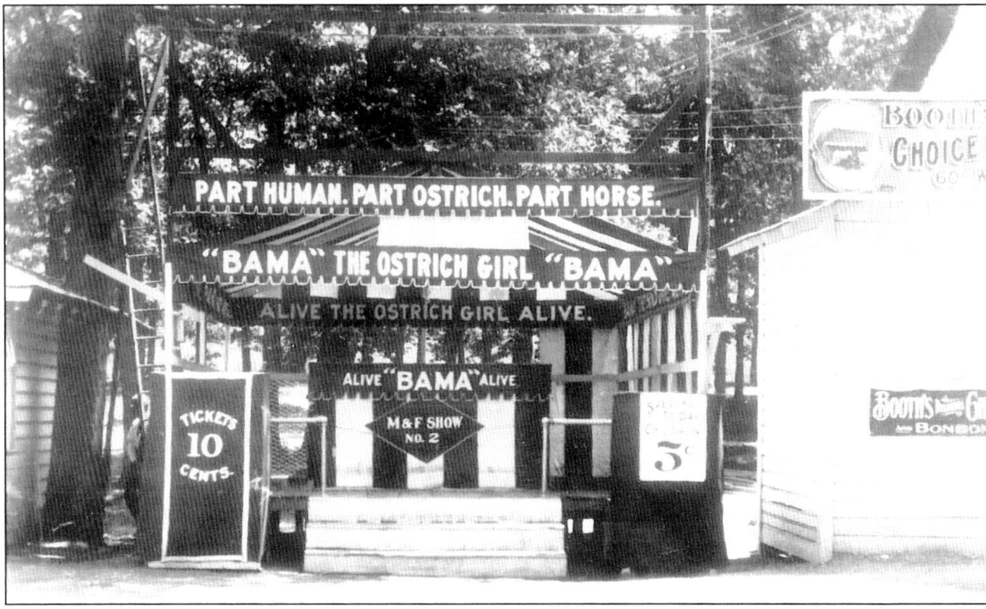

BAMA THE OSTRICH GIRL FOR ONLY A DIME! Children could get in for only a nickel. One freaky incident occurred at the park. A cannibal with one of the shows bit a Lansingburgh resident, and the local newspapers announced that the man would probably die as a result of the bite. The cannibal escaped; the fate of the victim is unknown.

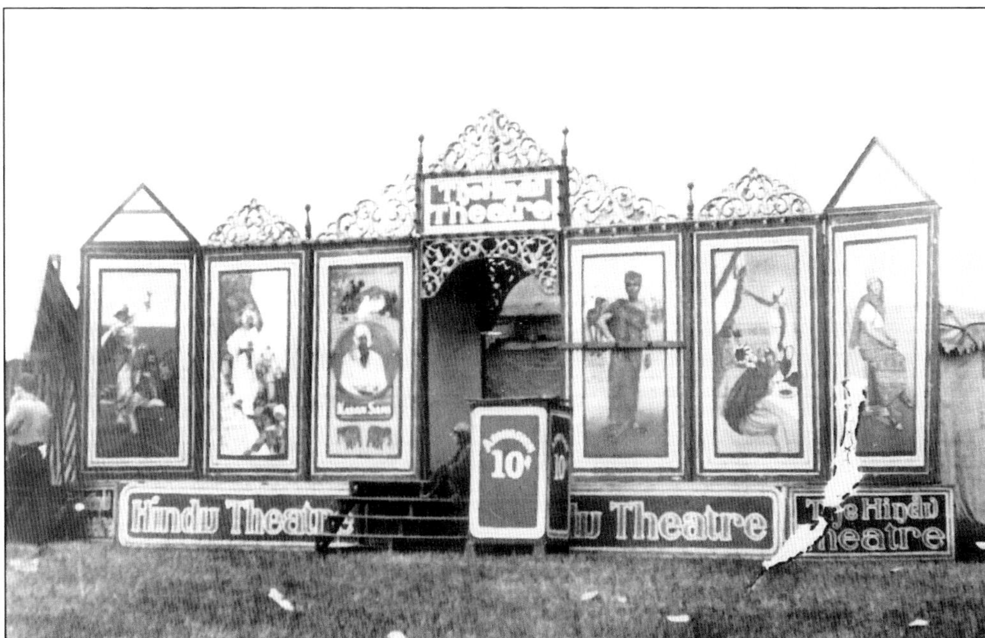

HINDU THEATER FOR ONLY A DIME! Amusement parks go back to medieval Europe, when they were known as pleasure gardens. The oldest operating amusement park today is Bakken, which is north of Copenhagen. It opened in 1583 and still amuses people to this day.

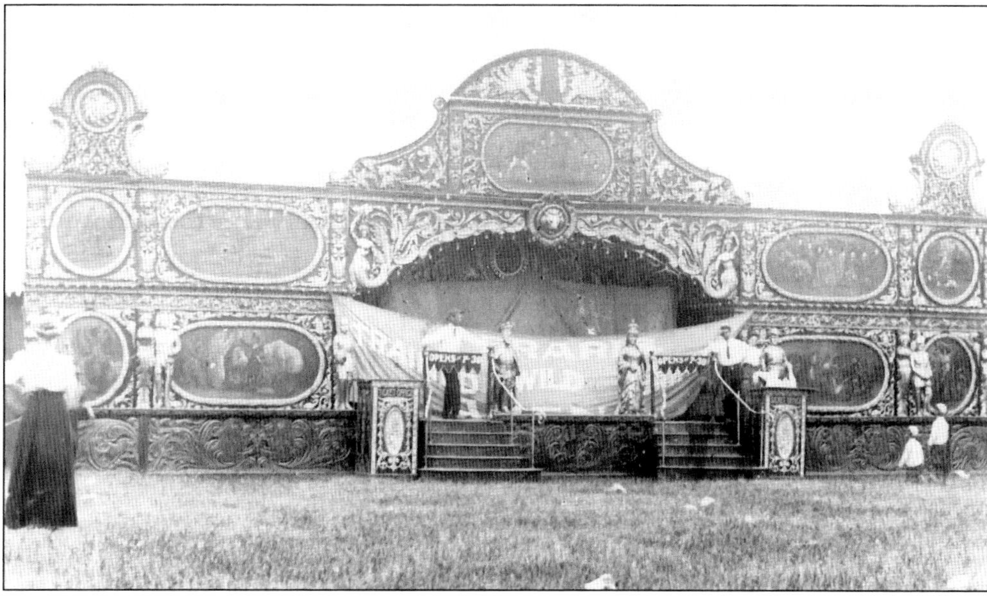

WILD SAFARI ANIMALS BEING TRAINED. In the back were cages of wild animals. This facade was used as an entrance to a variety of acts that occurred on the other side.

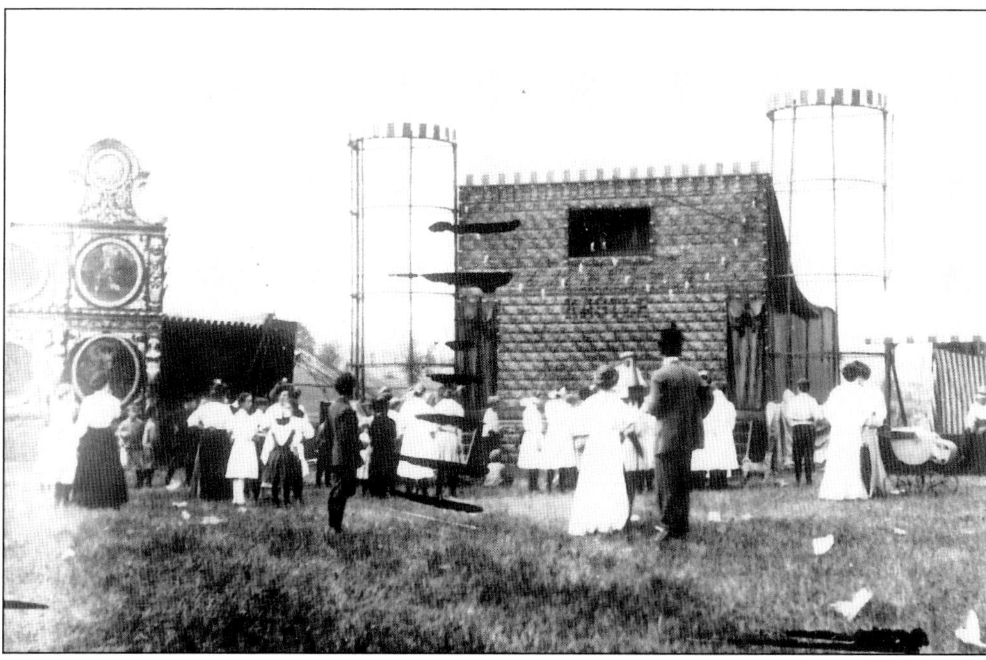

THE CASTLE! The golden era of amusement parks began with the introduction of the Ferris wheel at the 1893 World's Columbian Exposition in Chicago. Also introduced was the Midway, a combination of rides and concessions. This became the blueprint for all amusement park designs for the next 60 years. By 1919, at the end of Rensselaer Park's era, there were over 1,500 amusement parks in operation in the United States.

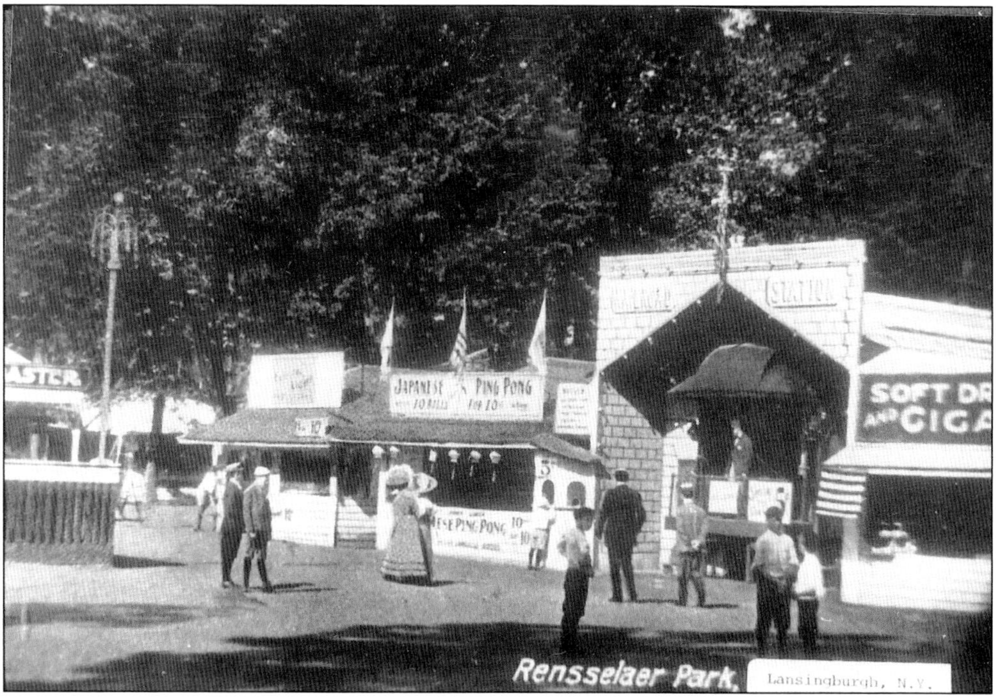

FOOD, DRINK, AND ENTERTAINMENT. The roller coaster was to the left. Note the interesting booth on the right where you could buy soft drinks and cigars. You could get your picture taken with an electric light for 10¢ next to the ping pong booth. The train ride was an artificially moving railroad car that gave the rider the experience of really moving down the tracks. A movie and sound system added realism.

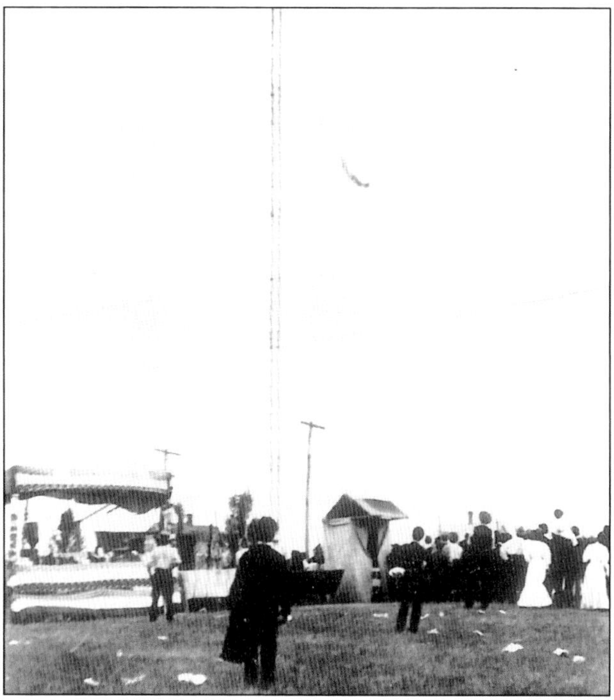

THE HIGH DIVE! Besides human attractions, Queen, one of J.W. Groman's High Diving Horses, performed here in 1908 and 1909. There was a lake in the southern portion of the park, within the race track area. The lake was created by damming a stream that flowed through the area. Park visitors could rent a boat; this was great fun for courting couples.

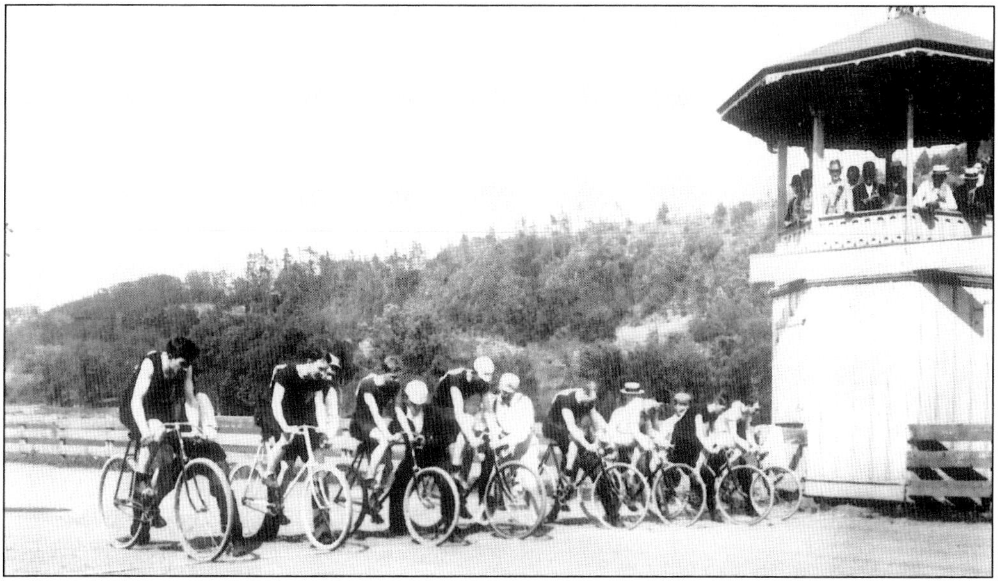

A Bike Race on the Track and the Judges's Tower. The race track was a popular attraction at the park. Horse, bike, and chariot races were held here.

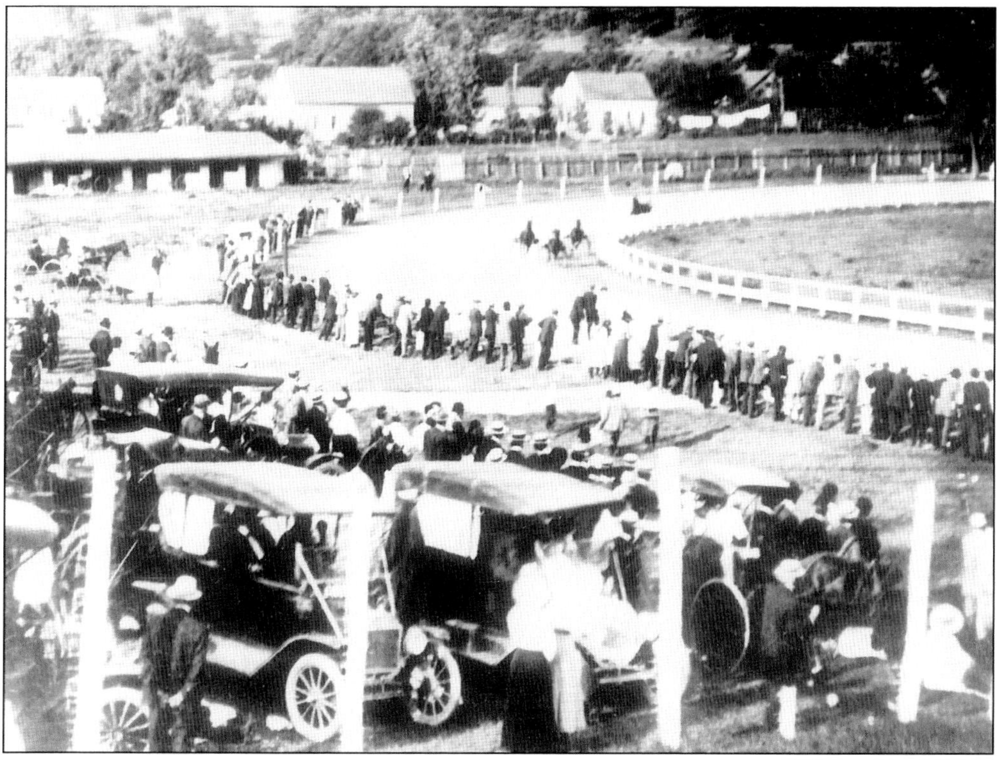

Watching the Horses! People have lined up on the northern part of the track and are watching a harness race. The Haymakers baseball team played at the park; in 1868, they played 14 games here and drew from 5,000 to 9,000 people. The park built them a U-shaped bleacher somewhere near the track. Park owners also built a secondary road around the track so visitors could stay close to the action.

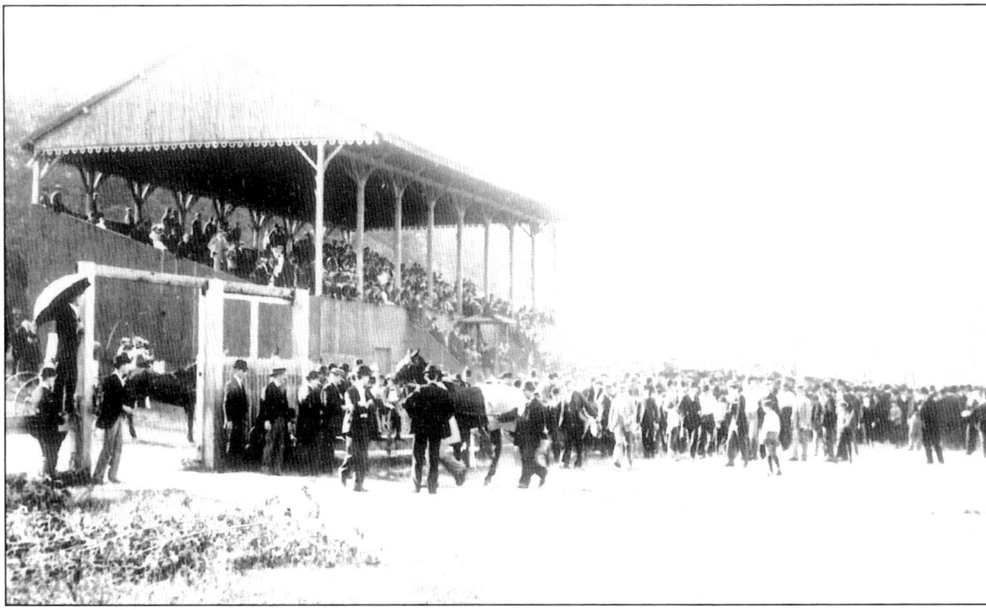

READY, SET, GO! The racing track grandstand and the half-mile track itself took up about half of the park. Harness racing was popular.

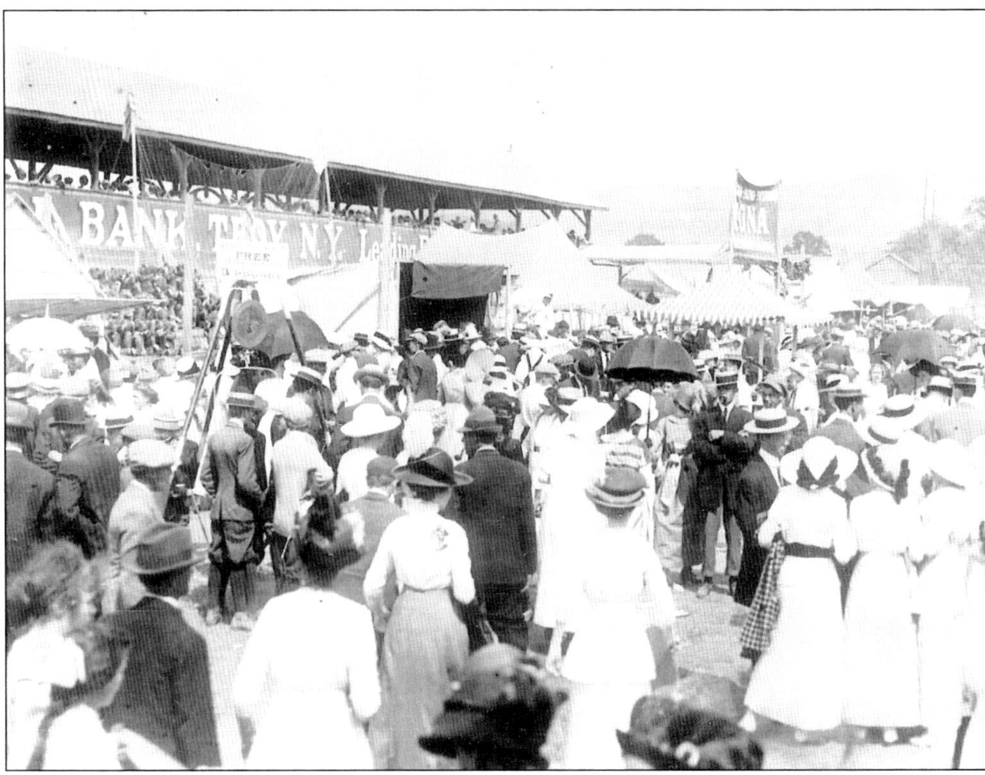

PEOPLE MILLING AROUND THE BACK OF THE GRANDSTAND, GETTING READY FOR THE RACES. Notice that almost everyone wore hats.

Seven

DISASTERS

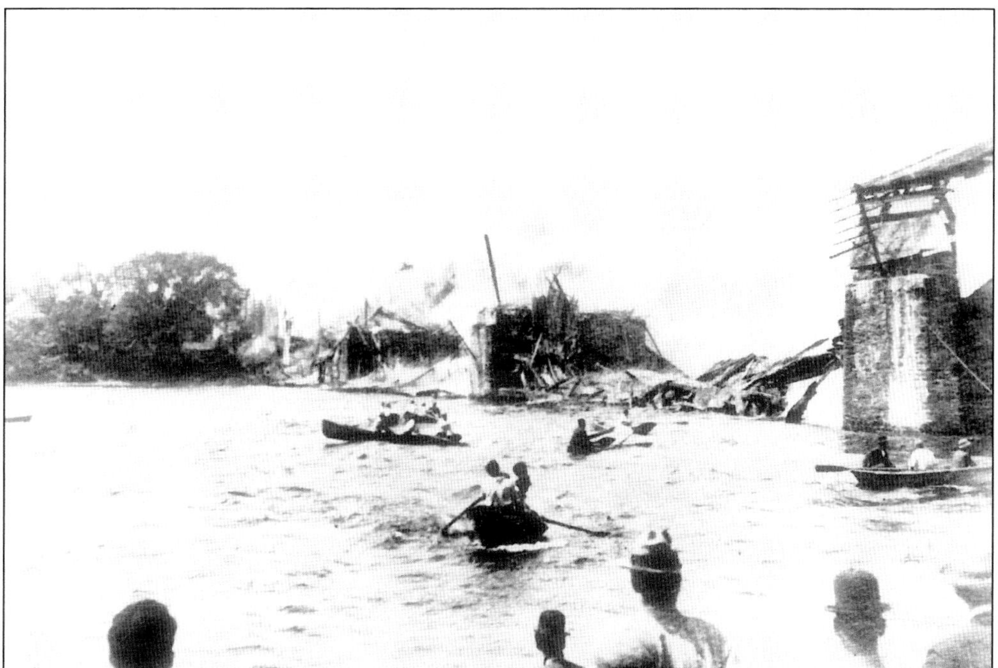

THE WATERFORD BRIDGE FIRE OF 1909. When built in 1804, this was the first bridge between Lansingburgh and New York City. A spark from a passing trolley ignited the oil-soaked floor. A steel structure was quickly built to take its place. Fires were a recurring threat to any residential or commercial area.

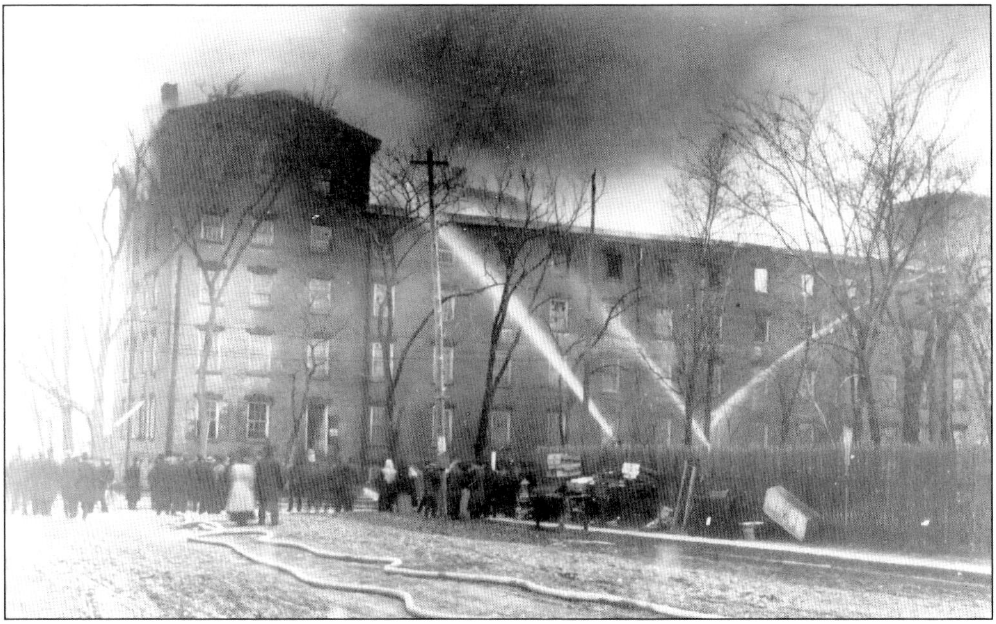

The Powers Oilcloth Factory Fire, April 22, 1907. One of the earliest industries of Lansingburgh went up in smoke. William Powers, a former schoolteacher, started this company in 1817. His widow, Deborah, and their sons carried on the name and were influential in many aspects of the village.

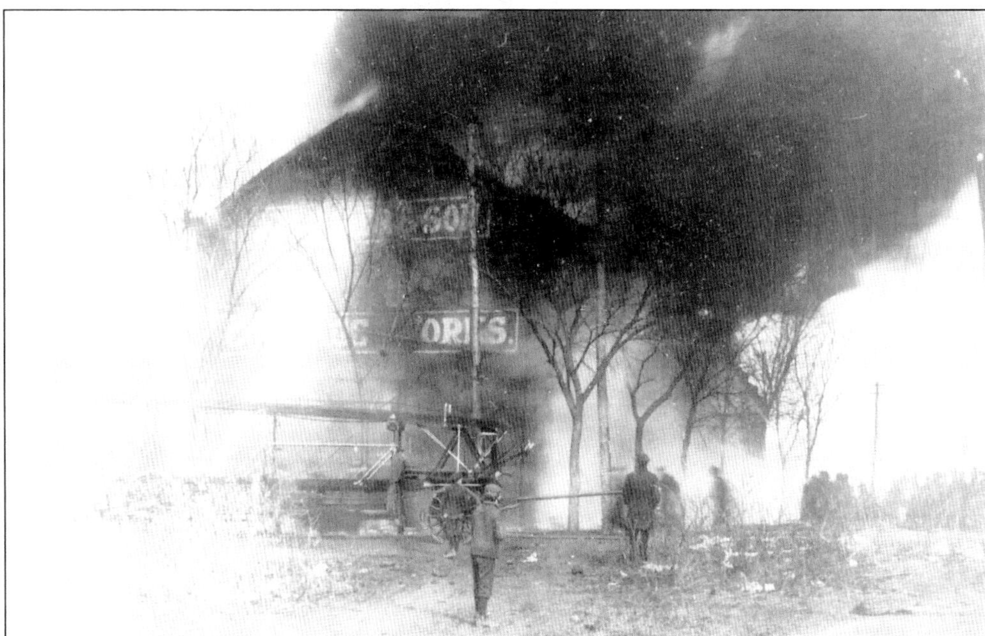

The J.J. Child Steamer at the Draper Cordage Works Fire on the Northwest Corner of 102nd Street and Ninth Avenue. Built in the mid-1890s, the building is still in use by Garden Way. Notice the hook and ladder there, as well as the crowd.

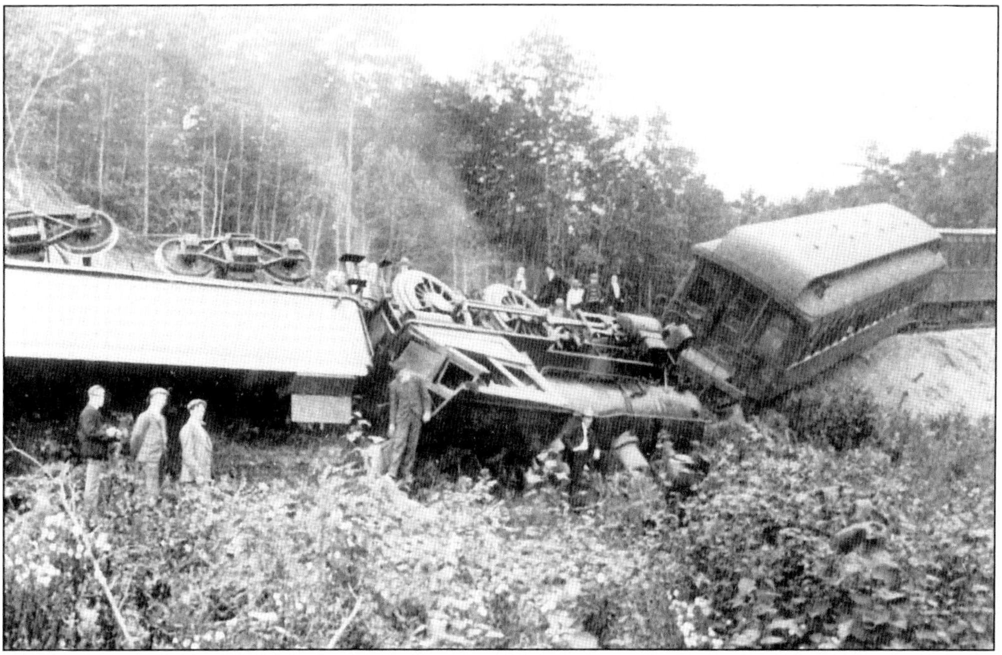

THE TRAIN WRECK OF OCTOBER 4, 1906, NEAR THE LANSINGBURGH TRAIN STATION AT THE FOOT OF 115TH STREET. A slow-moving train was struck by a troop train. Five people were killed.

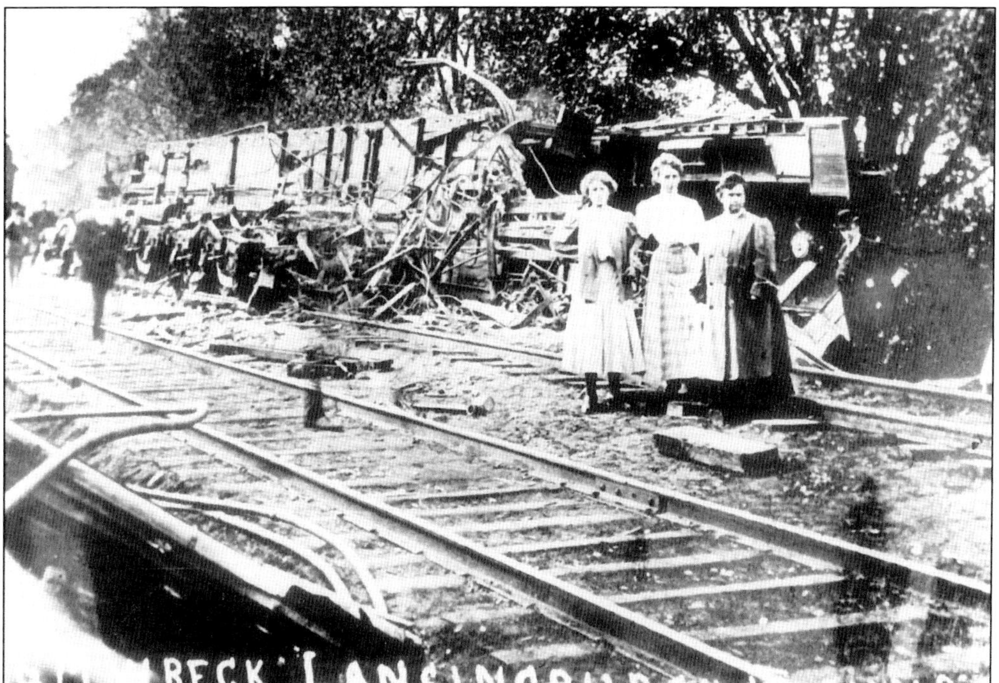

THE REMAINS OF THE SAME TRAIN WRECK AND A FEW YOUNG WOMEN POSING FOR THE CAMERA. Never let it be said that people didn't like a good accident to pose by.

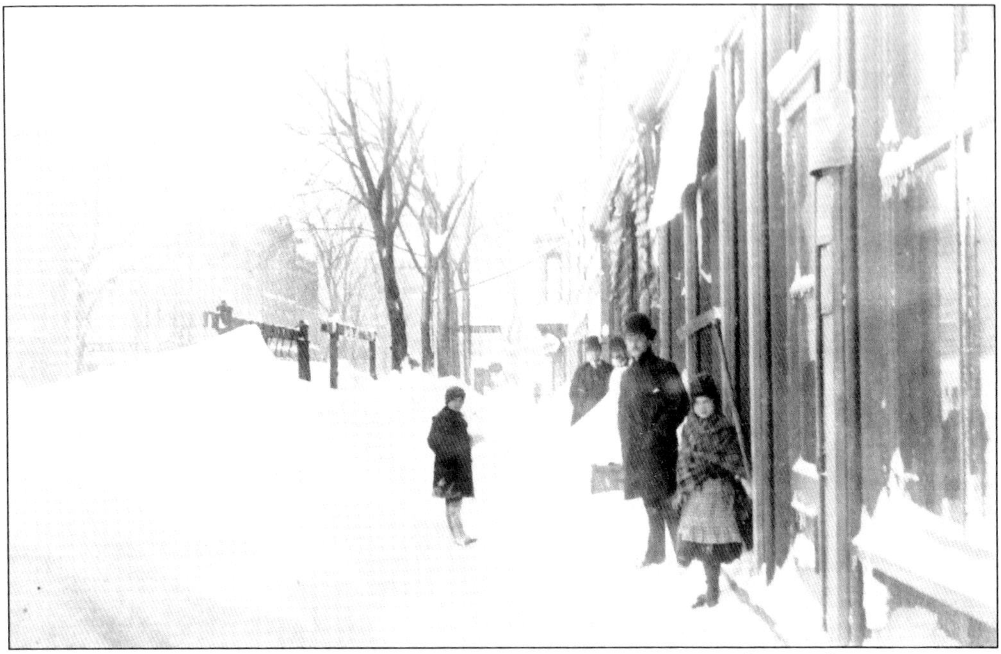

The Blizzard of 1888. Disasters aren't only man-made! This view of Second Avenue proves this claim. Over 4 feet of snow fell on the capital district on March 13, 1888, grinding the area to a virtual halt.

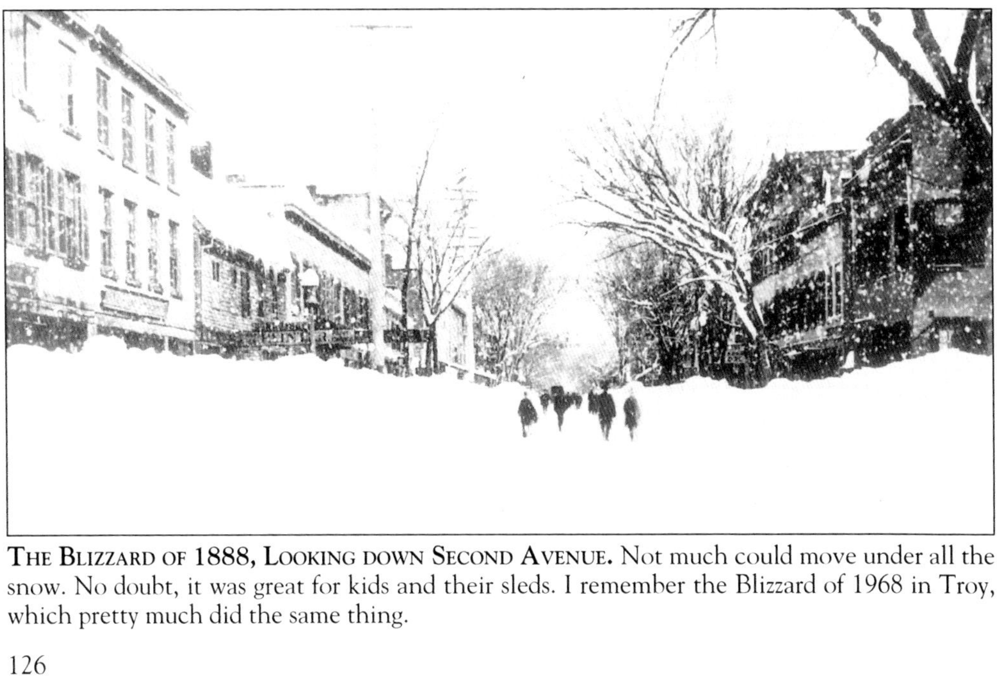

The Blizzard of 1888, Looking down Second Avenue. Not much could move under all the snow. No doubt, it was great for kids and their sleds. I remember the Blizzard of 1968 in Troy, which pretty much did the same thing.

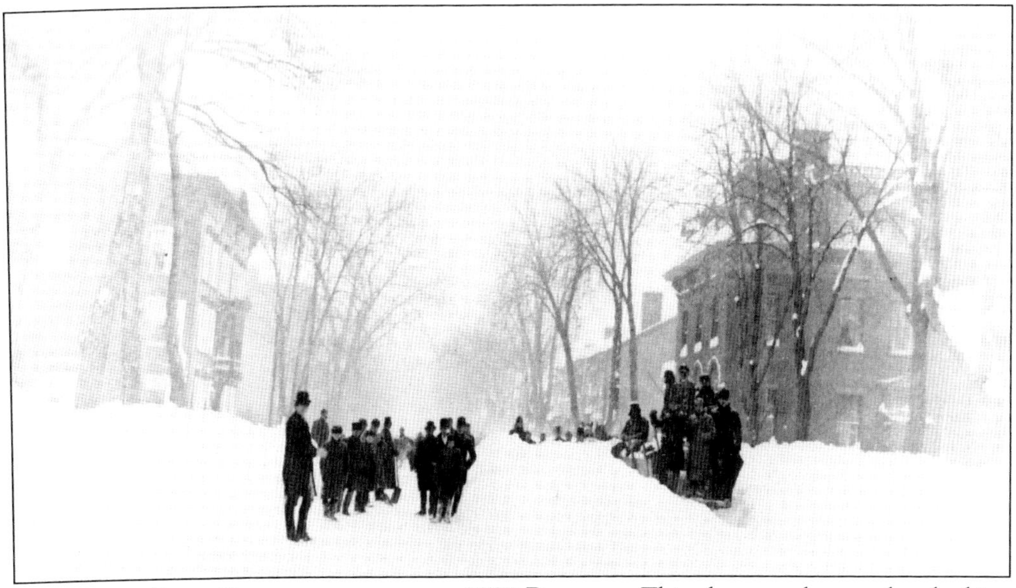

COMMUNITY SNOW REMOVAL DURING THE 1888 BLIZZARD. This photograph was taken looking south down Second Avenue at 114th Street. Without the cooperation of the citizenry, things could have been much worse.

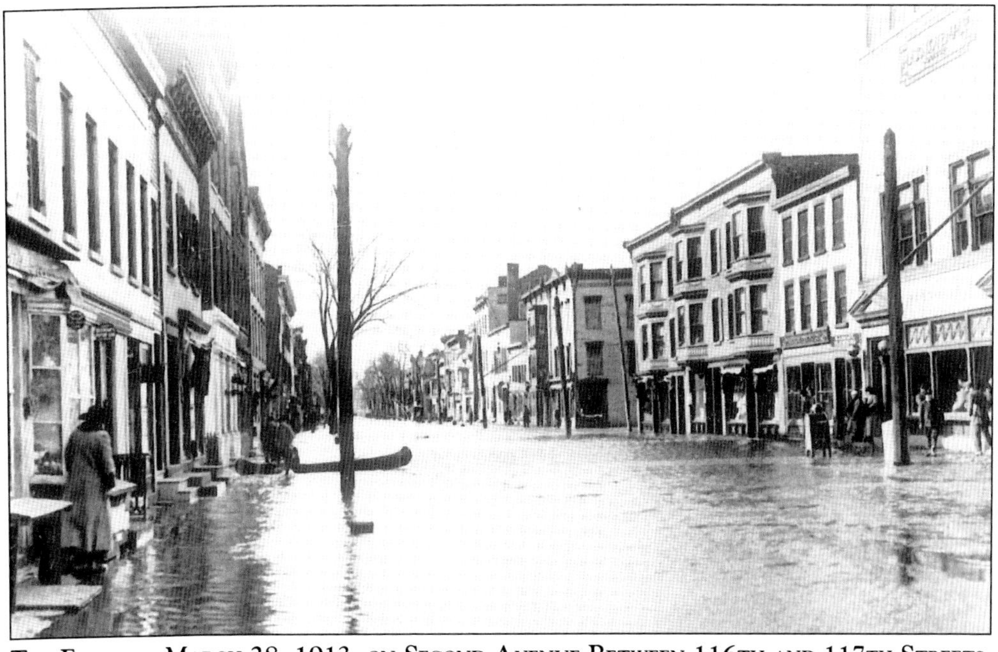

THE FLOOD OF MARCH 28, 1913, ON SECOND AVENUE BETWEEN 116TH AND 117TH STREETS. The police station and People's Bank are on the left; the post office (in the Masonic Temple) is on the right. The Flood of 1913 was one of the area's worst; the water level reached 28 feet above flood level. Another similar flood took place in 1936. Even with flood control, both Lansingburgh and Troy still get a good flooding once in a while.

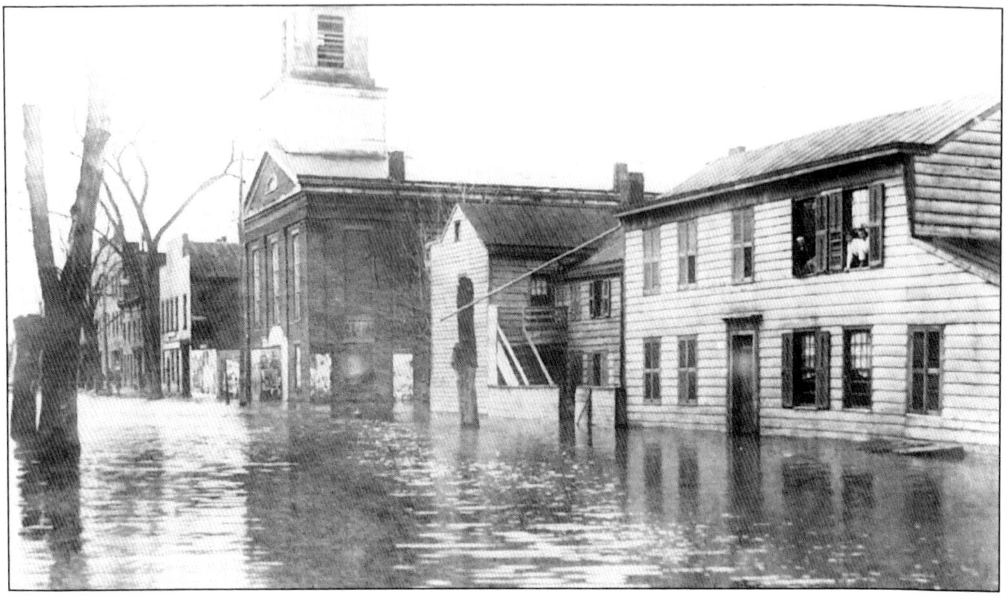

The Flood of 1913 at 116th Street. Notice the flooded Powers Opera House, originally the old Baptist church. Today, you would never know the building was a church; it stands as a one-story brick warehouse.

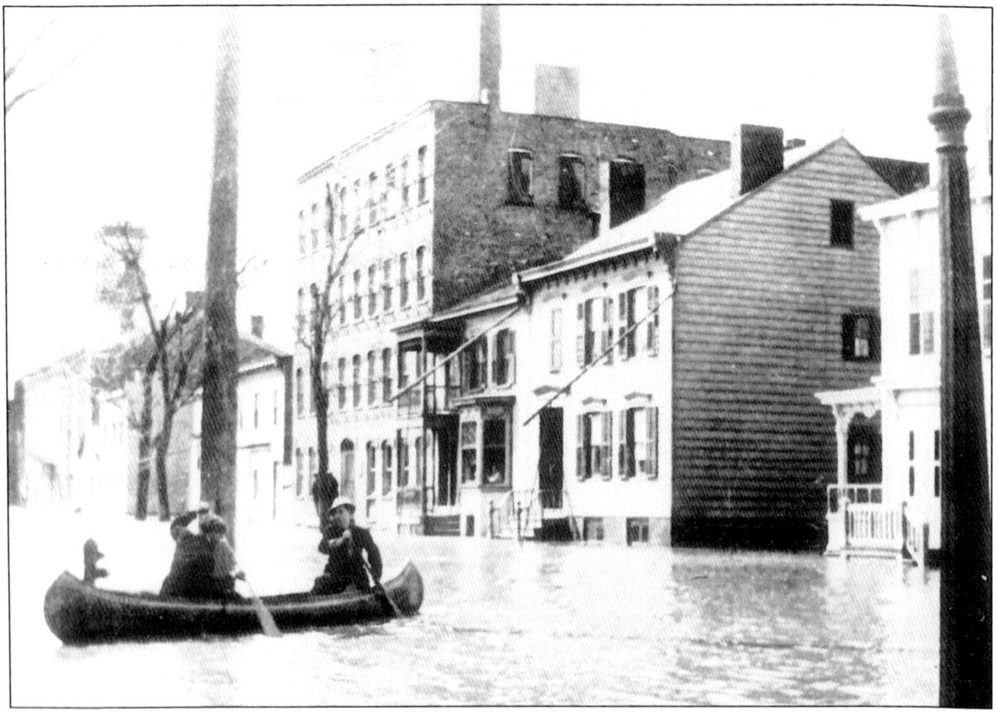

The Flood of 1913 at Third Avenue, South of 118th Street. The large Monarch Brush Building in the middle of the photograph is still standing at this location. The house second to the right of brush shop belonged to Rev. Tobias Spicer, a Methodist preacher. Spicer attended the General Conference of 1828 in the city of Pittsburgh, on May 1, 1828, as a New York delegate. The Powers Opera house is visible to the far left.